THE
BOAT OF LONGING

A NOVEL BY

O. E. RÖLVAAG

TRANSLATED FROM THE NORWEGIAN

LÆNGSELENS BAAT

BY

NORA O. SOLUM

GREENWOOD PRESS, PUBLISHERS
WESTPORT, CONNECTICUT

Library of Congress Cataloging in Publication Data

Rølvaag, Ole Edvart, 1876–1931.
  The boat of longing.

  Reprint of the ed. published by Harper, New York.
  I. Title.
PZ3.R6275Bo5 ₁PT9150.R55₁   839.8'2'36   73–11844
ISBN 0–8371–7069–9

Reprinted with the permission of Harper & Row, Publishers, Inc.

Reprinted in 1974 by Greenwood Press
A division of Congressional Information Service, Inc.
88 Post Road West, Westport, Connecticut 06881

Printed in the United States of America

10 9 8 7 6 5 4 3 2

The poems in this volume, with the exception of Astray *by Mr. Rölvaag, are adaptations of themes suggested by the original Norwegian poems, and are the work of Mr. Thomas Job.*

THE TRANSLATOR

*IT IS A MISTAKEN BELIEF
THAT THE IMMIGRANT HAS NO SOUL*

CONTENTS

FOREWORD

To those who may review this series of moving pictures I wish to say: It is not "types" which are drawn here. It is merely humankind. "Types" do not interest me greatly; the older I become the more I doubt the existence of such individuals. But I am interested in human beings. And there will scarcely be a life history which it would not be interesting to look at if it were singled out for scrutiny. Human portraiture has no end. It is as manifold and inexhaustible as life itself.

Through long association with the persons in these pictures I have learned to know and love them. It is, therefore, with a feeling of regret that I now part with them and send them out into the world. Take them in and be good to them. They need it.

THE AUTHOR

St. Olaf College, *October,* 1921

THE BOAT OF LONGING

I. The Cove under the Hill

THE place lay on the sea, as far out as the coast dared push itself, and extremely far north, so far, in fact, that it penetrated the termless solitudes where utmost Light and utmost Dark hold tryst.

In summer an idle sea stretched broad-bosomed and dreaming between skylines—for days at a time too indolent to stir more than just enough to betray its eternal restlessness. Across its glittering reaches wavelets, in sabbath mood, billowed lazily; finding an islet or skerry, they would rise, curious; then they would murmur on along headlands and around venturesome points, but purl more softly against the beaches of coves. The seatang and the long-stemmed kelp, peeping up from the soundless deep, would curtsy graciously to the moving softness overhead. . . . Summer night, glorious and big, listened intent.

Here the sea gull sailed and sailed on outstretched wing, now alone, now companioned, searching the deep. More often alone . . . silent . . . searching only . . . but gathering like a cloud above a school of saithe, where it would gorge itself tumultuously and set up a cry to drown man's voice . . . then, satiated, lifting again to resume its way aloof and voiceless out to the verge of the sea, there to listen to its riddle. Day and night the gull sailed. On . . . always on. Silent, high up, it cut its way into the storm, flew exultant into the face of a blast, or vanished like a phantom in fog and spoondrift, low over the billows. . . . Wherefore thus always on outstretched wing? Was it thinking to reach the source of the sea?

The Boat of Longing

And eider ducks rode the gilded gliders . . . the drakes usually in great flocks far out. There in summer they relived the good old days of their bachelorhood. Along the strands the wives swam alone, ducked for food now and then, and kept vigilant watch of a certain spot up on land the livelong day. The moment the sun shelved the western horizon they would waddle up the slippery rocks and head straight for the hidden nest.

And sun. Day and night—sun. Through the entire round of the hours it found nothing to do but pour splendour upon sea and sky, on steely crag and growthless rocks. Gold glittered, gold flamed crimson, and gold—dull and inert—glowed feebly, like dying embers. Everywhere sun. . . . Sunny too the moods of men at this season of the year.

But when winter came—! There where aforetime bright joy had reigned so strongly, gloom and a numbing fear set in. Then the sea ran terrifically. Storms might rage for a month at a time—aye, and more, the wave-roar never abating. Darkness hung like a pall over house and home. It was as though every evil genie had come abroad. Hideous to hear in the dead of night the hollow sobbings of the great breakers. The tempest piling the frothy water mountains high and hurling them thunderous up on land would bring men to cower in terror, for that sounded like the crack of doom. . . . Talk was little among people then . . . they only listened.

Such wild tales and queer legends went about in that far northern countryside. Of the many, one concerned a boat said from time to time to have shown itself out in the open sea. So phenomenal was the manner of its appearance that folk did not know what to make of it. It would come all of a sudden, float quietly in the sunlight awhile, then vanish as instantly as it had come. Not that anyone had ever been near

The Cove Under the Hill

it; but many had seen it at various times. At length it had crept into the stories and become part of the common lore. It availed little that now and then there came sensible persons who laughed at the silly old tales. The disdainful young, for instance, would affect to know better and would protest with their elders, insisting that there were no vessels plying these lanes other than mail-packets and boats carrying freight and passengers coastwise and to foreign lands. Still they could not quash the tale. No, not altogether. For just as soon as it seemed to have disappeared from the folk mind, it was certain to be resurrected; some one was sure to have seen it west in the sea . . . it was always west in the sea, where day couched and awakened. And therewith the story would gain new life.

Remarkable, incredible indeed, the tales about this boat.

Take what happened in Finmark that memorable spring when a storm claimed the lives of scores of valiant fishermen and left a trail of grief in its wake all down the coast. There were wives who never again saw their husbands; mothers with a son or two less; and fine lassies amany who were stricken for life because the lads upon whom they had pinned their hopes could never return. That time the sea, having risen to the full strength of its power, had taken more than its tithe.

During the summer which followed many were said to have seen the boat—both here and there along the coast. And small wonder that folk became visionary; for from every crag and hillock affording a clear view of the lane to the north there were so many eyes staring out into the open summer night. Everywhere eyes hunted the waters for boats expected, but never arriving. They searched and searched, filled with moisture, were wiped dry, and went on searching. . . . What was that? that speck out yonder on the skyline? . . . Wasn't it a boat coming? God in heaven, it was a boat, wasn't it? Hope fluttered tremulous . . . for it might

3

The Boat of Longing

be a boat—aye, it might! . . . But out there on the ocean rim the speck would grow and grow, become at last a sail rising out of the sea. By and by a hull would emerge to the view . . . only to scud briskly by into the south before the fresh north wind. When its passing was plain, the eye would fill with water, blotting out all vision for a while. . . . The great sea locks many a mournful saga in its bosom.

. . . Yet it was almost as though they could not leave off their staring, those many eyes. That summer many saw the boat—all the way from southern Helgeland as far north as Tromső it was said to have appeared. And not a soul in those parts but talked of it.

And there were other stories about the boat.

At Burness in Helgeland, in a parsonage situated high over the sea and commanding a clear view of the fairway, which ran directly by, lived the Reverend Munch and his family.

There was a child in the parsonage, the minister's little daughter Erla. Of her, folk averred that she was one of God's blessed angels come to earth, so much about her seemed not to belong to this world. Strangers who saw her for the first time were compelled to stop and marvel because of the unusual lovableness of her person. The Reverend Munch and his wife both moved about in the flood of sunshine which emanated from her being, bathed themselves in it and became very good on account of it. And time and again old Beggar-Kari, who so often came to the parsonage to ask for just a wee drop of milk and always went away with a pailful, would vow that that child was more than human. As if everyone couldn't see that!

In the spring of her seventh year little Erla took very ill with a malignant disease which no one could diagnose. A doctor was brought by boat from many miles away, and remained at the parsonage for several days. But the child did

The Cove Under the Hill

not mend. For all his examining and prescribing, she only wasted away, grew steadily weaker; her life was slowly ebbing out. The shadow of an unnamable sorrow began to lengthen over the lives of the Reverend Munch and his wife. Not all the power of their great love could bring life back to their child.

But unexpectedly, with the arrival of midsummer, she appeared to quicken. A strange ecstasy seized her, the source of which mystified the parents. In her singular cheerfulness of mood she would sing frequently, though with a voice too frail to carry its rich freight of joy. To laugh was not given her; she was too weak for that; but the smile never left her lips.

Then one evening she lay talking very sensibly to her parents, in curious question about the out-of-doors. Were there many rockroses in the meadow? she wondered. And had the eider ducks got ducklings yet? She would soon be well now, she assured them—she could feel it unmistakably. . . . The evening was one of surpassing beauty, and Erla pleaded with them to take her out into the garden, where she might look at the sun and the deep sea. 'Twouldn't hurt her, she implored . . . only do her good . . . she knew it would! Soon the summer would be so far spent that the sun would be hiding itself at night; then she'd have to wait another whole year before she could see its glory at midnight. Tonight it was warm and beautiful . . . they might know it would do her good to be out.

The father, fearful, threw questioning eyes upon the mother. But he found that she wished to please the child. So they carried her out, carefully wrapped in warm blankets, and propped her up on a garden bench which stood between two birches. From here she had a full view of the ocean. When they had got her seated, she became unusually bright and animated. She chattered and chuckled, and seemed almost to be her old self again.

5

The Boat of Longing

That night little Erla died. Death came very instantly. She was sitting between her father and mother, holding each by the hand and smiling radiantly toward the lowering sun. When it had dropped as far down as it would go, she raised herself up and, drawing her arms away, stretched them out like a bird about to take flight. Pointing seaward, she exclaimed in a high clear voice:

"The boat! See the boat!"

And then, sinking against her mother, she was no more.

The story of little Erla's death went out among the people and might often be heard, very probably because it concerned the minister's own child. But thereafter many claimed to have seen the boat that evening.

Then, too, there was the story about Johanne Ness. Years ago that was said to have happened; though the elders remembered it, as did some of the young—such of them as, walking under the affliction of a secret love, knew of life's dismay.

Ness is the name of a peninsula in northern Helgeland. There was a cotter's plot on it, which belonged to the Dunjarness estate; and near the extreme point, a fisherman's hut. A couple and their only child, a daughter named Johanne, lived there.

When Johanne was grown she went up to Dunjarness as a second maid. She was a comely and capable lass, and so faithful in every way that before very long she was the mistress's most trusted servant.

It was during her service here that she became betrothed to Per Tenholmen, the head hired man. Now Per was as fine a young man as had ever walked in through the portals of Dunjarness church; and Johanne, if anything, was fully as fine a girl. Self-evident, said folk, that life would be kind to the pair. And for two whole summers they had been lovers . . . and life had been replete with earthly happiness.

But with the third fall of their service a new head dairy-

6

The Cove Under the Hill

maid came to the place. She arrived directly from Salten, a large farm to the north. Her name was Katrine, but with Lapp blood in her veins, she soon got the nickname *Finne-Katrine*.[1]

She hadn't been at Dunjarness long before the tongues commenced wagging. It wasn't that her work was at fault, for, midget though she was, her quickness and skill were so great that the landlord himself had to own the dairy had never known a more competent head. Nor did she talk very much; inclined rather to keep to herself. But she smiled a good deal, and the word soon went round that there wasn't a man on the place could withstand that smile nor those eyes of Finne-Katrine. Presently, too, another whisper went round: Per Tenholmen was visiting the dairy somewhat more often than duties there, strictly speaking, required; and his stay, it was also observed, got at times to be rather long.

By the time spring was over that year gossip was rife. Katrine no longer slept indoors; when her day's work was done and the other help had retired she would disappear in the luminous night, and sleep abroad on the heath or in the wood, just like another wild animal.

Others too disappeared—she might have had followers aplenty, had she been willing. But only one ever found her . . . so it was whispered, at least.

At first the other help had viewed Per's infidelity lightly and teased Johanne about her rival. To think, said they, that she'd let a Lapp run away with her sweetheart. But such raillery soon came to an end, for when they saw how she grieved they at once held their peace; one and another among them thought he knew what it meant to feel love's hurt in his heart. And instead they had compassion for her who went among them so silent, hiding her sorrow.

Ill-will began to rise against the faithless one. Finally, several of the servants undertook to hunt down the pair who

[1] The Lapps came from Finmark.

7

The Boat of Longing

stole away into the woods and fields—they'd see what they were up to, all right. But that gained them no good . . . there were far too many grots and ravines and hidden meadow patches along the sides of Dunjarness Mountain. And most likely it did not matter, for as unfailingly as evening came and the sun had lost its glow, the two would disappear; and then when the sun once more cast slanting rays across the leas to the eastward, with folk beginning to stir, the two would be at their work. Not a soul on the farm but was stout in the belief that Finne-Katrine had bewitched Per Tenholmen.

Gossip grew and grew; finally the landlord had to speak to both Per and the dairymaid. But matters did not mend for all that. Per, impudent, answered his master as though he were his equal; gave the landlord to know that if his work didn't suit, he could jolly well say so . . . there certainly were other hired men to be got in the valley. Whereupon the landlord walked away. And when he came to Finne-Katrine, she smiled so bewitchingly at him that he clean forgot his errand, and only stood there joking with her.

With Johanne the affair was plainly working mischief. When the mistress saw that she was sorrowing herself ill, she dealt very kindly with her and, taking her in hand, tried to comfort and advise her as best she could. Then one day, calling her in privately, she counselled her to take her troubles to the minister the next time he came for services. On that occasion she talked long and very earnestly to Johanne; Johanne must by all means speak with the minister, aye, that she must, for it was common knowledge that that man had acquaintance with matters beyond the Lord's Prayer, that he possessed power over the forces both of good and of evil.

The Reverend Mr. Fredrickson arrived by boat on Saturday evening. And then, after folk had gone to bed and quiet had settled upon the place, and Johanne had watched from

The Cove Under the Hill

her window the lad of her heart strike out across the fields back of the house and disappear in the wood beyond, she sought the minister in his study. She knew his habit of sitting up late over the Word of God he was to expound on the morrow.

Now the Reverend Mr. Fredrickson was a man of stern mien, very large and imposing of stature, and so stric in his ways that Johanne feared to approach him with her trouble. But then it turned out to be very easy, after all. Her story, once begun, seemed to tell itself; it was as though she were standing in the presence of her Heavenly Father, her words coming like prayers. Only a wee opening in the door of her heart and all her heartache and sorrow poured forth.

The strange part of it was that the Reverend Mr. Fredrickson was not vexed in the least; rather, seeming somehow to understand, he helped her along, friendlily, until she had confided all. Her story done, he came to her, laid his hand on her head, and began to stroke her hair. What benediction in that touch! It passed like a gentle stream through her body.

He drew a deep sigh. "True, true, my girl," came the solacing words, "one does indeed learn to subdue the flesh in this world." After a moment he continued: "Fond of him, were you? Not easy for a young body like yours to relinquish its hold—not easy, no. We realize that, my girl. . . . *H-m-n* . . . *h-m-n!* So you don't think it's sweet love which draws him, but the devil's own mischief? You're sure she's a Lapp, are you, my girl? Very well! We shall see—we shall see if she is. Damnable all the witchcraft up here! Better go to bed now. And mind you don't forget your prayers; say them uprightly, too, I warn you. This is a matter for both prayer and fasting." Thereupon he edged her gently out through the door.

For a long time afterward there were rumours and curious surmisings as to what had taken place that night. But little

9

was known for certain, except that just as Finne-Katrine was about to slip quickly and quietly in through the cow-barn door on Sunday morning, the Reverend Mr. Fredrick-son, in full canonicals, stood ready to receive her. Taking her by the arm, he conducted her into his study, where she remained for nearly an hour. And did that place ever rumble and crackle while she was within! Well, folk hoped to tell that it did! . . .

The following week Finne-Katrine left Dunjarness; just where she went no one could say. Except that one must have known, for almost immediately Per Tenholmen also gave notice and left. The first wind that came of them was that they were married and had settled in Sandvær, where they had got themselves a fisherman's cot on an outlying island.

From the day of that rumour, Johanne was never her-self. She wasted away, seemed to be shrivelling up; and her eyes dulled. In the performance of her tasks there was prob-ably no difference, but there were times when she was most certainly queer. She might strike off and be gone for a day or two; then upon her return she would seem quite normal again. But she seldom talked to any one. The cross she bore she kept to herself.

At the end of her year she gave up her situation at Dun-jarness and moved home to her parents. Thereafter, the stories about her were many. On spring, summer, and early fall nights she was almost always to be seen abroad. A huge crag, familiar to fishermen as a landmark, terminated the peninsula on which she lived. On the one side it sloped gently into the sea, but dropped sheer on the other. This scar was usually her haunt on clear nights. On one occasion shortly after her return to Ness she had nearly frightened the life out of the cotter folk. About midnight she had come running and begun calling in through the window that they must hurry and come out. The boat was now lying out there,

The Cove Under the Hill

waiting for her. They must row her out, so she could get on board. When the people saw her they found her red-eyed and panting breathlessly; she talked fast and importunately. They must hurry, so she could catch the boat!

— Catch what? Where did she want to go?

— Where? Couldn't they see the boat lying in the lane, waiting for her? . . . She had heard them calling her a little while ago.

The cottagers looked and looked, scanned the waters in every direction, but they sought in vain. The sea was barren, save for the flocks of eider ducks which rode the billows beyond the reefs. Now and then a solitary gull would wing its way seaward, or a cormorant would lift itself ponderously from some outlying rock. But that was all. . . .

She was the victim of many such spells, during which she would see so much. But particularly the boat. When it got beyond the point of endurance, she would seek the cottager's wife at Ness and complain bitterly to her. And almost invariably it was about the boat yonder in the sea, which lay waiting for her. 'Twas the Lord had sent it, she said. It was to take her to the fair land of Love; aye, even now it was thither bound. It only waited for her . . . couldn't continue till she came on board. Wasn't it terrible to think that there was so little kindness among people that no one would row her out? When they knew so well that she was going to that country? Could they not take pity on her?

And the cottager's wife, humouring her, would nod "aye, aye," to all she said; then Johanne would find relief in tears and the spell would pass.

But one luminous spring night, when the wind blew hard from the north, and the scud drove nebulous before the storm at sea, when gull after gull sallied out across the racing sea-caps and the billows boomed hollowly, Johanne

The Boat of Longing

Ness disappeared. No one witnessed her going. No one ever found her. Seldom does the sea give back what it takes. . . . Truly, love's hurt is great in some hearts.

II

Then one year folk were startled by an occurrence up here:

Miles from the mainland in these northern waters lies a lonely little fishing station . . . where a few small islands and a lot of bald rocks have planked themselves down. In a tempest the sea will fairly inundate them. Round about, like a wreath, lie skerries and reefs. Upon these the surf breaks constantly; even in a dead calm long washings crawl up the rocks.

The station is not visible from any lower level of the coast; but if on a clear day one is willing to climb high enough, he may spy it rearing itself sufficiently above the water to be seen. Nor has it ever been inhabited. But there is a lone booth there, built for the use of those whose fishing-ground it is in spring and summer.

Early in the summer a company of fishermen coming up under the islands caught sight of a ship jammed in between two perpendicular walls of rock. They steered their course upon it, but found only the top wedged into the fissure. The bottom was dashed out; and the cargo, if there had been one, must long since have been washed away. The name plate, however, remained, and they took it with them. Then they went on to the station whither they were bound.

When the men came into the booth they were met by an even more baffling sight. There on a cot lay a human figure, that of a young woman. Her cheeks were sunken; her jet-black hair fell dishevelled over her forehead; her eyes were closed. Whether there was any life in the form was not at

The Cove Under the Hill

once discernible. Besides, the men's wits had been well-nigh paralyzed by the unwonted spectacle.

Finally one of the men recovered his senses sufficiently to go to the stove and commence kindling a fire. . . . If she who lies there is dead, he was reasoning, she isn't likely to harm us much; and if she is alive, she will certainly need the warmth of a fire. . . . Thereupon the rest also fell calmly to work. They were grave folk, these men, their constant battle with the sea and its terrible forces having accustomed them to not a little.

Before long, the warmth of the fire permeated the room, and they saw her eyelids open, disclosing a pair of large black eyes burning with a strange intensity even in their lifelessness. Having prepared some coffee, they succeeded in getting her to swallow a little of it, along with some milk. Food, manifestly, she could not take. Nor could they get a word out of her; either she did not understand their speech, or else she was too weak to talk. When the men had done for her all they knew how they went out to fish. They left the food on the table.

They stayed on the sea for many hours, it being late at night when they rowed landward again. Near shore, they were struck by a strange sight. On top of a headland, in lone silhouette against the sky, crouched the figure of the stranger, her face set toward the sea. The sight of her up there as they came rowing into the cove may well have been a disquieting one even to these men, who were not easily frightened. . . . There was so little of the human about her . . . she looked more like a great black bird with its wings folded. The men walked silently into the booth and attended to the evening's work. When they went to bed at midnight they noticed that she had moved up to the highest rock on the island. The sun now sat low on the horizon, shedding a dim, peculiar light; its wan rays seemed to be searching her out, transforming the black of her figure into a bronzed gold.

The Boat of Longing

In that manner the summer went on. No one ever got near her, for she kept away from the booth whenever the men were within; nor did anyone ever get speech with her, since she let no one come close enough. But that she must be entering the booth during the men's absence was plain, for the food which they left on the table would always be gone when they returned.

Late that summer, when it came time for the fishers to leave the station, they tried to entice the creature with them. They beckoned, gestured, and endeavoured in all kinds of ways to make her comprehend what they wished. But without success. Whether she didn't understand, or was afraid, or didn't want to leave the island, they were at a loss to know. Clearly, she must be deranged. A couple of the men were, as a matter of fact, uneasy. Whenever they followed and attempted by motioning and calling to coax her to them, she would back away, moving from rock to rock like a bird which remains calm under pursuit. Now and then she would utter a sound which to the men seemed to be neither word nor coherent talk nor song. Yet there was a sort of musical note in it, too—long-drawn out and plaintive, saddening the mood of him who heard it. It was like the cry of the loon on late fall nights when it complains against rain.

The men were, therefore, compelled to leave her at the station. But when they rowed away, their eyes never left her where she sat high on the crag, till their vision blurred and her figure, smalling with the distance, merged with the gray of the rocks. Evening shed a soft glow over the sea and the gradually vanishing station.

As soon as the men reached the village they reported the matter to the authorities, who prepared immediately to fetch her. Whether demented or not, she must be brought to people; they could hardly justify themselves in leaving her out there to die.

And a strange trip it turned out to be for those who

The Cove Under the Hill

undertook it! Halfway out a storm blew up, so terrible in its fury that they thought the boat like to go under, man and mouse. It must be counted a miracle that they reached the station at all!

And there she sat, high on the crag as before. Nor was she less difficult of capture; when the men came after her, she hopped from stone to stone like a sandpiper. It was only by stretching a net that two of them finally got her.

Once they had her in the boat, she sat very still, though terror of boat and water was written large in her face. Most likely it was fear kept her quiet.

Then, after they were well under way again, a fog so dense settled over the sea that they fooled around for two solid days. When it finally lifted and they got their bearings once more, they discovered that they had drifted far into the north and were miles from home.

III

Off-side, on a long spit of mainland running into the sea, a genial little cove had hid itself away well out of reach of the great ocean. Numerous low islands stretched themselves in front of it. Even when the sea raged at its worst it was the securest of havens.

Here, up in the hillside, lived a solitary fisherman's family: Jo Persa, his wife Anna, and their son Nils, a boy but recently confirmed. That was all. Folk commonly called the man Jo by the Sea, which appellation, in consequence, also often got attached to both the wife and the son, though the former was so kindly a soul that many called her Mother Anna.

When the fishermen reached the village, and the question arose as to what they now should do with their charge, it was Jo by the Sea who spoke up, saying that he could take her for a while at least; whether he caught enough to feed

15

three mouths or four wouldn't make any difference. It would have to be the sheriff's business to attend to the rest; the poor thing must belong somewhere. Jo had been one of the company who lay out at the station that summer, as he now was one of those who had made the trip to bring her back. He felt only kindliness toward the unfortunate one; surely everyone must deem it his duty to show a little humanity here, averred Jo.

It being agreed, therefore, that he should take her, Jo stepped forward and loosed the rope with which they had kept her tied ever since they caught her. A strange gentleness came into Jo's great hands that day; he worked with care, endeavoured to soothe her with strokings and kindly talk; his face, looking straight into hers, had a look of utmost friendliness. "You need never be afraid of me," said the eyes. "No, no one shall ever need to be afraid of Jo by the Sea!"

In the instant that she was free she showed signs of wanting to escape. But Jo hurriedly laid a gently restraining hand upon hers and said, quietly, "Come with me now"; whereupon she accompanied him good-naturedly.

For a while her presence created an atmosphere of strangeness in the fisherman's cottage. They not understanding her language, nor she theirs, she only glided in and out among them in silence. But no task was ever set her by Jo and Anna which she did not perform. Her early awkwardness of hand they simply ascribed to her not being used to such work, poor child; but she learned surprisingly fast.

What her age might be no one could guess; but with good care and plenty of food she was seen to increase so constantly in youthfulness that Mother Anna, who sat observing her one day, was startled into exclaiming, "Why, I believe she is actually only a child!"

Nor were they altogether certain that her mind was quite right, for she might act very irrationally at times—whether

The Cove Under the Hill

from pure childishness, foreign ways, or mental weakness it was difficult to determine. Still, it wasn't so much her queer doings which made them wonder; rather it was the peculiar far-away look in her eyes, reminding them of a room, vacant in itself, but adjoined by one from which voices are coming. It might happen that she would set about some task she had been appointed, suddenly forget about it, and stand with it in her hands, stockstill. Into her eyes would come the look of one striving to recollect some important matter which he had forgotten . . . a tendency far from natural in one so young, even though she had undergone terrible experiences and was among strangers.

At first, curiosity to see her whom the sea had cast up brought many of the neighbours to visit the cottage; and then all they found was a dark-skinned, quiet young girl, with whom they could not converse. After a time it came to be generally agreed that she was the sole survivor of the ship wrecked at the station, though how she could have saved herself when none of the others had was something no one could understand. But since the great sea hides so many a mystery from those who live beside it, folk soon ceased to think much about it.

IV

That Nils by the Sea was not exactly like other young folk was a fact which his parents had known ever since the boy came into the world. He was content to be with father and mother, and because he was seldom to be seen where the ways of others frequently fell, he acquired, even in his youth, the reputation of being excessively shy. And being of so retiring a nature that he never sought companionship outside of his home, he came to be left pretty much to himself all through the years of his growing up; hence also he got the look of one much older than he actually was.

The Boat of Longing

But a first-rate seaman he did promise to become. Even his father, who was himself acknowledged to be the most intrepid fisherman along this coast, preferred him in the boat in times of danger to anyone he knew; it gave him such a sense of security to have him there. He observed with what joyous abandon the boy would meet an overgrown sea, and it gladdened his heart . . . well-nigh made him think the lad a stranger to fear; already, despite his young years, he was like the most seasoned old salt. And fishing being the only means of livelihood these parts afford, it wasn't to be wondered that the father felt proud of a son who bade fair to become the coast's most able fisher.

The dreams which the sea cradles are many and strange . . . it was these filled the mind of Nils and gave him growth.

Besides the sea there was really only one other power which had any hold upon him:

Years ago, while he was still a little shaver, his parents had taken an old pauper to keep. He was a fiddler, the fellow, and so expert withal that those who claimed to understand such matters frankly declared that his equal for fiddling had never lived. It was from him that Nils learned to play, and to love music. At the time of the old crowder's death the boy had mastered practically all the dance tunes his teacher knew, and had already begun on some of his own. To fashion melodies which people liked and wanted to sing must, it seemed to him, be the most glorious experience on earth. Falling into this train of thought, he would sit for hours with his violin. His eyes would then take on a new look, dwelling upon something far away, beyond the border of any land. Jo didn't like this fiddling, for whenever Nils sat thus he would enter another world whither Jo could not follow. Still he couldn't find it in his heart to speak to the boy; but he would be sure to fetch him some work to do, if he sat too long.

And now, remarkably enough, it was Nils who came to have the greatest influence over the stranger. Under his playing, as she sat listening to him that first evening, a new being stepped forth in her, dispossessing the old. A rapt expression came into her face . . . some one had entered the empty room. She stood harking to the tones; yet not to them, either, exactly, her look more like that of one straining to catch faint, far-off sounds, uncertain just what they are. The music ceasing, she laughed, an altogether natural laugh, the first one since she had come into the house. Then she clapped her hands, her eyes taking in the room with the delight of one just entering it. After that evening, it was easier for them to make her understand their behests; and she showed more intelligence at her work.

Nils spent many an evening with his violin that winter. Among his tunes, one in particular seemed to have a power beyond that of any other to affect the stranger. It was one he himself had now struggled more than a year to make out of what he had heard his sea-dreams saying. He had not named it yet. Nor did he always play it the same way, for it would come so variously. But the motive never changed. Strangest of all, sometimes it would cry, then again laugh. Nevertheless, it was the same melody.

The first time he played it in her hearing was once in the dead of winter. The fog had hung thick for weeks, and the air had stood in sour and chill from the west. Late in the day the weather veered suddenly; a mizzle began to fall and the air turned balmy as a night in June.

"The sea will be bad now," said Mother Anna, gravely, her face showing deep concern. "God keep those who must be abroad tonight."

To which Jo gave no answer . . . only sighed heavily, and laid his pipe away.

19

The Boat of Longing

That evening when Nils took his violin to try the song of the sea the tone cried in pure dismay . . . cried and cried until it grew into a great threnody.

Before he had finished, the stranger was shaking with sobs. She let herself glide to the floor, buried her face in her hands, and began to moan like one in nameless anguish. This distressed the others greatly, for her grief was heart-rending.

"Merciful God!" exclaimed Mother Anna, "it must be the child bears a great sorrow!"

"Aye, she is deeply troubled," said Jo, quietly.

Nils rose hastily and hung up the instrument. After a moment of helplessness he left the house. Outside, in the dark, he remained standing for some time.

In a little the stranger followed; bewildered, he took a step toward her. Hearing the sound, she ran straight to him, caught him tight, and clung to him as a sick child clings to its mother. Crying seemed little by little to ease her, and she grew more quiet.

Nils, not knowing what else to do, stood stockstill; his left arm had instinctively come round her waist, and now his right hand was stroking her face and he was trying to calm her with low hushes.

For a long while they stood thus. Finally, she spoke; then, realizing that he could not understand her, she took him by the hand and drew him into the house.

The moment they were within, she pointed to the violin and spoke again. Seeing that he made no move, she went and fetched the instrument.

"She wants you to play a little more," said the mother, encouragingly.

Jo hemmed uneasily—as old people do when greatly agitated. At length he said:

"You'd better please her. Though you might choose another tune." Again the throat cleared.

The Cove Under the Hill

Nils complied. But a deep seriousness, of a kind he had never felt before, had now come over him; it said to him . . . unmistakably . . . "You are a man now, Nils."

The solemnity of a great festal occasion crept into his playing . . . transmuting it, welling out of it, passing into the mood of the listeners until they sat there as though in some holy sanctuary.

When he once more entered upon the song of the sea, he thought about all the wonder and beauty of which it had sung to him. A joyous ecstasy took him. He heard the low hum of summer morn at the sun's ascent from infinity; he heard the deafening chirm of the birds on skerry and island and rocking sea; and the waves' gentle susurration along beaches on sun-filled days. Never till now had he sensed so fully the bright joy of the sea. . . . The motive was laughing now, he noticed . . . a deep, hearty laugh.

He stopped playing after a little, and rose to hang up the instrument. The stranger rose with him. Radiant, she seized his hand and shook it. They had never seen her so happy . . . the empty room had been filled!

Thereafter the stranger was a different being.

She had no more than seated herself before she was on her feet again, singing to them. Her voice rose and fell in the melodious accents of some unknown tongue. Now and then she would gesture dramatically; and her body swayed under the rhythm of the tone surgings. At length the little room seemed filled with her notes. They were living, those notes; left a peculiar awareness to linger after they themselves were no longer audible. This drifted about in the room, had life and fixed itself on the mood.

First came songs telling of pain and sorrow, when the voice quivered and shook, yet, was so pure and sweet and full that the tones seemed not to be minding their burden of sadness.

21

The Boat of Longing

After a little the mood changed altogether. More joy came into it, sunshine-and-pungence-quickened, as though spring had suddenly returned after a long absence and begun tugging giddily at all the dormant earth things. The tones laughed loud in sheer gladness.

So infectious were the many songs which followed in this mood that Mother Anna, who sat knitting a mitten, dropped her work into her lap and had to break into laughter; even Jo, over his net-mending, had to smile, though he strove hard not to.

But Nils didn't laugh; only sat in open-mouthed wonder and listened . . . stared and listened; saw the stranger, not so much where she stood before him, as in the song places.

When, finally, she seemed to have sung herself tired, a peculiar impulse seized her and she walked straight up to Nils, threw her arms about his neck and hugged him, just as she had done outside.

Utterly confused by the sight, Mother Anna again dropped her knitting; but her face betrayed no annoyance—for the laughter remained in it.

Old Jo coughed gravely; it looked as if he wanted to get up. But he didn't. Once more he coughed:

"Have a care now, Nils!"

Nils sat dead still, in a soundless room.

. . . In that wise the stranger slipped into the lives of the fisher family. No one forgot the evening's episode, but it was never alluded to again.

. . . Thenceforward that winter Jo by the Sea was an unhappy man!

v

Thus the stranger came to be like one of the household. Mother Anna regarded her as a good child whom it had

22

The Cove Under the Hill

been given her to foster. Jo, too, looked at her often and had his thoughts, though he never spoke them.

Except for her inability to talk, there was really nothing peculiar about her. Nor was that to handicap her long; she soon caught the meaning of single words and phrases, and as the winter wore on learned many of the shorter expressions. At times her attempts to talk might become very amusing. If they then laughed at her blundering efforts, she would blush hotly and immediately change to another language, which, though wholly unintelligible to them, poured none the less as easily over her lips as water does over a falls.

They had never called her by any name; had only referred to her as *She* whenever they spoke of her. Then one evening, sensing plainly that it was herself they called *She*, she exclaimed, suddenly:

"Zalma! Zal-ma. Name Zalma!"

To the old people this sounded like a queer name indeed for a human; but to Nils it rang like a rich, meaningful violin tone.

The moment she had said it she gave an uproarious laugh; and when they tried to pronounce the word after her and failed because the foreign sound very troublesomely got stuck in their throats, so that they could reproduce only a piece of it, she laughed still more. Then she repeated the name.

That evening Nils sat very long with his violin, but, try as he would, he couldn't make the music come right. Finally he gave up in disgust.

Then something happened which Jo by the Sea did not like in the least. Twice he rose to protest, without doing it. . . . Not having these people in a boat, *how* was he to handle them? . . .

The incident was this:

23

The Boat of Longing

Nils, his fiddle put away, sat dismal as could be over a net he had taken to mend; Zalma was observing him. A couple of times she made an effort to speak to him, from which he comprehended that she wished him to continue his playing; but what further she might be meaning he didn't know, so he merely gave her a dejected shake of the head in answer.

Unable to make him comply, she laid down her work, went and seated herself on the floor beside him, putting her arm on his knee. She now made a third attempt, her large black eyes filling with a sunny joy as she looked up into his face. Then she began to sing, and kept on singing. That evening all her songs were happy.

When she was through, she again began chattering to Nils. Neither old Jo nor Mother Anna could understand a word of what she said; and as to whether Nils did, they were at a loss to know. But Nils stroked her hair gently and said, as though no one else were in the room:

"Oh, Zalma, there can't be anyone in the world who sings more beautifully than you do!"

A deep reverence was in his words. Letting his hand rest on her head, he bent over to have a full look into her face. As he did so, his eyes spoke a great "Thank you."

Immediately she gained her feet and brought him the violin:

"Play!" she begged, quietly.

Nils took the violin; but in place of acceding to her request he got up, returned it to the wall, and went out. He was gone a long time.

That night neither old Jo nor Mother Anna got much sleep. Jo was a man of few words who looked gravely upon grave things; when such as he reach a decision, they are not easily turned aside. He was now fully resolved upon Zalma's leaving. That night he said so to Mother Anna.

The Cove Under the Hill

But she set herself just as resolutely against it, saying that she could see no harm in the child's remaining. If the sea had cast her up on their very doorstep, it certainly wasn't for them to cast her out again. And the child seemed to be happy with them. Moreover, the time would have to come when Nils, too, would find some one to whom he would give his heart. Whether it was this child or some one else didn't much matter, did it? For one thing was certain—one would have to hunt far and wide to find a better heart beating in human breast than this child had. And it was goodness of heart that counted most in such matters, wasn't it?

This talk of the wife's angered Jo greatly. Could she, the mother, be wishing their only child so much ill? Was she really so indifferent about the boy's future that she could see no farther than that? Couldn't she see that all was not right with this person? Wasn't she going here practising her tricks on him, trying to bewitch him—if she hadn't already succeeded? Didn't the gleam in her eyes tell her that she was a sorceress? What? . . . Jo found speech difficult, his words coming by fits and starts through the dark.

But Mother Anna spoke up just as boldly, which made Jo all the more fearful. For he knew from experience that, once having made up her mind, she might be every bit as determined as he. From the witchcraft of that child there certainly wasn't much to be feared, she asserted. Didn't he see what a heart she had? Sorcerers and gipsies hardly proceeded in that manner—surely she was the one to know that! Besides, what was to be brought together, would, she supposed, be brought together for all of their interfering. The day would never come that she'd be a party to turning the child out of doors!

From that night on a peculiarly disquieting gloom settled over the fisherman's cottage. Under its roof went two good souls with diametrically opposite wishes for their dearest possession on earth. Fortunately, however, the conflict was

The Boat of Longing

so secretly waged that neither of the two whose welfare it concerned took any note of its existence.

VI

Finally, after a long winter spring came.

Tardy though she was in breaking through that season, once arrived, she lavished such dazzling sunshine upon hill and mountain that the eye, now unaccustomed to such prodigality of light, was almost blinded by the glare.

Upon every object here in the north she laid her hand. And she whom the sea had washed ashore was not the least to feel her quickening touch; she grew and unfolded like a bud; even the tawniness of her, energized by new life, took on an intenser hue, enriching itself to a warm brown.

Her songs, too, became joyous and strong. Moreover, she sang almost constantly: in the morning, at her work; at midday when she stood atop the hill, gazing after boats; but especially in the evening when the sun, blowsy and sated, lowered itself on the skyline. . . . Notes swelled and rippled with the morning breeze; rang jubilant through air quivering under the blue loft of noonday, but stole at evening more softly away toward the gilded sea, to be received and rocked by the waves.

The spring fishing had already commenced in these parts. Jo and his son Nils might now be away for days and nights at a stretch, coming to land only when the need of sleep overpowered them.

One morning when they were thus ashore, it happened that Nils got the start of his father. He slipped out-of-doors as soon as he was dressed. The air was still and clear; the day dizzy with the sun. Satisfied as to the weather, he walked down to the sea and began setting the boat in order. In a moment Zalma stood beside him.

"I go too!" she beseeched.

26

The Cove Under the Hill

The words transported him; and instead of answering, he merely gazed at her like one bewitched. "God in heaven, how beautiful she is!" he said to himself.

Impatient of his silence, Zalma grew insistent. "I too!— I go too!" she repeated, and started climbing into the boat.

"Aye, aye, as you say, then," he answered, his voice tense but filled with happiness.

He returned to the house to leave word with his mother and to fetch the coffee-pot and lunch.

"Tell Father that, providing this weather holds, he needn't look for us till toward morning," he said. "We're fishing redsnappers today, and trying for saithe tonight. Don't worry if we're long. I know this sea pretty well."

With that he was off. Having hoisted sail, they sped to sea before a breeze blowing cool from the mountains.

They fished all day.

Toward evening Nils rowed to some islands out in the seaway to the south. From the remotest of these, called Tenholmen, long reaches of banks extend northward. It was here that Nils meant to try for saithe. He put in to land, therefore. The boat beached, Nils immediately began supper preparations.

The primeval will rest upon an island lying thus alone in the sea. Nature's heart is felt throbbing in such a place. Here it smells of ocean, bird, seatang and kelp. If the vegetation is sparse, it has in compensation an aroma not to be met elsewhere in the world. Everything emanates a strong odour—even the snow-white shells upon the strand.

Life is fecund here, that which thrives above the waves; for in among the scrawny tufts of grass that have clawed a hold in chink and crevice the bird family has its home. More especially, the gull and the eider duck; but also the skua and the oyster-catcher, the duck and the goose; under the rock piles and in narrow cleft bottoms the black guillemot makes its nest. It will happen on such a holm that one may chance on grassy spots so studded with nests that there isn't space for a step. The intrusion of man's unquiet foot to molest the peace of this hidden domain will provoke an alarum which is truly deafening.

But all around such a kingdom, upon every side, laps and gurgles, splashes and washes, the restless sea. Eternally. Always. It is the song of the sea which is never silent.

Nils kindled a fire and set the coffee over it. Zalma meanwhile explored the island, carrying on like a child suddenly turned loose in a room brilliantly lighted and filled with the most novel toys. She shouted in sheer joy against the pureness of nature which came rushing so forcefully at her on every hand; she leaped from rock to rock, trying her strength; clapped her hands in delight at every new find. Why, this was fairyland itself with its countless wonders!

When Nils's simple supper was ready, he called to her; and she came skipping in complete abandon and whooping so that the whole wide sea fairly rang with the sound. She reached the supper place aflame, and began talking excitedly in a language which was so comical a mixture of her own and his that Nils had to roar with laughter. But he knew that now she was happy—he had never seen a human being so happy! And knowing it, he too became supremely happy . . . mood catches very quickly at times. In a deep bass, ocean-timbred, he joined her singing; whereupon she broke into rippling laughter, seized hold of him, and began dancing him around. Nils, bellowing, slipped his arm about her waist and fell in with her, romping as best he could with his sea-boots on.

. . . Out of breath at last, she halted. "That's all. No more now. My breath's gone!" she panted, putting her hand over his mouth to silence him.

. . . Then they sat down on the turf to have supper.

. . . Seated there, they fell into a strange stillness; had to be still . . . the ingathering Earth Spirit compelling it.

The Cove Under the Hill

It wanted quiet for the great miracle which it was about to perform.

. . . All sound died away. Even the red-billed oyster-catcher down on the strand had wearied of singing its ever-lasting *cheep, cheep*. He had tucked his bill under his wing, and now stood there asleep on a rock.

Their simple meal over, they walked farther in on the island, and up to its highest point. Here the island gave the appearance of once having been rent in two, a deep fissure in the rock running from the top down and widening as it neared the base. At some time or other a giant must have attempted to pull it apart with his fists without quite being equal to it. Spreading the floor of the fissure was a scrawny growth of grass interspersed with patches of sand.

"From here we could see the sun dance at midnight. Let's sit down," proposed Nils.

. . . And so they sat down on the grass, these two children of the sea, to watch the frolic of the sun upon the waters at midnight.

. . . Over their nameless joy had now come the deep quiescence of nature round about them.

. . . Resting against him, she began humming a song, softly and low, much in the manner of a healthy child about to fall asleep after its hunger has been satisfied.

. . . Meanwhile, deepening hues crept steadily, imperceptibly, into the lucent stillness surrounding them . . . rendering the silence yet more audible. . . .

. . . And the sun sank lower and lower . . . slipped insensibly but surely down upon the sea.

. . . Into the sun ball itself had come an untold diversity of colour tones. All of them vivid. And with all the light retained, but dimmed by their own intensity.

. . . Sea and mountain peak lay in a dull amber and rufous torpor; into which glided the gray rocks and crags of the island. Even they seemed to be dozing.

The Boat of Longing

. . . An eider-duck mother stepped slowly up the beach, and came waddling laboriously across the turf. It had its nest just below where they sat. Now it stepped onto it. Soon it too merged with the haze and was lost to sight, unless one looked sharp.

. . . Finally the glory ball out in the molten heavens had dropped clear down on the waters.

. . . And it looked as though the whole infinitude lifted to meet it, eager to embrace the treasure when it came.

. . . Billow after billow reared itself and stretched, kissed the sun and was showered with gold—to billow on, beatified.

. . . "Do you see, Zalma," exclaimed Nils, breathing heavily, "there dies Today? Soon it will be Tomorrow."

. . . Whether she heard him, he did not know. Perhaps she was sleeping. He could feel that she was resting heavily against him.

. . . But all the way from the sun out yonder and clear across to them a bridge of dull gold had been flung— shadowy at the ends, brighter in between.

. . . Nils was sure he heard a voice singing to him from the light out there:

> "Come now!
> Come now!"

The swells took the song and rocked it:

> "Come now!
> Come now!"

"No, not yet," was his answer. "Life is so beautiful now . . . life is so beautiful!"

. . . From the face lying close to his came the measured rise and fall of the breath. The child had had its full of play. Now it slept.

. . . Nils looked at the face. The lips were slightly parted. Bending over, he touched them gently with his own. In the instant her eyes opened and she threw them upon him with

The Cove Under the Hill

a wide, astonished gaze. Then her eyelids drooped again and she sank into a deep sleep.

. . . Nils laid the head down on the ground and got to his feet; he pulled off his coat and spread it carefully over her.

. . . Then he tiptoed quietly away to the boat. Supposed he'd better try his luck with the saithe for an hour or so! . . .

VII

When Jo learned that the two were gone off to sea that morning he reproached Mother Anna in a voice heavy with sorrow:

"That you should have prevented," he said. "You've gone and ruined your own child's chance of happiness now, that's what you have done! I don't see how you could wish him such evil."

Mother Anna gave no answer; she merely smiled to herself and thought:

"It isn't the worst that's ever happened in the world."

But Jo did not hesitate—he put on his coat and set out for the sheriff's at once. The girl was going; not a day longer should she stay in his house!

From the sheriff he learned that the authorities had without question been diligent in their investigation of the wrecked ship; they had tried to determine to what country it had belonged, as well as the probable home of the stranger. And their success was now practically assured, the sheriff added confidently—he was certain that they were at present on the right track.

That was all good and well, agreed Jo, but it didn't suffice for him. His demand was that the authorities come and take her at once.

To this he only got an answer so evasive that it might

have been taken to mean either *yes* or *no*. They at the
sheriff's didn't happen to be in a position just at the moment
to take a complete stranger into the household. The sheriff
therefore framed his words accordingly. He was of the
opinion that the girl, now that she had lived at Jo's so long
and had grown accustomed to it out there, would be better
off where she was until they could send her home. And he
would certainly see to it that Jo got proper pay for her keep.

Jo, thinking the matter settled as he wished it, returned
home immediately.

An interval of three weeks had probably elapsed before
the sheriff, accompanied by two strangers, also officers, appeared at Jo's to take Zalma away.

It was a beautiful day well along in summer. Neither Jo
nor Nils was at home, both having left a fortnight ago on a
three weeks' fishing-trip to the station. Desperate with
worry, Jo had finally seen no other way out than to get the
boy away from the girl.

The sheriff and his two companions came into the house
and stated their errand to Mother Anna. They had now
learned, they said, that the wrecked vessel belonged to a
Dutch trading company. It had been making a voyage from
Russia to England with a cargo of furs. A storm of several
days' duration had driven it out of its course; evidently crippled by some mishap, it had been dashed upon the rocks,
and had foundered.

The vessel had carried one passenger, they continued, the
daughter of a wealthy Jew, a goldsmith; not at all unlikely
that it was the very girl they had been housing this winter.
There was now an opportunity for her to get passage to
Holland. Tomorrow the fast mail-packet would be going to
Bergen; and from there it would be an easy matter to pro-
ceed. But it would be necessary to hurry, if they were to
catch the boat.

Mother Anna became so bewildered and dismayed that

The Cove Under the Hill

she hardly knew what she was about. Over and over again she asked the questions, just as old people do when a way of escape is not visible. Soon, however, she realized that there was none; Zalma would have to go. It would be a terrible sin to keep her from her own kin—poor child.

But to make Zalma understand what was happening proved to be an even more difficult task. They tried, as well as they could, to explain that they were helping her to get home. Apparently she grasped the word *home*; and when she finally connected it with herself, she looked like one suddenly come into the presence of a glorious light. She laughed, cried, clapped her hands, seized Mother Anna by the waist and whirled her round, as though storm-taken by an unexpected joy.

Then suddenly catching herself, she sobered and stopped short, every line and lineament of her betraying a terrific emotional conflict . . . her joy transformed into grief. Going over to the men, she commenced talking to them earnestly, yet commandingly, too, as though she were in the habit of being obeyed. Slowly and quietly the words came, but both voice and words had a persuasive power. They knew she was making some request.

Seeing that they did not understand her, she fetched a piece of paper, made some characters upon it which she showed them, talking excitedly and with much gesticulation as she did so. When this likewise proved futile, she looked about, as though in great distress. The men stood helpless, not knowing what to do; there was, moreover, that about her which involuntarily compelled respect for her wishes, whatever they might be. They marvelled that one like her could have got along in this humble fisherman's cot all winter.

Mother Anna, her hands folded under her apron, now came out from the chimney corner, where she had stood disconsolate and bewildered. Anguished heart understood

33

anguished heart, even though the spoken words were meaningless. In her simple way she told the men she thought she knew what the stranger was trying to say; supposed it was that the girl and their son Nils had grown fond of each other —though she really had no proof. Strange out here in this lonely place by the sea, she said, almost as if trying to defend them; very easy for heart to find heart when both were kindly. Indeed she did not know, she added, if it would be right even to take the child away before Nils came home. Though they who were officers must, of course, know what was best and right.

They hadn't much time to wait now, the sheriff explained, blandly; nor did he think her husband, Jo, would approve, if he were home. Besides, should matters be as she thought them, all would no doubt come right in the end . . . easy enough to get from one country to another nowadays.

But that leave-taking got to be a sad one indeed, both for those concerned and for the witnesses. The stranger threw her arms about Mother Anna's neck and wept violently; nor could Mother Anna herself restrain the tears, though she felt it embarrassing to cry before the authorities. And however it may have been, the scene became so pathetic for the officers also that they were unable to endure it and went outside meanwhile.

. . . But what must be will be!

At last Zalma was on her way. . . .

VIII

When the time arrived that the men's return from the station might be expected, Mother Anna was on the lookout constantly. The day they finally landed she was down on the beach, waiting for them.

No sooner had the men put to shore and Nils failed to find her whom his eyes sought, than he sensed mischief. Without

The Cove Under the Hill

tarrying more than a moment to strip off his sea clothes he leaped up the path to the house. The parents followed in silence. But the look that came into his face when he discovered she wasn't inside, either, terrified the mother. Going over to him and laying her hand on his shoulder, she said:

"Aye, my boy, she's gone now. But you mustn't grieve over that . . . she's gone home, you see—to her own people. Some day she'll come back; I'm sure she will. Pitiful to see her, poor child, she took it so hard."

Then Mother Anna began to explain, her utterance songlike, as is the way of Nordland speech, just how it all had happened; after which Jo remarked drily that they certainly ought to be glad she could be restored to her kin.

Nils vouchsafed neither an answer; only stared blankly into space. He left his food untouched. By and by he rose to his feet, went down to the pier, and began unloading the boat.

That evening the Boat again appeared west in the sea. Jo saw it. And Mother Anna saw it. But Nils was the first to catch sight of it.

It was a still evening with clear air. The hour approached eleven. Nils stood leaning against the wall of the summer kitchen, his otherwise erect and energetic figure looking listless and dull. Apparently he was far away.

Mother Anna came out and spoke to him, but received no answer. After a little Jo joined them.

"Beautiful this evening, too," he said, gently.

"Aye, if we only had eyes to see it," sighed Mother Anna.

All three stood watching the sun drop.

Of a sudden Nils was speaking, a strange distance in his voice:

"Now that's a queer boat!"

A chill swept the others.

"Which boat?" they exclaimed, with one breath.

The Boat of Longing

But Nils said no more.

The two fell to scanning the waters; then Mother Anna discovered it.

"Well, did you ever! If there isn't a white sail lying yonder!"

Then Jo got his eye on it.

Far out lay a vessel, right in the sun, where the eye would have difficulty in capturing it. Besides, it lay so extremely far out. It seemed without motion. Only the sails were visible. But they loomed very large and were of glamorous whiteness.

"Most likely a Finmark sloop bound for home," volunteered Jo drily.

"A Finmark sloop at this season of the year?" repeated Mother Anna, credulous.

"Aye! What else could it be?" answered Jo, his voice husky. Presently he went into the house; nor did he look to sea again.

The other two remained standing.

"What do you think it is?" asked the mother, moving closer to Nils.

"Hm!" A shudder seemed to pass through Nils. . . . "It's the Boat, Mother!"

"What boat?" she asked anxiously, knowing only too well what he meant.

"The Boat!" he repeated tonelessly.

"Oh, no, no, no, my son! That's only in old tales and such. . . . Come now, let's go in to bed; you'll have to be up early tomorrow, you know!" she pleaded with motherly concern.

Nils gave no answer; nor did he stir from the spot.

Finally Mother Anna had to leave him.

No sooner had she disappeared within the house than Nils made for the pier, jumped into the boat, and headed seaward.

Having attended to some kitchen task, Mother Anna came into the living-room, where Jo was preparing for bed. With-

36

The Cove Under the Hill

out making any remark, she went directly to the window for another look at the sea. Nils was already at the oars.

"Jo!" she cried out in terror. "Oh, Jo! Jo! come quick!"

Both father and mother stood staring speechless into the serene summer night. Nils, in the boat, was rowing furiously to sea, the spray spitting high before and a following wedge trailing the mirroring waters behind. It looked as though two lines tied to shore were being paid out from the boat.

. . . Straight on the Boat, discernible through the evening dimness, Nils seemed to hold his course.

. . . When he was lost to their sight, they still stood there.

Then Jo folded his rough brown hands and prayed aloud, earnestly, that God in His great might would protect the boy against all the damnable powers of witchcraft. Mother Anna, her head upon the window casing, was beside herself with crying.

That night was unslept in the lonely fisherman's cot. When dawn tinted the inland mountain tops the two were once more at the window, staring out. . . . It might be the Lord would again perform a miracle. It might be! . . .

The Boat was no longer visible. Just as the sun began floating upon the waters at midnight, the sails dislimned. The Boat did not sink. Nor did it sail away. A blur seemed to settle over the vision of the staring ones. When they again saw clearly, the Boat was not there.

In the morning the sea lay sleek. Not a billow rocked it. Only now and then a cat's-paw would whiffle across it, streaking a trail. But alongside, blue mirror-like stillness.

Jo and Anna moved about in haggard silence. Speech would not come to them; they had no heart for work; only pottered aimlessly.

Noonward they became aware of a tiny speck far out. Mother Anna discovered it first, but dared not mention it immediately. She was greatly agitated; besides, she might be mistaken.

37

The Boat of Longing

After a little, however, she grew more sure of herself and asked Jo to come and see, explaining very circumstantially just where he must look; then he too caught sight of it.

It must be a boat that was coming!

. . . Aye, it approached . . . it was nearing plainly . . . whatever it was out there in the sea! But why, then, did it dwindle so strangely when it was manifestly coming closer? The uncertainty was, however, quickly dispelled, and Jo fully convinced of its being a boat.

When he said so to Mother Anna, a fearful trembling took both of them, for they knew very well that no one but Nils could be expected in from the water. And prompted as by a common impulse, but without saying a word, they went down to the beach to receive him.

The nearer the boat came, the more puzzled they grew. They recognized the rowboat all right; and the rower obviously enough was Nils, the glint in his blond shock of hair betraying him. Still they were baffled—the boat rode very low; only the ends were sticking up. When it had come fairly close, they could see it was loaded.

Nils rowed in and pulled up alongside the little stone pier. And now it may very well be that both the father and the mother had cause to marvel. For the boat was filled from stem to stern with sleek, luscious saithe. Nils sat in fish to his knees; even the bow was half full. The boat barely floated above the smooth surface of the water.

Not many words were exchanged between the comer and the two on the beach. Both bade him, quietly, "Welcome from the sea!" to which Nils replied, just as quietly, "Thank you!"

"You certainly must have caught them at home last night," chuckled the father.

"Mercy on us! what a sight of fish!" exclaimed Mother Anna, slapping her hands on her thighs. But her voice had the quaver of tears in it.

The Cove Under the Hill

"I've often seen it worse!" responded Nils, calmly. "You've got some breakfast, I hope, Mother? I'm good and hungry now."

"Certainly there's breakfast, bless you! Come at once!" She was already ascending the stony path. But her heart threatened to beat out the walls of her breast, she was so happy for the boy whom the Lord had given her a second time. . . . And here he was talking as sensibly and naturally as though nothing in the world had happened to him.

Aye, and he asked for food! . . . The boy had actually asked for food!

IX

This is what happened to Nils that night:

The moment the mother was gone from sight, he was in the heat of a restlessness he could not master. He rushed to the sea, and before he knew it he was at the oars rowing, only one thought dominating him: "I must see that Boat." Goal other than those sails floating out there on the sea rim he did not have. It was upon them he held his course.

He rowed hard, yet seemed not to grow tired. Now and then he would rest the oars awhile and calmly scan the waters.

In this manner he continued until he had almost reached Baars Shallow, a vast bank lying west in the ocean. So far out does it lie that boats fishing there are beyond eye's reach from the low places on the coast. The old fishermen say that in a very turbulent sea the bank shifts. And so expansive is it as to become almost an ocean bridge.

As said, he was at the time near the shoal. Wanting to take his bearings before rowing farther, he stood up. To his utter astonishment he noted that with all his rowing he had got no nearer the Boat than before.

But he must of course be nearer; for he could see it bet-

The Boat of Longing

ter. . . . He stared in amazement at the marvel before him!

Out there in the sun the Boat lay. Aye, there it was, riding the ocean swells. The sails were plainest, sharing the peculiar whiteness of snow caught in sharp evening sun. They were even more dazzling, it seemed to him. The hull, too, he could now see more distinctly, if not altogether plainly, its colour tending to blend with that of the sun. The sails appeared to belly as before a wind, though there wasn't a breath of air stirring. And despite the great distance, he could actually see her dipping . . . up and down, up and down. This also struck him as being extraordinary, inasmuch as the sea nowhere showed any sign of a wave.

Still he couldn't discover that the Boat made any progress.

Nils gazed and gazed. And listened; strained till the blood whirred through his head. He was positive he heard tones coming from out there. . . . There! . . . No? . . . Aye, there they were again! . . . Not song. Nor yet the tone of an instrument. An interweaving rather of song and violin. . . . It came out of the sunglow. And from the sea. . . . It was there, and it was not there.

"That tone," cried Nils, "I must have!" A quick breath escaped him, and he flung himself down on the thwart and rowed till the foam frothed about the boat.

Just as he reached the spine of the bank he was brought suddenly to his senses by a deafening roar, breaking like thunder in front of him. The surface of the sea commenced to bubble. Completely dumbfounded, he lifted the oars and began looking around. And there the whole wide sea before him was teeming with saithe. The spray began spurting high about him, monstrous, beautiful fish milling the water. The sea in every direction fairly boiled with fish.

But then the fisherman in him awakened! Never, that he could remember, had the deep given up such wealth before, though he had seen a good deal for one of his years. In-

The Cove Under the Hill

stinctively he shot the trawl; he simply must see if they were biting, even though he was short of time. Sure enough, the bait no sooner struck water than the hemp began whining. To get that fellow over the gunwale would give him a tussle all right!

And then Nils, fisherman that he was, was seized with a love of battle. He could have shouted for joy!

Having landed the first fish, he immediately threw the line back, taking a stroke with the oars. Instantly another was on the hook, running away with the line even before it had straightened decently. Nils hauled in saithe till the perspiration streamed from him.

Yet in the midst of the wild joy of battle the consciousness of his goal stood clearly before him: he was heading straight for the Boat. "Just keep going, keep going," it told him. "You're soon there!"

. . . After a time he thought: "I must be nearly there now." Thereupon he threw line and sinker and let go.

He rose to look. Carefully his eye searched the sea rim. Not an object in sight anywhere—no, not so much as a chip! All he could see was a flock of drakes floating in the sunbridge. Now and then one of them would lift and flap his wings. . . . "How odd!" thought Nils. And he laughed, half in wonder, half in disgust.

He didn't, however, get much time for reflecting. A monster saithe snatched the bait the moment it struck water and started off with the line. Nils jumped up, stepped on the line as he did so, got his foot caught in the loop of it, and was nearly hauled overboard. That compelled him to collect his wits.

Having got the monster in, he gave a pull on one oar, swinging the boat just enough to enable him to keep an eye on the place out yonder. But the sea showed no object. . . . Still he wasn't greatly intent on it, either, his mind only dimly conscious of the distance. What really mattered now was to make the most of his time while the fish were biting. From long experience he knew they would go under when day took to coming in earnest.

. . . Thereupon Nils abandoned himself wholly to the mad joy of the fight.

x

Zalma was never mentioned again in the little fisherman's cottage at Vaag; the parents took care not to do it as long as Nils kept silence. But with him out of hearing, she was frequently on their lips; and it was always Mother Anna who began.

Nor did they ever allude to the Boat again, though Mother Anna could not get free of the thought of it; the sight had been too remarkable. Many times she caught herself on the point of asking Nils what he had been doing that night; but the question never slipped out, some strange restraint preventing it.

. . . Apparently all was as before. Events, so far as Jo and Anna could see, had not affected Nils; he bore himself exactly as he had always done. Mother Anna thought he talked less, that was all. Seldom that he began a conversation now.

It is late autumn and the beginning of winter, the season just before Christmas, when the gloom of awful, ingathering night begins to weigh heavily upon every object, that people mind most here in the north. It is as though some dark foreboding passes through nature and people alike, announcing that the sun is about to undertake a long journey from which it can never return. The fog is murkier, the rain more petulant and sour, and the storm wind more mournfully weird against the mountain walls. Even the gray cliffs get a more dismal look from staring into the desolation.

But when the darkness now began deepening in earnest,

The Cove Under the Hill

both parents could see that Nils wasn't the same. He was no longer the manly boy, with the kindly, intelligent face and sensible outlook.

A peculiar restlessness had come upon him. Not that he was less good-natured or kind than before; nor less brave on the sea. But a sort of indifference had got into him; he was so reckless in moments of danger. It actually looked at times as if he would like to see the boat go under, a spirit at which Jo, veteran salt though he was, shuddered. He knew that people exhibiting it were usually the prey of some unhappiness. That they seldom grew old he also knew.

One day late in autumn when father and son lay far out, pulling in lines, a terrible northwest tempest blew up. Nils was pulling; the father was manœuvring the boat. The moment the storm overtook them Jo proposed that they cut the lines and head for shore, but Nils wouldn't hear of it. This weather was no worse than they could manage. When, finally, the lines were in and they were ready to leave, the father wanted to take in three reefs. Nils insisted that two was enough, which angered the father. Still he was reluctant to betray any fear; besides, he knew that Nils could be trusted to handle the boat.

But that turned out to be the most reckless sailing Jo had ever done in his life. Repeatedly he had to warn Nils to be more careful; whereat Nils only grinned exasperatingly and steered the boat straight into the most overgrown sea, nearly losing control. Time and again it happened. He thrashed the boat as though it had been an angry dog.

"Stop this nonsense! It'll never do!" cried Jo, enraged, once when the boat on its craziest course threatened to slew round into another sea.

"Ha, ha! 'S that so? Look now, aren't we going?" Nils righted the boat and let it hurtle. Then he tightened the sail a trifle more. And the grin on his face widened.

It was precisely what Jo saw in Nils's face that terrified

The Boat of Longing

him. From that day Jo by the Sea took fright. He had seen it so plainly, in an instant. The boy had gone mad! He was trying to sink the boat! When the worst blasts came, Jo would grab the sheet with both his hands in order to relieve the press.

The second time the father did it, Nils spoke to him in wrath. That had never occurred before. And Jo never forgot it. For it hurt him more than anything he had ever known.

They reached shore safely, however, though wet as ducks. Neither had spoken a word after Nils's reprimand of his father. Come safe within the cottage, they sat down to coffee. Nils's face then had a bored look. Seemed almost as though he chafed.

From that day forth Jo by the Sea went about with fear in his heart for the one object he loved more than all else 'twixt heaven and earth. But though his unhappiness mounted, he never confided his fears to Mother Anna.

With the growth of the dark time these spells of restlessness became more and more frequent with Nils. They were particularly noticeable in periods of extended lay-ups, when the weather was bad. The bored look would then come back into his face. He would seem weary even when he had done very little. He might upon a sudden notion throw aside his work and go out; striking the path, he would follow it to the top of the hill just back of the house, and stand there for long spells, gazing seaward. Upon his return his face would look more cheerful; but there was scarcely a word to be got from him.

. . . Otherwise, life went on as before with these three.

One day shortly before Christmas, when the storm spell had been unusually long, Nils, flinging down his net-mending, remarked that he guessed he'd make a trip to Vik. Vik was their nearest trading-place and lay a three hours' walk distant.

44

The Cove Under the Hill

The father glanced up, but offered no comment. Mother Anna appeared to be pleased, and helped him get ready. Fortunate that he wanted to go, she said; she was needing a good deal for the house just now, so that either he or the father would have had to go soon, anyway.

It got to be late before Nils returned. When they were seated about the supper table, he talked gaily and looked happier than he had in a long while. Conversation actually grew merry among the three and it seemed unusually pleasant within the cottage.

Then Nils announced that he was going to Lofoten that winter.

"Are you going to Lofoten?" gasped the parents, in one breath. Incredulity left them staring, open-mouthed.

"Aye. I'm going to Værøy with the Jörgensen schooner," he continued, in a happy voice. "We'll be leaving right after New Year's. I'm to have two hundred crowns and my keep till April 20th, which is a lot more than I could earn at home. Not a penny to be earned here, anyway, in the middle of the winter. Every bit I make will be yours, Father. And the work will be easy," he went on in the same bright voice. "You see, all Jörgensen intends to do is to buy fish and sell supplies to the islanders. What do you think of it, Father?" he asked, his face glowing with childlike happiness as he sought approval in that of the parent. But the latter's wore a closed look.

"What do I think?" Jo repeated the question: "What do I think?"

Then he lapsed into silence, and the shut look on his face became still more shut. Pretty soon, shoving his plate aside, he rose from the table and crossed the room. Having stood awhile in thought, he said, quietly:

"Doesn't matter a great deal what I, your father, think, does it?" A pause of some moments followed. Then, "Only I want to tell you this much, Nils: in my day young people

45

The Boat of Longing

looked before they flung themselves recklessly away." That was all; and he sat down to his net-mending.

Mother Anna didn't take the news any more cheerfully. A moment ago all had seemed so pleasant to her; it had been as cozy in the room as on a fine summer day. Then in an incredible instant all had changed . . . the bright coziness had fled, the room gone dismal and lonely. Here sat the boy, in whom their sun had risen and set for nearly seventeen years, announcing his intention to leave them soon. The light went out of her life. Finally the sadness of the thought became so overmastering that she had to lay down her spoon and leave. Out in the kitchen she sat down on the hearthstone and began to cry. . . . She remained in the kitchen for the rest of the evening.

It distressed Nils that his parents took this so ill, and his face again assumed the old melancholy look of weariness and boredom. For the first time in his life he felt bitterness in his heart toward human beings—toward his own parents, moreover. When Jörgensen in Vik had made him this offer, he could have danced for joy, and had accepted at once. It hadn't occurred to him that his parents could object to such an offer. Nor could he for the life of him see why this which was his one and only chance of happiness should look so utterly impossible to them. They were plainly unreasonable; didn't have his welfare at heart. Didn't they understand how he felt, or know what he was struggling with? Did they really wish him to stifle within these narrow limits of home, when his whole soul was crying out for escape . . . not to mention all those strangely disturbing forces which so gripped and bewildered him?

. . . Well, it couldn't be helped; now that he saw the way out, he meant to take it!

After they were in bed that evening, Mother Anna broached the subject to Jo. Ought they really let him go? When he was so young? . . . And in such a frame of mind?

The Cove Under the Hill

Jo didn't answer. But upon her repeating the question, he answered quietly that he could not see that it was a matter for them to decide. The boy was grown up—they couldn't very well compel him to stay home. And since he was discontented, they'd better let him try for himself. "Life seems to be that way," he added, wearily.

Such comfort was small help to Mother Anna—she could not dismiss the thought from her mind. Shortly after midnight she got up, dressed, lit the lamp, and went in to Nils. . . . He was not sleeping, either. She placed the light on the table, crossed to his bed, and seated herself on the edge of it. Then she began stroking his hair and face. She stroked and stroked.

. . . Her tears fell fast. The sight of them unmanned Nils completely and he turned his face to the wall and wept like a child.

An indescribable tenderness came into Mother Anna's hands. . . . She sat thus a long while. Finally, she got up to go. Not a word had passed between them. But they had found each other, nevertheless.

Shortly after New Year's Nils went.

XI

The Jőrgensen schooner lay in the Rőstnes Harbour of Værőy that winter.

Among her crew was a light-hearted, hail-fellow-well-met chap, a couple of years older than Nils. Peder Hansen was really his name, though he didn't actually go by it. He had, in fondness, been dubbed Per Syv by his parents, because he was the seventh child in the family; then others had picked up the name, and now everyone called him that. And it pleased Per better; of late, he had even begun to write it that way. "For," argued he, "it's never been known to happen that anyone with so ordinary a name as Peder Hansen ever made any mark in the world. What's more, the Bible History doesn't have any such." This last he usually offered as an explanation.

Almost everyone liked the boy. He was kind and very jolly; and he had a remarkable talent for telling stories.

All that he related, no matter what it might be, seemed to take on the stamp of personal experience. Wherever he thought it would fit, he would supply generously from the rich storehouse of his own fantasy. People would, therefore, often accuse him of lying, whereat Per would take no offence whatever; only dismiss the accusation with the explanation: "You don't understand this, you see; that's why it sounds strange to you," and then go good-naturedly on with the tale.

Nils and Per Syv became friends. They were the youngest of the crew, bunked together, and were otherwise thrown much in each other's company. Certain qualities in Nils attracted Per. His heart was kind; moreover, he was the most willing listener Per had ever had; Nils, on the other hand, was fascinated by Per's cheerful spirits and amazing yarns. No matter how long the yarn, or how much Per wove into it of his own invention, Nils never objected or found fault. And when Per finally did stop, Nils would usually put him a quiet question, and immediately start him going again.

Per had a brother, Otto, who had emigrated to America about a year ago. According to Per's trustworthy account the brother had done exceedingly well. He was now laying the foundation for a most glorious future for himself and Per; next summer Per would be joining him—that was altogether assured. After having made things hum for a couple of years, they would come back and would then be twice as rich as Jőrgensen in Vik. Their plan was to purchase a steamship and return with a cargo of American merchandise for market in Lofoten. They might, of course, do a little trading in fish while they were there, though he hardly expected they would. Most likely they'd make it purely a pleas-

The Cove Under the Hill

ure trip. . . . There really wouldn't be any need of them going into the fish business, you see.

The winter brought two letters from Otto, which, together with those he had previously received, put Per Syv in possession of an acquaintance with America that was truly astonishing. He would relate the most incredible achievements, both of his brother and of the country, particularly when he and Nils were alone, because Nils always listened so attentively:

— Otto was now in a tremendously large city by the name of Minneapolis, a city so unconscionably big, asserted Per, that one could, on his life, walk for half a year and never reach the end of it. For that reason the inhabitants had had to build railways in the streets! You see, they had to have some way of getting from one part of the city to another, and for them to walk such distances was unheard of. Adjoining this city was another equally large. Simply unbelievable what might and power there was in America!

"But don't people get lost in such a city?" asked Nils.

"Certainly not! We couldn't get lost. You see, there's a big building in the middle of the city with an enormously high tower on it, reaching clean to the sky. And in that tower there are chimes that play tunes."

"Chimes that play tunes, you say?"

"Sure. You see," said Per Syv, a quiet fervour in his voice, "we've got to have some landmark to go by, or we couldn't find our way. All we need to do is listen to the chimes and look for the tower, and we'll know where we are."

This about chimes which played tunes impressed Nils as being very singular, and he lay awake far into the night, thinking about it.

— And it was so ridiculously easy to earn money in America, Per Syv informed him.

49

The Boat of Longing

— Well, was he so certain about that? Nils wanted to know.

— Certain? You bet you! It was in Otto's letter, and Otto wasn't the fellow to be telling fibs, he needn't think. Times were very good over there just now. In one of his letters Otto said that this fall he had earned more in two weeks than Per would be earning this whole trip. And then there was pay day every single week. As soon as Saturday afternoon was over, you had your money in your pocket. "Be no begging and waiting for our pay when we get there, I'll tell you," vaunted Per Syv.

Nils came to hear a great deal more that was remarkable about America and the city of Minneapolis, where Otto Hansen was making such strides. Nearly all of it surpassed the most extravagant fairy tale in wonder.

— Take, for example, all those curious people one would see and mingle with: Chinese and Japanese and Jews and Russians, even Redskins and Negroes. Germans and Frenchmen were so common they weren't worth mentioning. In his last letter Otto had said that he had had a Negro shine his shoes for him that day. Those people were so black themselves, explained Per Syv, that it was easy for them to do such work. "You can see that, can't you, boys?" he added, confidently.

The time Per told this story to the whole crew in the cabin, the men swore he lied, or that his brother did. They certainly knew Otto Hansen, and unless they were badly mistaken Otto would have to black his own boots if he wanted it done!

Per Syv willingly forgave them for calling his veracity in question. It wasn't to be expected they'd know what eminence Otto had attained in Minneapolis, or what a figure he himself would be cutting when he arrived next summer! Per Syv merely laughed genially at their scepticism, and was straightway off upon other matters.

50

The Cove Under the Hill

—Verily it must be a land of wonders past all belief, Per Syv would often remark to Nils. There the most beggarly pauper could snap his fingers right in the face of the richest big-bug and do it with impunity. You bet you! Otto had himself done it many times. And it could be done simply because there one man was just as good as another, whether he had ten cents or ten millions. No bowing and scraping nor any such nonsense in America. Don't you ever think it! Here Nils could just see what Otto had written about this skipper of theirs—Jőrgensen. Per Syv went directly to his chest and fetched the letter to show Nils:

"Had that stuck-up merchant in Vik been in this country he'd have been hanged before the day was out for his airs. He simply wouldn't have been tolerated."

"Seems funny they can treat people that way, doesn't it?" asked Per Syv naïvely. "I'm not going to treat them like that when I get over; that's really almost mean, I think."

Nils, too, thought it strange. To him, Skipper Jőrgensen seemed a pretty decent sort; and he knew that his father was of that opinion, since he had on several occasions heard him say so. Certainly peculiar that such men would hang in America!

—And drinks could be had on every street corner in the city! Oh, but it was a splendid place, Nils might imagine. Men would stop on their way to work in the morning and have their pails filled with beer. People drank beer over there just as freely as they did water in Norway. It belonged to the order of the day; in America one was a free person. And the inside of these saloons was so beautiful that even the homes of counts in other lands couldn't begin to compare with them; and here they were frequented only by poor people.

"By poor people?" repeated Nils astonished. "How can there be any poor people in America?"

"Oh, you see, Otto probably means only such as haven't

51

The Boat of Longing

been there long enough to lay up a fortune yet," Per Syv explained. "For there aren't any poor ones, of course, such as here; Otto has said that repeatedly."

. . . "I'll tell you what, Nils," said Per one day, "when Otto and I come back with our ship, we'll just take along a few hogsheads of that beer which they claim is so good. Food, too, is better over there. Everything is. And they have such fine clothes and shoes. Imagine how struck the girls will be on us when we get back! Though I, for my part, don't intend to have anyone but Beret Ness!" he added, with a stout loyalty.

. . . "But the best of all is," said Per Syv one day they were down in the hold, salting fish, "that in America one always gets to be somebody—becomes great, you know! Look at Otto, now, who can talk English already—well, and all those other languages, too, for that matter, though he hasn't mentioned that exactly. But what I wanted to tell you was that Otto is now debating whether he should become a minister or a lawyer. Doesn't care to be either a doctor or a business man, he says. Have to suit himself about that, of course, but as for me, I want to be a doctor when I get over!"

These reports of conditions in America took hold of Nils's mind and began occupying his thoughts. He was busy with them by day, dreamed of them by night. Was Per, he enquired one day, quite certain that a person could become what he liked in America?

— Certainly, of course. Why, that was easy! Anybody could be just whatever he wanted. His brother Otto was now living with a fellow who was a poet. And that fellow, mind you, had come from Norway without a penny in his pocket—just like them; and with not a bit more schooling than they. And now he'd got to be a great poet! Wasn't it as though the place were enchanted?

— But could they be so sure it was all true? questioned

52

The Cove Under the Hill

Nils, quietly. Per Syv had no idea what a ferment he was starting in his comrade's mind.

Called upon to prove, Per Syv grew eloquent:

"True? Why, certainly! You don't think for a minute I'm standing here lying, do you? That poet's name is Karl Weismann, if you want to know it. I'll show you, so you can see for yourself, when we get down in the cabin. And to think that Otto, who was such a fiend for books, should come to live with a fellow who actually writes books himself! The kind people read, mind you! Isn't it queer? You can imagine Otto learns a lot that way—being the friend of a person who writes books! Isn't it just like a fairy tale, now? I intend to live with a good doctor when I get over—with one of the best ones!" he confided with great secrecy. "And then I'm coming back to Norway to cure all those who suffer. Be a little different from hanging round here salting fish for Jörgensen, I'll tell you."— Per's joyousness was truly infectious.

And Nils learned many another remarkable fact about America and the enchanted city, Minneapolis.

There were, in addition to Per's stories, other circumstances which helped foster Nils's longing to escape that winter:

The village of Röstnes had a very good fishermen's library, of which Nils, immediately upon his discovery of it, became a constant patron. His reading, however, turned out to be a veritable hodge-podge, since there was no one to give him advice. Some books he could understand and grew to like; others touched his very soul and would not leave him; others left him wholly indifferent. There were, for example, the romances of Ingeman; they played with his mood, like fairy tales. For Sir Walter Scott's *Ivanhoe*, not even two readings sufficed; he had wanted to read it again, and returned it reluctantly. But not until he read *Arne* and *The*

53

The Boat of Longing

Fisher Maiden did he find books he genuinely loved; and once he had read them, he possessed them for life. *Synnöve* and *A Happy Boy* shared some of the witching power of the two former, yet had it in less degree. The poem "He Could Not Get Leave," in *The Fisher Maiden*, he read very slowly. Come to the end of it, he went back to look at it a second time; then laying the book aside, he pondered its meaning word by word. Thereafter, the poem frequently ran into his thoughts. While he was at work in the hold one day, salting fish, the poem came to him along with a melody for it. Impelled to see if it would fit, he began humming it.

In exchange for *The Fisher Maiden* he got Carlyle's *The French Revolution*. But with it he was helpless, ran himself into a blind alley. He thought it provoking to have to bring the book back without being able to say, in honesty, that he had read it. Besides, the old codger from Vega, in charge of the lending, had the annoying habit of asking the young fellows questions when they came in with a book. Could he depend on their having read it? If anyone confessed that he hadn't, he would immediately have the book returned to him with the command that he'd jolly well have to take it again and read it through; when that was done, he might come for another. There being no way out of it, Nils set to work with a will, plodding his way laboriously through part after part. The book, strangely enough, had a certain fascination; when at length he found himself at the end of it, he felt constrained to reread some of the portions, and did. The book impressed one fact clearly upon him, namely that a whole nation could go stark mad, could lose its senses completely. He shuddered at the terrible thought.

All the books were alike in one respect: they took him away upon long journeys. He sped over mountain and sea to distant lands and strange peoples. Even *Synnöve* bore him out—Björnsen probably more so than any other writer.

Besides, there was his violin. Only rarely did he bring it

The Cove Under the Hill

out, for he was too bashful to confide in it when some one was listening. But whenever the crew was ashore and he was alone in the cabin, or only he and Per Syv were there, he would take it out. The tone would then seem to him richer and fuller than before; and he could get more mood into it.

One evening as he sat playing thus, Per Syv burst out:

"Depend on it, Nils, if you ever get to America you'll make a name for yourself. All you've got to do is to go around and give concerts and you'll be a millionaire right off! Americans haven't got time for such stuff, you see."

To this Nils gave no answer, only looked flustered and bothered, like a young girl who, having just come from a secret meeting with her lover finds herself suddenly discovered. Thereafter Nils never played while he and Per Syv were alone.

XII

Though Easter fell late that year—not till April was nearly over—spring had come betimes, so that when it arrived all of the lowland and most of the mountains were bare of snow.

The day broke with splendour . . . tranquil and clear. The Westfjord lay too languid to stir in the pleasant sunshine.

Most of the crew made ready for church. Now it is a good Norwegian mile[1] from Rőstnes Harbour to where the church lies in Nordland, but that fact deterred no man, even though he might have to tramp the whole distance in sea boots.

At a couple of points the road bears well upward into the mountains. On a clear day these places will permit to the eye a view sufficiently unhindered to let it take flight. Which some let it do; others get it fixed on the scree. It all depends on the temperament they have. . . .

[1] Seven English miles.

The Boat of Longing

Per and Nils were trudging upward together.

With their approach to the heights and the whole of the magnificent panorama beginning to unfold itself to them, Per's head began fairly to seethe with ideas and he found no end of matter for talk. Nils, contrariously, walked abstracted and silent. . . . What must not the top of the mountain promise with the view thus vast and fine already here, marvelled Per. Nils wondered, too. They then agreed upon the climb for the afternoon; that is, Per proposed and planned it; Nils simply listened and nodded assent.

They had reached the church.

There it stood, paltry, weatherbeaten, and hard-looking, with its silly little pretext of a spire, staring at an endless sea. The whole mighty ocean spread before it; and just as far as it very well could, the church had gone out to meet it.

. . . Within there was silence and the solemnity of a great festal occasion. The place was thronged with people. Men jammed the aisle from the outer door to the front pew. Beyond that point none dared go; it was not for any save the elect to approach the choir. Those farthest in front were embarrassed at being so much in the public eye. Their heads were so shrunk into their shoulders as to give their figures a hunched appearance when seen from behind.

. . . But today there rested upon the weathered countenances a look of childhood contentment, and of simple, unquestioning faith. Easter joy kindled in the blessed warmth of the spring sun. Death was vanquished, aye, death was vanquished! The thought gave comforting assurance to those who fought with it daily. God's own Son from eternity had wrestled with death and had conquered. Aye, the Son of God had conquered! Hence, no more need to fear! —

. . . On the strand below, a hungry surf kept rolling in from the mystic depths of the Arctic. It sighed heavily, and tugged tenaciously at the long-stemmed kelp and the seaweed.

56

The Cove Under the Hill

. . . Sea gulls hovered above, listening awhile ere winging their way outward.

. . . The redolence of spring hung sharp in the air under the blue-vaulted heavens.

. . . The sun scattered a glitter of sifted silver upon the pearl-grey mountains.

. . . And within, under the low beams, the tones of the hymn,

> "He is arisen! Glorious word!
> Now reconciled is God, my Lord;
> The gates of heaven are open,"

rose and fell from many throats.

Nils sat near a window through which a shaft of sunlight broke so brightly that he had at times to close his eyes. The hymn stirred him. The sermon, too. The theme, "Life's triumph over death," seemed in the simplicity of its exposition to bear him forcibly upward and onward to great heights where all was peace and contentment. When the sermon was ended and the others rose to go, Nils continued to sit in a deep reverie.

Returned to the ship, and with dinner over, Per Syv had no longer any zest for the climb. Nils didn't object; was, on the contrary, glad. Today he preferred going alone. He went to the skipper and asked leave to take the jolly-boat. By rowing to Sőrland, he could shorten the distance one-half.

That Easter Sunday afternoon Nils went into the mountains alone.

Værőy Mountain, from the Sőrland side, is not so steep as to be difficult of ascent, the trail running at a gentle diagonal across a broad expanse of grey scree, which disappears from sight far upward in the blue sky.

Nils had already got a good way up the mountain-side. At the last human habitation down in the valley he had tarried

57

The Boat of Longing

a moment, fascinated by the peculiar hominess of the place. Sidling close to a wee cottage stood a tiny cote, no bigger than a dwarf's house. In front of it was a little paddock, where a shaggy ram and four sheep baked leisurely in the young spring sun. The horns of the ram came nearly level with the roof of the cote. Now and then the ram would stop chewing its cud, turn its head, and stand blinking up at the sun.

Nils had halted beside the paddock. The animals seemed to have addressed him, and so he was chatting with them in a low, warmly intimate voice.

Then he had gone on, and had by now reached a fair altitude. Stopping at intervals to have a look round, he could notice that breathing was growing easier and easier; it was as though some power were lifting him from beneath. The higher he climbed, the more majestic became the view. The mountain he was ascending, which from below had appeared to tower above all the others and to dominate them, now sank into insignificance and seemed almost levelled out. It was, to be sure, still there—he could feel that; but the grandeur which increased mightily with the ascent quashed it down into itself.

. . . A thin cloud flitted past the sun. The day round about him grew chill and grey—the mountain below looked still smaller and meaner.

. . . Higher and higher he went. Perspiration anointed his body as with the smoothest oil, making his limbs and whole body very lithe and supple.

. . . Then the sun came back. The shine of it sent a warm, trickling sensation through him, pleasant to feel even if he was perspiring.

— At long last he gained the summit and infinitude. The sight oppressed him; made him feel like a speck. He breathed heavily.

. . . Off and on whiffs of air sped by from the southwest;

The Cove Under the Hill

like harbingers of summer's solar breezes they came. But
Nils did not notice them; the spectacle before him bore in
upon him too strongly from every direction:

Rising up to meet him in the endless reaches of the north
were the Lofoten Mountains. Moskoe foremost, in the middle of the sea. The Arctic dispatched a heavy undertow up
toward him to enquire what manner of fellow he might be.
In the south stalked the Rőst Peaks. Already in the lighter
purples, they were advancing on the deeper.

. . . Two thousand feet below him spread the fretful
Arctic . . . heaving . . . billowing . . . endlessly following. . . .

. . . Wisps of cloud hung low over the sea in the distance.
Nils sat on a mountain boulder and stared at them. That
must be Ut-Rőst, the Enchanted Isle! Aye, it *was* land he
saw there—drifting and dreaming!

. . . And were not those sails? Surely they were! Their
shape was indistinct, but they were white—looked as though
they stood veiled in mist.

. . . Nils felt small, and very strange. He gazed and gazed.
He must be close to God now. Aye, the Deity could surely
not be very far away. . . . His hands came folded, more
reverently than they had done since childhood.

. . . As he sat there on the rock, a terrible longing gripped
him, a longing to get out to the great and the sublime, to the
imperishably beautiful.

. . . And he cried. Aye, he sat there crying, not knowing
that he did it.

. . . And he prayed to the Being who had created all
things and had made the world so wondrously big and beautiful—prayed that He would let him go out to the great and
the sublime, so that he might live it.

. . . Unconsciously he stretched out his left arm and
crooked his fingers; his right hand began making movements
as though he were drawing the bow of his violin. Never before had he felt such need for expression in tone. Sitting

59

The Boat of Longing

thus, swaying his head, beating time with his foot, fingering imaginary strings, it was as though mighty flood-gates hitherto locked had suddenly burst open. Like an overwhelming torrent it came. And he heard tones in this mountain place, purer and stronger and more exquisite than any he had ever dreamed.

. . . He sat till the sun sank into the sea. When he went down, he walked as in a daze.

Nils sat in the jolly-boat, rowing out of Sörland Bay, clear star-night round about him.

The spell of the sublime lay over him still; yet he was busy with many thoughts.

— "When I get back home again," he was promising himself, "I'll go to Father and tell him frankly that I want to go to America. I'll have to say it, since I must go. And it'll be better to say it directly, once and for all. About the only way it can be done. . . . Father will take it ill when he hears it, won't answer for a while. . . . And Mother? Aye, what about Mother? When she's alone, I'll tell her. She'll see it. She understands better what it is I am struggling with. . . . After a while Father will say—'No, this you must not do, Nils. What do you want in America? We've got boats, and gear,' he will say; 'besides, we're not exactly destitute otherwise, either. What do you want to go to America for? Whom shall I get to handle the boat, if you leave? And what's to become of us two, if you desert us in our old age?' "

. . . Nils slackened his speed. He kept turning the words in his mind, examining them closely.

After a bit he found a solution:

"I'll answer: 'Father, you are now so far along in years that you ought to stop slaving your life away on the sea. You've no longer any need to. What you and Mother want to do is to hire some good girl to stay with you, one who

60

The Cove Under the Hill

will look after you and be kind to you. I'll send the money for paying her—aye, every month I'll send it, so you'll not require to use your own.' That's how I'll answer Father.

"And then I'll tell both of them that after a time I'll be coming home again; I've certainly no intention of staying for good—I like the sea much too well for that. But I'll have to become what I want to first." . . . The oars were still again. "Though I needn't mention that yet. . . . There can be no harm in my withholding that from Father, surely?

. . . "Nor shall my being gone make the least bit of difference—that, too, I shall tell them. It will be exactly as it would be with me at home—or, as it has been while I've been away this winter. Every week they'll have their letter, so they'll know all about me—providing, of course, that I get on fairly well.

. . . "After a couple of years I'll most likely return; and then if it's in the power of anyone on this earth to make life pleasant for others, I'll, make it so for Mother and Father—I certainly will!" Nils gave a vigorous tug at the oars.

. . . "Perhaps I'd better leave in the evening, though . . . I needn't say the precise hour, of course. That's not deceiving, surely? Leastways not when they know that I'm leaving? Be easier that way."

Nils's thoughts kept running in this vein as he rowed back to the ship that night.

XIII

The joy of Jo by the Sea and Mother Anna when Nils returned from Lofoten late in April was so great that it would have done the heart of anyone good to see it. Cheer and a genial warmth now filled the cottage round which spring had already begun to hum softly.

Mother Anna trotted about full of chat and questions;

61

The Boat of Longing

prepared the food she knew Nils liked the best; stole into his bedroom early in the morning those first days to have a peep at him while he slept. It seemed almost as though it were difficult for her to believe that this strapping fellow who lay there so tanned and weathered by wind and sun was her own boy. "Dear me, how handsome and splendid he is!" she sighed as she tiptoed out again. "May Heaven bless him and make him happy!"

Four months had wrought great changes in Nils—that both the mother and father could see. The old Nils, the one they had known, was there, and yet he was not there. A newness clothed him; but it was like a diaphanous garment through which the old Nils could still be seen and recognized. His familiarity or unfamiliarity all depended on how one took him. The truth of the matter was that living among strangers had matured him greatly and made him more manlike.

But if the mother was proud and happy, then the father was even more so, though he didn't say much about it. An extraordinary impatience to be on the sea was over him—he wanted to fare it constantly, whether there was fish to be had or not. And Nils seemed pleased enough. But one never saw the father take the seat in the stern now. Oh no, that place belonged to Nils. Thereby Jo showed his son the greatest honour one fisherman can show another; because that was recognizing him as a superior. Not that Jo hadn't let Nils take charge before; but it had always been for the purpose of teaching him. Now the motive was altogether different: the father took his place in the stem as the lesser of the two. Nils, understanding, grew under the privilege. Yet he was bothered by it, too, and on one occasion when they stepped into the boat he bade his father take his place aft so that he himself could try his strength on the fore oars. Jo wouldn't hear of it! "No," said he, "handling oars will be about all I'm good for now; that's why I'm leaving the

The Cove Under the Hill

rest to you. . . . You could perhaps find a spryer man than I to assist you in the boat, if you wanted to; but you'll not find one better acquainted with these waters. And that's somewhat, too, I can tell you," he added, proudly.

Nils could feel how genuinely happy his father was, for it was seldom that he spoke this much of himself.

They seined and they trawled. Their methods failing in one part of the sea, they would move elsewhere. Every time the father hit upon a new idea, Nils would immediately say, "Aye, let's try it!" And so they did. Father and son lay there splashing and tossing exactly like two happy school-boys on the jolliest summer holiday.

When they pulled in to shore, Mother Anna was almost certain to be standing on the beach to bid them welcome from the sea. She was like a child in her joy over having such a husband and son. Up in the cottage the coffee-pot would be simmering on the hearth, waiting for them; and there was always some goody or other in reserve for them. Jo, noticing it, would chuckle contentedly, "I can't but think you intend to have us eat ourselves out of house and home, Mother!"

"Well, who cares about that?" she would counter, laughing.

Happiness like it had scarcely been known within that fisherman's cot these eighteen years—not since the memorable day when Nils was born.

. . . Then, caught up on sleep, father and son would set out again.

. . . Gradually the seam of light began to work its way upward. Spells of rain and drizzle became shorter. Days lengthened; nights grew luminous. It was as though life's purest joy had hunted out this fisherman's cot and set up his quarters there.

The spring's catch was not of the largest, and Nils complained at times. Then Jo would rebuke him, saying: "Don't

63

The Boat of Longing

complain of this fishing; it could easily be worse. As long as the boat keeps the pot boiling at home we've no right to grumble."

Matters had lasted thus for about three weeks when a change set in and a peculiar uneasiness began to take hold of the parents. Jo got it first, but he made no immediate divulgence. Then Mother Anna gave in to it. And the warranting circumstance was such a trivial one—only that chest of Nils's.

The chest was still at the quay in Vik, where Nils had left it upon his return from Lofoten. Having carried it into a corner, he had asked Jørgensen if it might stand there meanwhile. "Certainly," the merchant had said; "leave it there till next year's trip if you like. With the chest on board I'll likely get the man too!" he had jested. The skipper had evidently been well satisfied with Nils and would like to hire him again. He later said so to Jo by the Sea in the presence of several.

Then one drizzly afternoon, about three weeks after Nils's return, Jo hinted that it might be just as well to make a trip to Vik and get the chest. It wasn't so heavy but that they could manage between them. And then they'd have it . . . just the job for a day like this. Were they to fetch it by boat, it would take them a good half-day, which they couldn't afford in fair weather. Old Jo laughed as he said it.

Nils turned the proposal into a joke. "Oh no, Father. I'll not haul that empty chest over hill and dale, don't you ever think it! Wouldn't we two cut a fine figure dragging that thing! No, today I want to stay home and be lazy."

That dismissed the matter for the time being. But Jo was a man of precision, and careful of his possessions. The thought of the chest, therefore, came to his mind again and again.

Later, on a still evening when father and son lay just beyond the skerries, setting lines, a neighbour chanced to come rowing by; he was on the way to Vik with a boatload

The Cove Under the Hill

of stockfish. Resting on his oars, he greeted them and enquired about the catch. It thereupon occurred to Jo that
this would be an excellent chance to get the chest home; the
neighbour could toss it into his boat and set it ashore on his
return—he would be passing directly by their pier, anyway.
Without consulting Nils, Jo simply asked the neighbour to
do them this favour.

"No," called Nils, incisively, "don't you bother about that
chest! Just let it stand. I'll likely be going in by boat myself
one of these days, and then I can bring it."

Jo was at a loss to understand. Why didn't Nils want the
chest? Even more puzzling, What errand might he be having
in Vik with the boat?

"Why must you go to Vik with the boat?" he enquired,
astonished, as soon as the neighbour was out of hearing.

"Oh, I just thought it embarrassing to bother a stranger."

The father took a sidelong glance at the son in that instant
and thought he looked ill at ease. A premonition flew through
him. After that evening Nils was very taciturn.

Try as he would, Jo could not rid himself of the premonition. It was with him constantly, sat like a shadow back in
his consciousness. Before he was aware, it had augmented
greatly and darkened his whole life.

. . . He simply could not fathom what the boy might be
having on his mind. . . . Did he have something bad in the
chest? . . . Or what then could make him so opposed to
bringing it home? He certainly must know that the chest
would have to be brought sooner or later!

Now it really wasn't this which Jo feared at all. Far from
it. But the suspicion which alarmed him most he resolutely
said nay . . . steadfastly refused to entertain. Still it
wouldn't away, the insidious thing!

. . . Where could he be wanting to go, if such was the
case? The other day, when they had talked of a herring trip,
Nils had declared emphatically that he wouldn't think of

The Boat of Longing

seining! . . . Well, there was no place else they could go.
. . . And even if there were, why shouldn't he want the
chest home? His agreement with Jőrgensen last winter had
been specific enough, hadn't it? Why then all this considera-
tion now?

For several days Jo by the Sea went pondering the matter.
Dread gripped him and grew into a terrible anxiety which
tortured him night and day. And the more unreasonable the
conclusion he came to, the worse and more unbearable became the fear.

Finally he brought it to Mother Anna one night after they
had gone to bed. But his way was round about.

"You'd better speak to Nils about bringing the chest
home," he began. "It can't stand in there all summer. And
if we go out to the station later on we'll need it. . . . He'll
be having some clothes in it, too, I expect?"

— Oh, the chest was safe enough, no need to fret about
that, contended Mother Anna. It would get home sometime.
. . . No, his clothes were home. They'd be about all he'd
have in it, she guessed.

"Aye, but there'll be no harm in mentioning it. I have already reminded him twice, and I don't care to do it again.
The chest can't stand there, that's certain; it's the only large
travelling-chest we have, and I shouldn't like to see it
ruined."

Now that Mother Anna came to think of it, she, too, found
it strange. Moreover, she could so easily understand Jo's
reluctance to speak of it again, especially since such a fine
relationship had sprung up between the two. The man went
about fairly idolizing the boy. She promised, therefore, to
mention the matter to Nils.

Then at the dinner table one noon Mother Anna announced that Lorents over at Straumen would be making
a trip to Vik by boat in a couple of days after a supply of
flour. Why couldn't one of them run over tonight and ask

him to put the chest in his boat? Then they'd get it home and be done with it.

"Now what do you want to do that for?" remonstrated Nils. "Why bother others about that miserable chest? Can't it stand where it is until we ourselves go in by boat? It's safe enough, I'm sure!"— All afternoon Nils was curt.

From then on Mother Anna grew suspicious, too. But Jo no longer doubted—the boy was keeping some secret from them. Could he actually be planning to desert them?

. . . Another circumstance helped quicken Jo's dread. He noticed that Nils never missed an opportunity to send enquiry after a letter in Vik. And he knew of at least two letters which Nils had received of late. These, together with the ones he seemed to expect, Jo, therefore, connected with the chest. Thus it came about that Jo worked himself into a gloom which no ray of light could penetrate; and despite his strong and innately reticent nature the burden became heavier than he could bear. One evening he spoke somewhat of his fears to Mother Anna, though by no means all, for he wanted to spare her as long as he could.

And then Mother Anna lay piecing facts together and trying to look at them, until at length it became quite clear to her, too, that Nils was trying to hide some secret from them.

"But," she answered, in her direct and practical way, "it surely would be strange if his companions on the trip wouldn't know it, if he means to leave us for the summer. Why not go and ask Jörgensen in Vik tomorrow? He'll tell you, if he knows."

This was more easily said than done. But one must take the road that lay open; so next morning Jo announced that today he would make a trip to Vik.

Then came Nils's turn to be frightened.— What? Go to Vik on this fine day? When they had lines to take in? . . . The decision was certainly sudden. It nettled Nils.

The Boat of Longing

But Jo set out, and Mother Anna went with Nils to help pull in the lines.

Just as Jo was leaving, he stopped to remark, "I may as well strap the chest to my back and fetch it home, then it won't need to stand in there any longer. I can manage that much of a load."

Then Nils became alarmed in earnest.

"Oh, let that chest stand there now, Father! You know I don't want you to go carrying that heavy thing alone. We don't need it yet, and I'll be responsible for getting it home." The entreaty betrayed more than a concern for the father; and both parents divined it.

"Very well," laughed Jo, bitterly, "as you please, since you insist on having it there!" He turned and was gone.

Now there is scarcely any situation more effectual for bringing two human souls close to each other than that of sitting together in a boat of a fine day. In such a circumstance the one mind finds it very easy to unfold to the other . . . the two come forth to meet, as it were—seeking understanding, finding it, and being made more calm thereby.

It was thus with mother and son that morning. Mother Anna manœuvred the boat; Nils pulled in the lines. During the work both were too occupied for many words to pass between them.

But when they sat there in the quiet, rowing toward land, Mother Anna asked point blank:

"Are you thinking of leaving us, Nils?"

"Of leaving you?"

"Aye. Are you going away from us?"

"No. Not away from you, exactly."

"But you are going away?"

"Well, for a while I am."

"Do you intend to hire out?"

"No, that I'll not do."

68

The Cove Under the Hill

Mother Anna gave a sigh of relief. Such not being his intention, it couldn't be so bad, after all.

"Is it a seining trip, perhaps?" she came back, lighter voiced.

"No, it's not that, either." A brief inner struggle. Then, baldly:

"I'm going to America."

"Where, my boy?" Mother Anna held the oars; the blur made it almost impossible for her to distinguish him, though he sat directly opposite her, aft in the boat.

"I've decided to go to America," said Nils, quietly. His face was blood red.

Neither could muster a word. A barrier of leaden inertness filled the space between them.

Then Nils manned himself.

"You see, it's this, Mother, that I must go."

"You must ——!"

"Aye. . . . Because life is not in this place."

"But we're happy here," cried the mother. "And we're certainly not poor. . . . Whatever you want you can have." . . .

Nils became eager:

"It's not that, Mother. Even if we had a million and lived in a palace, I'd have to go. This to me is not life."

But then Mother Anna corrected her son, for to her his words sounded like blasphemy.

"Life not here, you say? It's wrong of you to say that, my boy. God has scarcely given a better spot to any man than the cove has been to your father and me! Especially when you are there."

Nils stopped rowing; his face puckered; then he said, penetratingly and very quietly:

"It's not that, Mother. Far from it. Nor do I quite know how to say it so you will understand. But life is not in this place—not for me—no, not the whole of it. . . . Not yet at

The Boat of Longing

least. . . . That's why I must go out after it. For it is that which one must find."

The silence again grew oppressive between them. She pondered deeply what he had said; as did he. Then after a little, quiveringly:

"And you'll stay over there, then?"

"Stay there? How you talk! . . . Haven't you noticed that spring returns every year? No more could I, in the long run, remain away from this place."

Another interval of silence. Mother Anna was not crying now, but the teardrops trickled close. She rowed with even strokes. By and by her words came back:

"What is it you are going to become, then?"

Nils was glad of the question—though he couldn't tell why; nor did he know precisely what to answer. His answer getting to be tardy, she repeated:

"What is it you are going to become, then?"

"Oh—that which is highest of all."

"The highest?"

"Aye." It came very naturally.

The heart of Mother Anna swelled at the words. They made it ache as well. When she did not answer immediately, he added:

"And I want to see the most beautiful. And live that, too. . . . Then I'll come back!"

"God only grant it won't be too long for us to wait!" Veering suddenly, she brought a question from an entirely different quarter:

"Are you still thinking of Zalma?"

"Oh ——"

"Do you think you will find her?"

"I have a feeling that I shall meet her."

"But she'll not be caring to come back and live our simple life now. She was plainly not of ordinary folk."

The Cove Under the Hill

"Zalma wouldn't change. The good was in her, and that can live anywhere."

. . . When they stepped out of the boat the mother said:

"Well, you must do as you like. If you've made up your mind, you'll go; but the day of your going will break your father. . . . You are all his life, you see."

Nils gave no reply.

. . . Meanwhile Jo by the Sea stood inside at the merchant's in Vik. When all the other customers were gone, he approached the counter and began ordering small articles. He took plenty of time about each.

The procedure was, however, natural enough, for Jŏrgensen was a great talker.

— "Well," began Jŏrgensen, when Jo seemed to have got all he required, "what has Nils decided to do?"

"Nils?"

"Aye. Think he'll strike out for America?"

Jo had quite mechanically set his elbows on the counter and was leaning forward. His chin now sank into his hands. A grim, furrowed look came into his face. But not a muscle contracted.

Jŏrgensen had to take notice of him. The man was looking downright pathetic today.

"You're not feeling well, Jo," he said, sympathetically.

Jo did not answer immediately. After a while he said:

"No—I've been a bit poorly of late. I'm getting old, you see, and the rheumatism plagues me. . . . No, I can't say that Nils has definitely made up his mind yet. But I think likely he'll be going."

"Per Syv and he talked of it last winter, I know. And now Per comes in every day the mail arrives to look for his ticket. Too bad, Jo, that boys like Nils leave the country. With fellows like Per it doesn't make much difference. But how can you stop it? When the fledgling is grown, it will take to its wings."

The Boat of Longing

"I suppose so. I suppose so," came wearily from Jo.

"Is it to Minnesota he's going?" There were no other customers in the store, and Jőrgensen enjoyed talking.

"To Minnesota? . . . Aye, I expect that's the intention."

Jo by the Sea was looking so worn today, that Jőrgensen advised him to consult Hoben, the physician. When Jo turned a deaf ear, Jőrgensen invited him to a cup of coffee. But Jo said, "No, thanks," he'd not have anything. . . . He'd be all right in a moment . . . just felt a little achy, that was all . . . as folks did when they got along in years.

Thereupon he started homeward.

He didn't reach the cottage until almost bedtime. Nils and Mother Anna, after having waited and waited, wondering what had become of him, had finally begun to fear that some evil might have befallen him. Then just as Nils was getting ready to look for him, he arrived.

Save for the worn look on his face Jo betrayed no inner disturbance when he entered the house.

— No, thanks, he wasn't hungry. No, he'd not have any supper.

"Aren't you well?" asked Mother Anna, concerned.

"Oh, it's nothing. Just a queer feeling that came over me out there on the road. It'll pass."

With that he went to bed.

Mother Anna looked at Nils. But Nils didn't meet her look. The accusation was plain enough, anyway.

The moment Jo was out of view of Jőrgensen's buildings that day, he had sat down by the roadside. Like one death-sentenced he had sat, all his bright dreams shattered in a single blow. How could Nils cause him this sorrow? He simply could not understand. And how happy and comfortable they were in every way! He could not fathom it; no, that he could not. Nils—who was such a good boy! Did he not see that both the mother and he were growing old? And

72

The Cove Under the Hill

that they had no one but him? How could he bring himself to do it?

After a little the bitterness seemed to leave him and he took his eyes off the ground.

. . . And there on his knees in the heather, lay a tempest-tossed old sea dog, beseeching God to bless the child he loved beyond all measure. He prayed, he bemoaned, he implored . . . and prayed again that God in His mercy and almighty power would turn the thought of the boy away from his folly.

But no heavens opened to Jo by the Sea and no angel descended . . . no, not just then!

XIV

The night passed without either husband or wife having mentioned what each knew. But in the morning, when all were seated at breakfast, the father brought up the subject by saying, very casually:

"You are going to America, I hear."

Both mother and son looked at him. Neither of them found words for an answer.

"Though I should hardly have thought it necessary for me to learn it from strangers," he went on. . . . "It's not very much I have denied you these eighteen years; and now I couldn't if I wanted to, I suppose."

There was in reality no reproach in Jo's words; nor did he want that there should be. But there was unspeakable sadness in them.

"Well," said Nils, "since you take it that way, I suppose I can't go." He gave his plate and the other dishes in front of him a shove.

"Aye, aye, we can talk it over and see," counselled Mother Anna, conciliatingly.

. . . "It's just this," continued Nils, brokenly, "that I

73

The Boat of Longing

feel I can never live my life completely unless I get leave to try. . . . You must understand that I kept still in order to spare you—and not from indifference."

Nils bent over the table and commenced to cry.

Then something happened in that little room. Something unexpected. It was as though all the obdurate in Jo had of a sudden vanished. He rose, went round the table to Nils, and laid his hand on the boy's head in benediction.

"No," he said, his voice now wholly natural except for its deepened timbre, "you are all your mother and I have in this world, which we really love. And since you cannot see life in any other way, then you must go. What has been ordained, must be. But it will be lonely for us two here in the cot."

"Now I cannot go. I can't bear to!" Nils shook violently under the touch of the hand on his head.

"'Twill come out right enough," Jo continued. "All day yesterday I went thinking about it. You must try what you've set your heart on—there is no other course. Better to have it go wrong that way. None of us shall go to the grave knowing that Mother and I ever put a cross in your way. Have you money enough to get started? And what about his clothes, Mother? Have you begun to see after them? We can't be idle now, if we're to get him off properly!"

Such volubility on the part of her husband so astonished Mother Anna that she had to glance at him repeatedly. And she liked him so well at this moment that she wanted to put her arms about him. But in that she did not succeed, for by the time she was up Jo was already outside the door.

. . . Now it turned out that Mother Anna and Jo both vied with each other in getting the boy ready for America. Old Jo himself rowed in to Vik after the chest, and Mother Anna took charge of the packing. She arranged and re-arranged—packed and repacked many times—before she finally got it all to suit her.

In a week's time Per Syv came to the cottage to enquire

The Cove Under the Hill

if Nils now actually wanted to join him. He had just received the ticket. With departure thus assured, the boy's enthusiasm knew no bounds. He talked joyously and continuously, and harked for the most part only to his own bright thoughts.

"Certainly, Mother Anna, we'll be coming back! What the deuce should we stay in America for, after we've earned all the money we want and have made what we wished of ourselves? Never you fear we won't be back! I intend to come in my own steamship, you see." Per's eyes gleamed with pride. "And then Nils can come along, if he's ready and wants to."

Per's happy spirits infected Mother Anna. Putting him questions, she got more information, a happiness Per Syv gladly gave her. Encouraged, he began telling about his brother Otto, who had done so well in America; and about the great city of Minneapolis with its wonders incredible of people and splendour, of food and drink. In the midst of which glory he and Nils were now presently to alight.

. . . Per Syv rattled on until the mind of Mother Anna fairly whirled with it all; until, indeed, she began to feel it almost incumbent upon herself and the father to do all in their power to help Nils reach this enchanted place.

When Per Syv was ready to leave she begged him earnestly to look after Nils; he must help him all he could, he who was practically acquainted over there already!

The day before the departure, the chest, packed and ready, was brought to Vik, in order that it might be there in plenty of time.

— But they'd better not come with him all the way to Vik when he left, Nils remarked to his mother—the trip would only tire them.

Mother Anna understood, all right. So she mentioned the matter to Jo and they agreed to arrange it that way.

The weather turned out to be very miserable the day Nils

75

The Boat of Longing

left. The boat not being due before eleven at night, he did not have to start from home until seven in the evening; even then he would have ample time.

During the afternoon the wind, which throughout the morning's drizzle had been from the south, veered to westward. And judged by the flow of the sea there was a bad storm brewing. The rain drove heavily.

At supper no one felt like eating. The table stood filled with tempting delicacies; and yet it was only to please Mother Anna that father and son sat down. No one would take more than a cup of chocolate, and that mostly for the sake of appearances.

"You'd better not come out in this rain," remarked Nils, pushing away from the table. "I can put on my oilskins and sou'wester and leave them at Jörgensen's, and you can get them sometime when you go in."

"Aren't we to be allowed to take you a way?" exclaimed Mother Anna, in a brave voice. "What sort of talk is that?"

Jo, without a word, put on his boots and oilskins.

Nils dressed quickly and stood looking about the room. Strange how its every object and aspect seemed suddenly to have become endued with power to compel awareness—not only the object, but its very position seemed fairly to come at him. There stood the stove. There the table. There the chairs. Over there was the door opening into the little bedroom. He knew precisely the spots where the paint had been scrubbed off, though he wasn't seeing them just now. On the long wall hung a picture of the thorn-crowned Christ, in a frame. Directly across from it hung another, also in a frame. It was of a ship, full-rigged, all sails set, cutting its way through an angry sea, toward a coast which lay veiled in a thin fog, alluringly mystic and hinting the gateway to fairyland. Infuriated breakers exploded against it. Beneath the picture was printed in bold Roman letters: THE VOYAGE OF LIFE.

The Cove Under the Hill

He had been uncommonly fond of the picture ever since boyhood. Bound up with it were all his imaginings about the mysterious craft which haunted this coast. For several moments his look lingered on it; and then, after a circuit of the room, came back for a second look.

In the wall, just under the picture, stood a clave,[1] half full. Beside it on a chair lay a coil of dry lines. In the window corner, near the table, was Father's Sunday pipe, propped aslant, just as it had been every blessed day since he could remember. Nils was aware of every little detail, though he really saw nothing.

Presently all three were outside in the rain. A little way up the path Nils had to turn around for a last look at the place and the sea. He stopped.

"Better tie the boat more securely, Father; she'll be bad tonight. Or would you like me to do it? We've plenty of time."

But the father didn't stop, and so they walked on.

From the three trudging figures there came no sound save the steady beat of their footfalls. The west storm screamed about their ears. The wet heather pasted itself stickily to their legs.

Within sight of Jörgensen's store Nils drew to a halt.

"You mustn't come any farther," he said.

"No," replied Jo.

"No," echoed Mother Anna, hollowly, "we'll not go any farther now."

Nils stretched forth his hand—to the father first.

"Thanks for—!" But that was all he could muster. From the strong face before him two gleaming eyes peered at him through the rain. So stolid and shut was the look of the face in that instant that to say what thoughts worked behind it would have baffled the most expert reader of minds.

---

[1] A wooden instrument formed like the prongs of a fork for making up a fishing hand line.

The Boat of Longing

The father took the hand, locked it hard for a moment, then dropped it; but not a sound escaped his lips.

Nils offered his hand to his mother. She grasped it, clung desperately to it, could not let it go. The hand not being enough, she seized his arm, caught him close, and began to cry so convulsively that she sank upon his shoulder.

"Oh—my boy, my boy! . . . My blessed boy! . . . God reward you for the comfort you've been! . . . And God be—!"

Nils held her until her crying, having stilled itself, came more easily, like a child's.

Then with a wrench he tore himself loose and went.

Having got a little way off, he had to look back. This he had not wanted to do, but he couldn't help it.

And there through the shrieking storm and driving rain he saw the figure of his mother, plain as could be against the murky sky; but not his father's. The mother was holding her right hand high. . . . He walked on, only to turn again. The figure had not moved . . . stood there as before, pointing skyward. The gloom and the rain were now so thick that the hand could no longer be distinguished . . . only the arm reaching up into darkness.

"I wonder if Father has left her?" thought Nils; he could not see his father now, either. But not daring to tarry longer, he went down to the store.

That evening many had come to Vik, as commonly happened on boat days.

Nils felt ill at ease and wanted to hide himself. But people whom he knew caught sight of him and came up to greet him and wish him good luck and a pleasant crossing; some soberly, others with much joking and laughter, saying they would soon follow. Plague take it! why should one go slaving here in filth and poverty? You bet they were coming! A couple asked him to write and tell them how he liked the country and how much he was earning.

The Cove Under the Hill

Nils said little to anyone; he stood and looked out across the harbour. If only the boat would arrive! But there was no sign of it yet.

Then an old man came limping toward him. He was halt and walked with a stick. A sou'wester drawn low over his head made him look even stubbier than he was. He was Ole Hansen, the father of Otto and Per, or more strictly speaking the stepfather of Otto, his wife having had that son before marriage. . . . Slowly Ole Hansen made his way toward Nils; extending his hand, he greeted him quietly:

"Is it you who are Nils?"

"Aye."

Once more the man, peering up into Nils's eyes, seized his hand and said,

"They say you are an uncommonly fine boy."

Nils only shook his head.

Ole Hansen's voice sank lower and came like sheerest music through the rain:

"Be so kind as to look after Per! Please do it . . . he's . . . he's so irresponsible, you see. And Otto never writes home, though you'd think he might remember his mother . . . For the sake of an old man, won't you have pity on me and promise to look after our boys? I can see you're dependable!

"Come a little farther over on the quay, so we can talk in peace," begged Ole Hansen, starting to walk. Nils followed mechanically.

"You see," continued the old fellow, "Per is so scatter-brained. And Otto's pretty wild, and he doesn't write."

There was that in the man's concern which was so compelling that Nils could not tear himself away. Dread sat gaunt in it.

Presently he continued:

"It's this way, you see: Otto likes drink so well. The Lofoten trips are to blame for that. Did Per do any drinking

79

The Boat of Longing

this winter? No? Well, God be praised! Drink is supposed to be easily got over there. And now Mother and I are afraid of Otto dragging Per into the mischief. That's how we got to thinking, Mary and I, that maybe we could get you to look after our boys—being you're such a fine fellow yourself." ——

Nils stared hard after the boat. . . . What had become of it, anyway? . . . Must be long past due now? . . .

"Mostly this we wanted to ask you, Mary and I," continued Ole Hansen, "if you wouldn't be so good as to mention a little about our boys every time you write home? Not so far to Vaag but that we could get word. I could go out; so could Mary. Won't you please do two old people this great kindness?"

Nils said that he would.

"I can depend on you, then? We'll never hear from Otto. And Per is such a scatterbrain—though he means no harm by it."

Nils had to do violence to himself in order not to walk away from the man; the contagious fear in the man's voice clutched at his throat and made it difficult for him to speak.

"Why, certainly I'll write about your boys, since you ask it!" Having manned himself once more, Nils spoke with much resoluteness.

"Would you give me your hand on it?" asked the old man.

And Nils did give Ole Hansen his hand on that promise.

"God richly bless you! I know He will. All Mary and I need do, then, is to go to Jo for news? For you will write; aye, I know you will!— Well, I declare, there comes the boat. If only Per doesn't fool around till he misses it now!" With which remark Ole Hansen hobbled off in quest of his son.

. . . About a quarter of an hour later Nils stood in the bow of the little fjord steamer just at it was about to pass

The Cove Under the Hill

the point and plough into the open sea. Beside him stood Per Syv, puffing a pipe. Per was in holiday humour.

"Here we go, boy!" he exclaimed, jubilantly, slapping Nils on the shoulder.

But Nils didn't answer. Nor did it look as though he would. Wherefore Per restrained himself a moment. Then suddenly he burst out again:

"Well, now, what's that out there, do you suppose?"

Per Syv pointed. The steamer was directly in line with the headland.

Nils followed the direction of Per's finger. And there up on a crag, square in the face of the west-wind storm, sat a hunched figure, leaning forward.

Per in his bright spirits quickly forgot the figure. He had now begun to remember that there was drink to be had on board; and Nils not replying to his invitation, he went below and drank alone.

Nils remained in the bow until the figure on the point became one with the rocks and the rain and the storm.

. . . And long after, he stood there! . . .

II. In Foreign Waters

I

IT WAS almost noon. The great clock in the Court House tower pointed a quarter of twelve.

Nils Vaag swung off Cedar Avenue and on to Fourth Street, heading for the little delicatessen shop just round the corner, where nearly all sorts of food were to be bought. He turned in there, walked forward to the counter and ordered a loaf of white bread and fifteen cents' worth of American cheese. Having gained the door again, he stopped abruptly, as though arrested by an idea. "Well, let it go," he said to himself; "the coffee that's there will probably last till tomorrow."

He continued up Fourth Street. A few blocks on he caught sight of a flock of boys at ball in the schoolhouse yard ahead. Directly he came in line with them he broke into a run, letting his heels make time until he was well past them. Peals of laughter followed from one of the boys. Another shouted a remark after him which he didn't understand; but he could hear that there was much profanity in it.

Nils fairly went cold. . . . Mercy! those American balls were hard as rocks. . . . Past his understanding how anyone could find pleasure in playing with such; a chance hit by a bullet like that and a fellow would be stone dead! . . . No regard for life at all in America! . . . Was he, too, going to become like that? . . . He wondered if he would. . . . He couldn't see that his not caring to be killed outright just now was so much to laugh at. . . . He wished, though, that he'd put on a bold front and walked by as

In Foreign Waters

though he hadn't seen them. . . . Tomorrow he would take the other side and pretend he didn't notice them; then they'd not be so likely to recognize him. . . .

Presently he drew up in front of "Babel," a rooming house on the corner of Fourth Street and Thirteenth Avenue South. The sight of it brought a bright look into his face, as if from a certain joy of recognition: it was his lodging-place—his oasis in the great, strange city. For three months now it had been his home, and he had already come to regard a section of the street thereabout as in a sense belonging to him.

Sounds of a children's quarrel came to him from the direction of the narrow gravel path on the Thirteenth Avenue side of the house—an infernal racket of screams and shrieks. Nils hurried round the corner to see what was up.

There within the court, in a solid heap, lay a flock of children, a tangle of kicking legs; most of them coal black and glistening, but in between, an occasional nut-brown one. And there were arms protruding—tearing, pinching, hitting, wherever opportunity permitted. Up above, at the head of the narrow back stairs leading to the second story, sat little Ralph Pinsky, saucer-eyed and surveying the scene. Judged by his face, he must have been crying hard and long, for it was streaked with grime and water. But no sound escaped him now other than an intermittent and prodigious hiccough. From out the open windows of the adjoining house came sounds of talk and laughter.

Nils bethought himself a moment; then walking up to the heap, he plunged a firm fist into it and began disentangling it. The task was not easy, for the moment he had extricated and separated a couple from it they were all for flinging themselves right in again; he succeeded, however, in pacifying them sufficiently to bring them to their senses; there were more Negroes than others. Finally he reached bottom; and there lay a strong-limbed blond girl on top of a big Negro boy, clutching him by the throat—her thumbs pressed in good and deep.

"Why, Annie! Are you the one who is fighting?" Nils took her by the shoulder and lifted her.

"Let me go!" she whined, the touch angering her; thereupon coming to her senses enough to see who it was, she rose very painstakingly, holding the Negro boy down as long as she could before letting him go. Released, the latter shot up like a rocket, bolted round the corner of the next house, and disappeared within the third, where he belonged.

To appearances, Annie, as Nils called the girl, was about twelve or thirteen years of age, or more probably fourteen; she was sturdy and well set up, though short; barefooted, bare-armed, and brown as a berry. As she now stood there, the incarnation of fury, she looked ready to have at him at any moment.

"Come along, Annie!" he said, quietly, offering his hand.

"No, sir!"

"Yes, do!"

A look at Nils's face completely disarmed her, it was so genuinely friendly.

"Whew!" she panted, open-heartedly, thrusting her chubby warm hand into his, "that made me hot!"

"Do you fight often?" Nils enquired, in a grave voice.

"No, I don't!" she flared. "Abe Jones took Ralph's piece of bread, if you want to know it, and I promised Mrs. Pinsky I'd take care of Ralph while she's out washing. The dirty niggers! Ralph's little, and Mrs. Pinsky hasn't got much food." The girl fairly sizzled with indignation as she trotted alongside Nils.

At the door Nils stopped to find the key.

"Did Abe take all of Ralph's bread?"

"Bet you—gobbled it down one, two, three!" she mouthed, demonstrating the noisy avidity with which the Jones boy had devoured the bread. "Pushed him, too, so he fell on

In Foreign Waters

his nose. . . . But then didn't he get it! Gee! how I pounded him!" she exulted.

"Say, Annie, go and fetch Ralph, and then the two of you come to my room, will you?"

"Shall we? And then will you play for us?" she cried, her voice just as intense in eagerness now as in anger a moment ago.

"We'll see," was Nils's rejoinder as he let himself in. "You run along and get him."

Presently, Nils stood within the corner room to the right of the hallway. The room was spacious. A large round table, disorderly with stacks of books and magazines, writing-materials, small piles of paper—several of them—a good-sized glass tobacco-jar and an ashtray upon which lay a couple of pipes, occupied the middle of it. There were, besides, two beds, separated by a screen; a small dining-table in one corner; and a stove in the next. The walls were papered, but their hue was at present so uncertain that it would be difficult to say just what the original had been. Upon them hung numerous pictures, of famous authors, for the most part; the remainder were landscape paintings. And then there was an enormous bookshelf, which, running nearly the entire length of the one long wall, seemed to require the lion's share of space in the room. The *Kingdom of Spirits*, the "Poet" called it.

Nils crossed the floor to the smaller table and put down his packages; then he hung up his cap and coat; thereupon he unwrapped the bread, cut two slices from the loaf, and covered each with a ridiculously thick slab of cheese. This done, he began preparing his own lunch.

A moment later the door opened and Annie trotted in with Ralph on her back. Without ceremony she walked straight to a chair and plumped him down.

Nils silently handed Ralph the one piece of bread, and

The Boat of Longing

Annie the other. Ralph stared at his a moment, wide-eyed, then grabbed it with both hands and fell to.

But Annie said, "No, thanks," she wouldn't have any. She had now become bashful.

Nils gazed at her:

"You won't have any?" He felt almost offended.

"No," came the answer, trailed by an audible sigh. "Mother says you're too good-hearted; you'll never get rich in America. Course," and here Annie cast longing glances at the great slice, "I'd just as leave eat it if you want me to. You can get some from me when I begin earning. That'll be pretty soon now."

"So I can," laughed Nils, handing her the slice. "And by what do you intend to get rich?"

Annie threw her head back proudly:

"Dancing!"

"Dancing?"

"Uh-huh!" The nod of her head was so positive that the matter must be regarded as settled. "Like they do in shows and the movies on Washington," she went on to explain, looking at Nils. "It's real nice, I tell you. Haven't you seen it? My, you ought to! I'd just as leave take you if you've got the money." She talked and munched simultaneously.

Nils had also sat down at the table. He was eating bread and butter and cheese, and drinking water. Wouldn't have coffee today, since he was having visitors. He could very well do without it. Right now Nils was in topping spirits. Annie was such a dandy youngster; so straightforward in every way and easy to understand; and so full of fun. She was, moreover, the best English teacher he had found. It was possible to ask questions of her; and she never got stuck, nor did she ever give up till he pronounced a word correctly. If he was having difficulty, she would place herself on the floor in front of him, screw her round mouth

86

In Foreign Waters

into shape, and then enunciate so slowly and distinctly that he caught the sound.

"Aren't you through yet? My, but you're slow!"

"Think so?"

"Uh-huh. Got to hustle up now and play."

"Any hurry?" asked Nils, rising from the table.

"Yes, there is. If my mother finds me here when she comes home, I'll catch hell."

"What's that you say?"

"Oh, never mind! Don't you know what that means—a big man like you? Well, it's the same as a licking in Norwegian, I guess."

"Why doesn't your mother like you to come in here?"

"She's mad at the Poet."

"That so?"

"Yes, he wants her to marry him—the mean old thing!"

"You don't say!" exclaimed Nils.

"Ugh, he's nasty! Ugly, you know."

Nils was so completely taken aback by this revelation that he nearly lost his speech; but Annie promptly brought him to again by demanding that he begin to play now pretty quick.

"Play a piece that's lively and pretty—one that's got streams of light trickling out of it. Then I'll dance it for you."

"Can you dance?"

"Start to play now." Annie, having already taken the middle of the floor, stood holding her short skirts out from her hips in imitation of the professional dancers on Washington Avenue.

Nils, keeping his eyes on the girl, began very cautiously with a jolly air he had picked up one evening.

Annie, meanwhile, darted back and forth across the floor, dancing on her toes, spinning round like a top, and finally finishing in a mighty kick.

The Boat of Longing

Nils stopped, incredulous. "No, Annie, that you must not do. That isn't nice."

"You just go 'head and play, and I'll show you somebody that can dance nice." The girl was aflame.

When he now drew his bow across the strings for a few measures, she picked up the hem of her skirt and, holding it even with her hips, went into a pirouette; in another instant she had kicked a second time.

Again Nils stopped playing. This was serious. "No, Annie," he remonstrated, "if you're going to dance like that, I won't play for you. That isn't nice for a girl."

Annie was mortally offended.

"Oh, you're only a greenhorn; you don't know anything. You ought to see 'em over on Washington! But," she continued, her voice becoming milder because of great self-confidence, "I'm 'most as good as they are now. My mother says so, too. Only, my skirt's in the way. When I take it off I can do it much nicer."

"Does your mother know that you do such things?" asked Nils, embarrassed.

"Course she does! I've danced noons a lot of times this summer over at Melone Lumber Company. And I got a whole dollar from those people every time."

"Didn't you have a skirt on then?" Nils looked away from her when he put the question.

"Course not!"

Nils rose and put his violin away. Annie followed his moves with tinder in her eyes. But Nils did not look at her. Could not.

"That all you're going to play?" she cried, angrily.

"Yes," said Nils, his voice very low and bashful.

Thereupon Annie grabbed the young Pinsky so roughly that he began to cry and flew out of the room with him. "You fool of a newcomer!" she blazed as she banged the door behind her.

In Foreign Waters

II

Depressed of mood, Nils sat right down, staring moveless into life for a long time. Then recalling that the bread and cheese still stood on the table, he got up to put them away; afterward he gave the table a good scrubbing.

This done, he put on his cap and coat and went out, sauntering up Fourth Street as far as Nicollet Avenue. No need to hurry; the afternoon was before him . . . he didn't have to go to work until four.

Up on Nicollet all was beautiful; there was so much that was attractive to look at in the shop windows. Yet it was not these that drew him the most; rather it was all those comely and happy-looking human beings.

Nils liked letting himself glide into the great human stream coursing Nicollet at noonday, to be borne along with it. Only he would hold back ever so little, to keep from going too fast; in that way the current gaining slightly upon him, he could see more people. At Tenth Street, where the stream always thinned perceptibly, he would swing round, glide into the down stream, and let himself be carried by it as far as Washington Avenue, though that did not happen often. All the comely and happy-looking ones disappeared between Fourth Street and Washington. A couple of times he had ventured as far as the riverside; largely, on the last occasion, for the sake of getting better acquainted. But he had decided not to go there again; for it was like getting into a different world . . . the faces were so worn and hideous, as though they had never known happiness. Besides, there was that in their look which frightened him. They reminded him of the west sea when it lay sleek far out, with cloudbanks above it, boding not even the weather eye of the most experienced old sea dog could say what. Some of these faces were so shut and stolid-looking. Others he

The Boat of Longing

felt he would like to speak to and entice with him up to Fourth Street, in order that they too might rejoice over all the beauty up there.

. . . Up there, yes! Between Fourth and Tenth it was like fairyland. In the windows were to be seen every curious and exquisite object that money could wish to buy—yes, and more. Nils would often stop and stand gazing at them, deciding in his mind that this he would buy to take home with him, and that, and that. Yes, and that! One day he really had to laugh at himself. Why, he'd be having a ship-load, were he to buy all that he liked.

. . . Still, it was not the window objects that he looked at most. No, it was the people. Well-dressed nearly all of them; and so beautiful of countenance that they could never have known adversity. Goodness and joy shone in their faces, as though sorrow did not exist in the world! It seemed to Nils that he also could catch their intoxication just by gliding into the stream. Could he, too, he often wondered, become like these—as good and as happy—could he become one of them?

. . . On . . . on . . . on . . . ceaselessly on ran the stream. Especially when noon came, and for a couple of hours into the afternoon. Then the blue smoke of cigars bore through the air in clouds. Through the street whirred two endless processions of motor-cars, backs disappearing, fronts appearing. Like running the undertow in Nordland to get past them. But the main current, that which interested him most, ran forth and back, back and forth, upon the walks.

Having walked himself tired, he would station himself in front of a door or a window and stand there watching the stream. Occasionally, though rarely, his eye would detect a face which seemed not to fit with the others, or a body less beautifully clothed. Usually he let such go instantly and busied himself with the others. And then, standing thus,

In Foreign Waters

he would pray that some day he too might enter this world and become as good and as happy as those whom he saw.

Today it happened that Nils chose to stop right at the entrance of a five-and-ten-cent store on Nicollet. His attention was presently arrested by the hitherto unobserved fact that every now and then some individual would be shunted out of the great throng of well-dressed, happy-looking human beings, and enter the store. The stream continued as before, up and down, up and down; that some slipped out it seemed indeed to make no noticeable difference in it; only now for the first time he began really to be aware of them. Some were young like himself; and, in a way, they too looked happy; and the majority were well dressed. Yet it did seem as though the person were worn in some way—like a new garment which has just lost its first freshness. Most of them were women; at times, older women. Nils stood there, every sense alert. If he were any judge, some of these had rowed against the wind all their lives. "Did you ever see the beat?" he said to himself. "There are such folks, too, in the stream!"

Deeply absorbed in the discovery, he began counting those who went in and out of the store. A couple of short-skirted, tittering girls chancing along, he would leave them out of the count; no need to bother about them . . . there'd be enough, anyway, he saw that plainly.

Suddenly he drew a startled breath. Two middle-aged women came drumbling along and headed for the door. One of them was crookbacked and walked with a cane. She had the identical look of Ole Hansen as he had stood there bidding him good-bye on the quay at Jörgensen's three months ago! That woman made number three hundred thirty-four.

So excited was Nils by the sight of the woman that he forgot his counting and followed the pair into the store. He felt embarrassed about going in when he had no thought

The Boat of Longing

of buying, but he went, anyway. Very unlikely that all who went in made purchases.

He walked up behind the two women at a toy-counter. "They're certain to be rich folks—looking at such finery!" he concluded.

"Find what you want, Oline?" The companion of the crookbacked woman had gone a little farther forward, and was now returning.

"Well, yes, I'm looking at this rattle. Be nice for Ole's Kermit, though I really can't afford it. But I guess maybe I'd better take it, anyway."

Their talk was meaningless to Nils; he only saw that the one held a novel and a very pretty object in her hand. But as he now looked at her a still greater wonder began to take him: She no longer resembled Ole Hansen, but his own mother!

"What about you?" asked the crookbacked one. "Did you find anything?"

"Some playing-cards, yes. It's so lonesome for John to sit alone when I'm out washing that he's got to have some sort of pastime. Think I might as well buy him a deck. He's played with the old one over a year now, so you can hardly tell hearts from spades any more. And his eyes are so bad. I ought to take him to a doctor, if it only didn't cost so much. And now he's saying it's no use bothering." She whose name was Oline let a heavy sigh escape as she walked away to purchase the cards.

Nils began to look about him at the articles which were for sale; and then he made the extraordinary discovery that no article cost more than ten cents. There were leather soles, combs, toys, toilet articles, tools, finery, writing-paper, and goodness knows what not. Priced alike at ten cents! Only ten cents! Here on Nicollet, mind you, right in the very centre of wealth. And from the outside this building had looked no different from the others. Nils hurried about from

92

In Foreign Waters

novelty to novelty, from counter to counter. But when he also found a violin and picked it up to look at it, he became disgusted. Plain as day that there could be no music in such trash!

When he turned round, the women were gone. He hastened to the door, but he was too late—they had already been swallowed up by the stream. Joyously it flowed, as before. Yet strangely enough, his interest in it had waned.

III

A manifold world indeed that he had been plumped down upon just three months ago, mused Nils. The dream scene! And now the reality that he could see and touch! How infinitely different the two! Still, he had not let go of the dream. No, not yet. Only now it always fixed itself somewhat farther up in the heart of the metropolis.

Some one had dubbed the rooming house he lived in "Babel." Just when, or through whom, or why the name had originated no one knew, not even the Poet, who had lived there longest. But Nils's supposition was that it must have been on account of the variety of tongues which had been spoken by its occupants. That situation obtained now, too.

Upstairs, in the left-corner room, lived the Widow Andersen and her daughter Annie; that is to say, the woman passed for a widow, though, strictly speaking, she wasn't one. She and her illegitimate daughter had come to this country from Christiania eight years ago. Her language was a curious mixture of cultivated Norwegian and Christiania slang—mostly the latter when she really got going. And she was easily started, for her troubles had been many. To begin with, she had been shamefully deceived by a Christiania scamp; and now over here she had been waging a six-year warfare with a Dane she had been witless enough to marry. A more worthless fellow than that Dane (accord-

93

The Boat of Longing

ing to Mrs. Andersen's version of it, and she said it often) had never walked in two shoes. Now, thank goodness, he had actually left. Where he had gone she hadn't the faintest idea. But he was gone, and that was enough for her!

Across the hall from Mrs. Andersen lived the Pinskys: the wife was a Russian Pole, so recently a newcomer that she could speak no English; and the husband was a Jew who kept a small shop on Washington Avenue. The wife worked out whenever she could get anyone to take care of Rudolph—or Ralph, as all "Babel" called him; which wasn't, however, easy, since Ralph cried a good deal and wouldn't talk to people. If she could find no one, Ralph would get tied to the bedpost for the day . . . at least that's what Mrs. Andersen said.

In one of the front rooms upstairs lived Mrs. Sarah Hoffmann and her two grown daughters, Sarah and Martha, who among themselves always spoke German. All three worked in a shirt factory. Fine folks, the Poet said. Mr. Hoffmann had died of sunstroke the year after the family came to Minneapolis.

The other front room above was occupied by Per and Otto. Formerly, Otto had shared a room with the Poet; but when Per and Nils came, the brothers had taken this one together, and Nils had gone in with the Poet.

On the first floor there lived, besides the Poet and Nils, a man named Gustaf Söderblom, a Washington Avenue bartender. Söderblom was married; had five children, and a wife who wept daily to think that she who had come of such good family in Sweden should be doomed to such squalor in America. The Poet had in an inspired moment composed a lament about her, which he called "The Disconsolate Wife in the Tents of Babel." Whenever, upon occasion, the Poet was drunk and he happened to hear Mrs. Söderblom's sobbings, he would open the door and sing the song to her.

In a small back room lived two young ladies, Dagny Hals

In Foreign Waters

and Marie Gundersen, both clerks in a large downtown department store. They rose late in the morning and came home late at night; and even though they did live in "Babel" they dressed as well as the finest ladies uptown. Little was known about them; it was only Mrs. Andersen who seemed to have any information at all. If they were mentioned in her presence, she would snort contemptuously: "They, yes! Looks fine so far; but just wait till the show wears off, and they'll wake up some sweet day and find themselves stuck in the dirt they're groveling in!"

But in two small rear rooms on the other side of the narrow hall dividing the structure into two parts lived Mike Sullivan and his wife Maria. They were the owners both of "Babel" and of other shacks along this section of Thirteenth Avenue. In these two cubbyholes they sat drinking cheap whisky and taking care that the rent was paid on time.

These, then, were, for the present, "Babel's" tenants. And they were well off here, especially in the spring and fall, when the temperature out-of-doors was about right. In the smallest rooms, with their single window, it might, of course, become unbearably hot in summer; but then "Babel" was a corner building, and its inhabitants were still so near the simple ways of innocence that they left their doors and windows wide open at night. Thus all could get the benefit of whatever breath of air might be stirring without. . . . But in winter it was worse! The cold might then become so severe that it was almost impossible to live there. And wood and coal being expensive, poor folk had to be as sparing of such items as of kitchen to their food.

Taking it all in all the place was not bad. The occupants of one room never troubled much about their neighbours' affairs so long as they themselves were left in peace. And for that matter there was little to trouble about. In a general way, each knew the life history of the other—with one

The Boat of Longing

exception; namely, the Poet's. His life was the enigma which baffled them all; not even when he was drunk as a piper did he disclose a thing. Where he got his money no one knew. And since no one had ever known him to do a day's work, the conjecture was that he must have inherited, or that he had in some way made a great stake. Be that as it may, he had money. For which reason they also found fault with him. Why, if he had money, did he stay around here? Why didn't he betake himself uptown, where he belonged? . . .

IV

It was not quite two o'clock when Nils returned from his noonday ramble.

On the way back, just as he rounded the corner of Nicollet and Fourth Street, he encountered Otto Hansen arm in arm with a fine gentleman. Both looked very happy. A wave of resentment passed through Nils at the sight of Otto. What right had he to intrude into this bright world on Nicollet? The flushed happiness of his face was not the sort he had just been looking at. He didn't belong there, he who sold whisky to poor folk the livelong day.

Nils walked down Fourth Street, as bleak in mood as a rainy day. The thought of his last letters home came to him. Three times running now he had ended them with: "Greet Ole Hansen and tell him that both Otto and Per are working." More than that he had not been able to say, for to have done so would hardly have given joy to either Ole or Mary. He remembered those eyes of Ole Hansen's; they'd not twinkle to know what Otto and Per were doing. Some slight peace of conscience he had got by securing Per's promise to write himself and tell how matters were going. Per's promise had, however, been easy, and the peace short-lived; so his dread had continued to mount. What was he to tell? Last Sunday he had omitted writing altogether, simply be-

In Foreign Waters

cause Otto and Per had not come home till far into the night and had then caused such a commotion as to disturb the entire household. And now he couldn't get rid of the eyes. They haunted him!

Nils was doing the janitor work in eight Cedar Avenue business places. Four were saloons, in which he swept and washed floors. The others were stores.

And he rated himself prosperous. He was now earning nine dollars a week, and the work wasn't hard, either . . . except that it kept him up late nights. The stores he always did early in the morning, and was then through with them for the day. The saloons were worse, for they required two cleanings daily. The first of these he gave them in the middle of the afternoon, when the customers were fewest; the other, late in the evening at closing-time. It was most disagreeable on days when he had to wash the places . . . a saloon might become revoltingly filthy after a ribald Saturday night. Nils couldn't understand how people could make such beasts of themselves; they scarcely resembled human beings any longer—no, not even animals. And they were Norwegians, too, many of them. At times he wanted to cry over all the wretchedness he was compelled to witness toward the end of such a Saturday evening. Again and again he would say to himself that he'd never touch strong drink.

. . . It was Otto had secured him this work; the somewhat grander job of tending bar in the saloon along with himself he had reserved for his brother, Per Syv.

In the beginning Nils had earned only four dollars a week; whereas Per had earned six. But having after a week's time hunted other jobs until he had eight places in all, he had now got it up to nine dollars weekly. Per had got no farther than seven. When, however, Nils had tried to persuade him to look for other employment, Per had simply turned a deaf ear.

The Boat of Longing

"Just wait till I've learned the business, and I'll be earning twice your wages!" he had replied. And so it had been left at that.

Nils counted a saving of twenty-two dollars this last month. Neat enough, it seemed to him. Together with what he had previously laid by, it made forty-eight dollars and fifty cents. But then he had of course lived as cheaply as he possibly could; only his evening meal that he had taken at the boarding-house on Seven Corners; breakfast and lunch he had prepared himself.

His greatest concern now was to find employment for those spare hours in the middle of the day. He simply must earn more! It wasn't this kind of life he had come to America to live . . . oh no! It was the fairer life uptown. It must be possible for him to become somebody, too!

He entered his room to find a gross hulk of a man engaged in pacing the floor. The posture of the figure was so forward that it affected the look of his whole body. His waistcoat dangled unbuttoned, and his arms were crossed behind his back. Heavy pouch-like folds of ruddy cheek helped to augment the massive look of his face; his hair hung in unkempt locks around his neck; but the top of his head glistened like a dome of silver. His breeches were rolled high, showing legs bare from the ankle. He had house slippers on. It would be impossible for anyone to say how many years the figure bore: perhaps seventy; perhaps only fifty.

Nils came in, hung up his coat and cap, and immediately flung himself down on one of the beds. The man, taking no notice of him, continued his pacing. Quiet pervaded the house. Through an open window Nils could hear Ralph whimpering up above, and now and then a voice talking to him—Annie's, he thought.

"Hum!" grunted the pacing figure. Nils sent him a look,

In Foreign Waters

not certain whether it was safe to interrupt the cogitations yet. But after a little he ventured cautiously:

"How goes it? Can you make it work today?"

The figure kept on walking. His eyes, rolled upward, had no life. If they were seeing at all, it was not immediately apparent in the face.

All of a sudden the figure came to a dead halt. The eyes were now wholly lost to the distance. Hurrying to the great table, he sat down and began to write. Nils could no longer see the head on account of the mound of books; but he could hear short, gleeful grunts. Presently these trailed into silence and there was an interval of no sound. Then a whistle, long-drawn-out and joyous, followed by a peremptory summons to Nils from behind the book-pile:

"Come hither, lorn sea dog. What does your crude heart think of this?"

So infectious was the sound of the deep bass voice that Nils was out of bed and at the table in a single leap.

The face he now looked down into was not the same as the one he had seen a short time ago. All the lifelessness had vanished; even the pouchy chin seemed aquiver.

"Sit down and listen!" The Poet rose from his chair, shoving it over to Nils; he himself leaned against the table. The hand which held the paper was shaking violently. He began to read with much spirit:

> "Now if your hair were golden,
>   How the moonlit pearls
> Of dew in your dancing
>   Would gleam in your curls!
>
> "Oh, if your hair were golden,
>   When the sunlight falls
> You'd be a crownèd empress
>   On high castle walls!
>
> "Aye, if your hair were golden,
>   Walking in the meadow,

The Boat of Longing

You could spread your hair and catch
The sun's gold shadow.

"But if your hair were golden,
   Then I couldn't care
For a silly lassie
   With dark-brown hair!"

The poem ended, he fixed his eyes on Nils for a moment like one about to offer a child a pretty toy; then he handed him the paper:

"There you are! Now you may send that blessed chuck of yours up there at the North Pole these Goldenlocks stanzas. Heh, heh," he chuckled. "And you may at the same time convey this greeting from me that we're not all bulldog materialists in America, either!"

Nils accepted the poem in unconcealed admiration.

"Now this is beautiful! Did you make it up while you were walking the floor?"

The Poet looked into Nils's face with the expression of one having unexpectedly received a poetry award.

"Uh-huh!" he nodded. "The idea has lain in my mind for some time, luxuriating itself. It just now sprang into blossom."

"How do you go about making poetry?"

"Go about it? Oh, you infant, you infant! Or shall I say whale cub? or seal pup? Why don't you ask Earth how the flowers grow? Flowers come of themselves, you see. On a balmy spring day a tender green shoot will peep up from the ground, glance about itself, and wonder; then it will stretch a little, until one fine day it has become a lovely flower! You must learn not to ask such foolish questions, Nils. We're a pretty smart lot in America, I'll tell you! You must be more careful, my boy, more careful!"

Nils only smiled, his face glowing with admiration.

That seemed to please the Poet. Leaning forward, he became intimate:

In Foreign Waters

"Remember that young woman we saw in the park last Sunday night? The one who sat waiting for somebody who didn't come? Remember how restless she was, how she kept looking about, and how her eyes stared? And do you remember how bitterly she cried?"

Nils indicated that he did.

"Well, that same Sunday night when you were snoring away in bed I made her a poem. No one has a right, of course, to cast pearls before swine, but I'd better read it to you, anyway, since it is an undeniable fact that there are actually swine who like pearls." The Poet fetched a paper from a loose pile on the table. "I've called it 'Astray.'" He began reading once more, sombrely,

"Astray

"Weep, child, weep.
The day is on the wane
And the road is rough and long
With never a cabin to cheer you.
Though footsore and in pain
Hurry up and hurry on—
I thought I heard a rustling near you?
Weep, child, weep
And you'll not hear the forest moaning.

"Weep, child, weep.
The moon fell from the sky,
Bears ate all save a wee tiny rind—
The big bears a-roving are hungry!
If you be passing by
And the littlest bit you find,
Don't let the eating delay you!
Weep, child, weep
'Cause the night thickens fast in the forest.

"Weep, child, weep!
Should it never dawn no more
And day forever dead and gone,
At home you've no one waiting,
Gnomes will pick you up

The Boat of Longing

As soon as you're down
Or a bear will come to get you.
Weep, child, weep
Your eyes must be good for something?"

Nils had fallen into a brown study and was far away. Before him lay a desolate ocean in a murky gloom of dusk and rain. He thought he saw a lone black bird lift wings and sail out.

"What are you gaping at?" snapped the Poet.

The query brought Nils back with a start.

"Oh, it was what you read. . . . It was so strange."

"That so?" The Poet looked at him as though he would bore a hole through him.

"For being a mere whale cub you're not so foolish!" cried the Poet.

But the Poet didn't know what thoughts excited the mind of Nils.

"What will you do with this one?" asked Nils, holding out the poem.

"Add it to the rest. It has already accomplished its purpose, as far as that is concerned; it has given you and me a happy moment. The Lord Almighty can't do more, even when He calls all His omnipotence to aid. To me that seems a great deal." The pursy eyelids dropped so low that Nils could not see the eyes.

"Must be fun to be able to make such beautiful poems!" exclaimed Nils.

"You bet it is! No pleasure in the world like it. For it's what the Ancient of Days Himself felt when He stood at the dawn of things, letting worlds drip out of His meditations."

To Nils the explanation was somewhat dark; but his veneration was now so great that he didn't dare ask questions.

102

In Foreign Waters

The Poet resumed the conversation in a voice and mood wholly altered.

"All told there probably aren't in the entire city of Minneapolis more than, say, two souls to whom such verses can give a moment's pleasure; wherefore we two are fools. It's only the fool who can go into peals of laughter over sheer nothingness! . . . Yes, that's the way it is. For here in Minneapolis live the *élite* of Minnesota's Norwegians! . . . Ugh!" An expression of infinite loneliness and sadness crept into the face. The features sank. The whole figure took on a hideous look.

"Fetch me that whisky-bottle under the bed," he requested, drearily.

Nils didn't stir. After a moment he said, almost humbly: "It was so beautiful here just now. And the whisky ——"

"Is so ugly," the Poet finished. "When I say *go*, you go, you mooncalf. You'll not get a drop of it, anyway."

"But," protested Nils, "it hurts me to see you drinking that beastly stuff."

The Poet's face grew demoniacal.

"Fetch that bottle, boy," he growled, "or, the devil smite me, I'll heave you out through that door neck and crop!" And he lunged forward as if to carry out the threat immediately.

Nils rose reluctantly and brought him the bottle.

"The glass, too! I don't drink out of a trough like a swine!" he raged.

Nils went to the little kitchen cupboard and got him a glass. That done, he jerked his cap and coat from the hook and started for the door.

Just as he reached it the Poet bawled out:

"That's right, hurry up! And you needn't trouble about coming back. Fine gentlemen like you need finer company. I and Karl Herman Weisman can get along first rate without you. Hear that, you half-wit?"

The Boat of Longing

Nils stopped—stood still a moment. Then, turning, he went back to the Poet and held out his hand.

"You must forgive me if I've offended you," he stammered. "I didn't mean to. I was only feeling that it was so beautiful here with you reading that poem, and—" There was more he wanted to say, but he could not utter it.

"Go along with you now, go along, you big simpleton. And in case you don't find another place to stay for the night, you can come back here!" he growled.

Nils could hear that the Poet was no longer dangerously angry. But he had no more time for talk.

v

Late autumn in the Middle West will usually bring a spell of fine weather, with cloudless, languidly still days and unseasonable heat. It is as though the Earth Spirit had bethought herself and desired to return from the grave into which she had just descended; and then a rare beauty may lay itself over all in nature which has just died, for it will have in it so much of the mysticism of life and of death. Indian summer the days are called.

It was early Sunday morning the second week of November. Day had come. Nils rolled away from the light and tried to steal another hour's sleep. Convinced after a couple of unsuccessful attempts that it was no use, he got up and dressed. Then he made himself a little breakfast. The Poet was still snoring peacefully over in his own quarter.

Breakfast finished and the food and dishes cleared away, Nils went first to one window to have a look at the weather, then to the other. The sky was cloudless and pale gold in colour, without any of the more vivid hues even this early in the morning. The sun hung stupid, shedding a feeble glow; today it sent forth no rays; only wan, yellowish light. By the air at least one could tell it was the Sabbath. The city, too, lay very still. Now and then one could, to be sure, hear a wagon rattling along on the pavement, its noise spreading wide, since there was nothing to hinder it; but soon it, too, would die away.

After a little Nils was standing on the street corner below, debating in what direction he had best strike out. From the Milwaukee Railway Station came the roar of rolling trains and the uncanny hoots of whistles. The everlasting whorls of black coal smoke were rising above the house-tops. Today they would not mingle with the still, yellow air, but slunk away in patches and heavy clouds.

In "Babel" it was fairly quiet yet. Nils had stopped in the hallway a moment on his way out. Up above he had heard the sound of a child whimpering, and the voice of a woman, also tearful, hushing it. The Söderbloms, he had reflected. Outside he saw little Ralph Pinsky perched at the top of the back stairs, holding a big piece of bread in his hand. Otherwise "Babel" lay as if altogether lifeless.

But despite its seeming so quiet and desolate now, there had been bedlam enough during the night, though perhaps it had not been greatly worse than usual of a Saturday night.

It had started in Otto Hansen's room a little after midnight. Otto and Söderblom had come home together, both on a merry pin. Nils, asleep by that time, had not been sufficiently disturbed at first to come wide awake; he had, instead, been roused into a half-doze, in which he lay dreaming about a cormorant which sang. The fact had puzzled him, for he had never, that he could remember, heard a cormorant sing. But was it actually a cormorant? In his half-doze he had concluded that it must be a sea gull. Yes, it was a sea gull, sure enough. Satisfied of it, he had been on the point of slipping over the borderline into a sound sleep again, when all of a sudden he had been startled by a terrible commotion in the hallway above. A barrage of

The Boat of Longing

curses from the Poet cracked the air like forked lightning. Nils, now thoroughly aroused, began comprehending, if only hazily, what was going on.

It had happened thus: When Otto and Söderblom came into Otto's room, they had decided to have a last swig together—a parting drop, as it were. It and several more had made the two of them well-nigh as fuddled as it is possible for two men already drunk to become. But they were at the time fairly quiet.

Trouble had, however, finally arisen. The question was whether "Terje Viken" was not the greatest poem ever written, which Otto swore beyond all doubt that it was. The contention had at first met with no real objection from Söderblom. So eloquent was Otto in "Terje's" behalf that all the Swede could manage to say was:

"Sure—sure. "Terje" is a beautiful poem, all right—as you say, no doubt. But," he thundered, bringing his clenched fist down on the table with such a blow that it set the glasses clinking perilously, "can that poem be sung?"

Otto Hansen howled with laughter. "Terje Viken" be sung? Whoever heard of "Terje Viken" being sung? Had Söderblom gone crazy? Why, certainly not, "Terje" couldn't be sung!

— Well, sir, then it was not the greatest poem, Söderblom protested, much offended. Every Swedish poem could be sung, even "Goodman Noah"! The mere recollection of that convivial ditty being enough to set him going, he launched into it forthwith, singing at the top of his voice.

It was then matters had broken loose up there. Never had the greatness of "Terje Viken" been so manifest to Otto Hansen as it was at that moment; let no Swede even dare mention it in the same breath with such trash as "Goodman Noah."

Though no battle had been waged aboard the wreck,[1] there

[1] In the poem.

had been one in the hall of "Babel" that night, which ended
in Sőderblom's committing Otto to the foot of the back stairs.
There Otto, on the bottommost step, had continued to ponder
the singability of "Terje Viken." If it were possible, then
that Swede would at last be treated to a song that was a
song. Intent upon establishing the superiority of "Terje,"
Otto had begun trying all sorts of hymn tunes to it; but
without success. He simply could not find one to fit. Overcome with grief, he had begun to cry. . . . What a shame
that "Terje" couldn't be sung! Unthinkable that it couldn't.
Everyone knew it was the greatest poem. Hence it must be
possible to sing it! Again he tried, with exactly the same
result. To think that he couldn't find the tune for "Terje"!
Overcome by the thought, he had bawled like a baby.

Before sleep overtook him, however, he had recovered his
senses sufficiently to grovel his way up the stairs. In the
dark he had unluckily mistaken the doorway and staggered
into the room of Dagny and Marie. In that place he had
encountered more persons than convention would, strictly
speaking, permit at this hour of the night. For Otto, however, the circumstance had been fortunate, one of the number having come to his assistance, hushed him up, and helped
him to bed in his own room. There he had lain sobbing and
experimenting with tunes for "Terje" till he fell asleep.

Per Syv hadn't come home at all that night, which was
the first time it had happened; as a consequence, Nils had
spent the rest of the night awake, looking into those eyes of
Ole Hansen's. It would be impossible for him to write home
hereafter. No, he couldn't even write his own parents!

And so a melancholy lay upon Nils as he walked down
Fourth Street that Sunday morning, which even the beautiful Indian-summer sun was powerless to dispel. He passed
the Norwegian Evangelical Lutheran Church; read the name
mechanically, as he had often done; and got a vague feeling
back in his consciousness that he ought to go to church today.

The Boat of Longing

But it would be some time yet till services began; he'd better take a long walk first.

Having reached Cedar Avenue, he turned the corner and proceeded along that street as far as Seven Corners; thence down Washington to the bridge. Across the river lay the university, beautiful in the serenity of the Sabbath; most likely thither he was bound, though he had no distinct notion of it.

But he halted when he came to the bridge. Below, in the depths, a group of boys were playing in the trestles. They appeared to be having great sport, scaling the lattice-work in the trusses with the agility of cats, and then laughing and whooping high over the abyss. Instead of crossing the bridge Nils began descending the stairs leading to Bohemian Flats—mostly for the sake of watching the boys.

The houses in the pit, viewed from above, resembled black scorch flecks in the bottom of a huge kettle. Nils had often wondered how human beings could endure living down here.

He went clear to the bottom. Finding himself presently at the head of the narrow principal street, he followed it until it ran square into a perpendicular cliff wall; thus brought to a halt, he crossed to the opposite side and returned to his starting-point. There he stopped. He looked down the row of little houses, at the tiny front gardens enclosed with picket fences, and at the chickens and ducks, yes, even geese, poking about in them. So this is a place where folk and fowl live together, mused Nils. Now and then he would see some person moving quietly about. Not even children made noises here—except those boys up in the air. Nils's eye followed the long stair he had just come down. Obviously there were oceans and whole continents lying between this place and the one up above, even though only a bridge separated them.

On the corner where he stood, a low house squatted on

In Foreign Waters

its haunches. It looked as though it had come scooting down the cliffside, heading straight for the river; and then, having hooked itself fast just in the nick of time, had remained there. He could see that the curtains in the little windows were spotlessly white. He also thought he glimpsed a human form watching him from behind them. For that reason he moved on to the river.

Down there he almost fell into a fine humour; his gloom seemed to fall off by layers. He was a boy again—felt like a human being once more. An old Nordland melody began running through his head; his lips shaping themselves unconsciously, he commenced whistling it.

The closer he got to the river, the more powerfully it drew him. Taking the remaining distance in a couple of long leaps, he landed way down on a strip of flat sandy beach. "Sakes alive!" he exclaimed, "here's a sand beach just like ours at home!" Imagine having lived near this all these months without knowing it! He immediately started skipping stones, gaily whistling the Nordland melody as he did so. Like the youth he had been, he hunted flat pebbles and tried his skill at skipping them clear across the river. Now and then he glanced at the boys playing in the air, and was almost tempted to join them.

During the moments that Nils had stood on the corner surveying the place, a thin, elderly woman had been observing him from behind the curtains. Struck by something in his appearance, she had kept on watching him; and when he had walked down to the river she had gone out and continued to gaze after him. The tune he was whistling seemed likewise to be exerting some strange influence over her; for she was trembling so that she had to sit down. When she saw him begin to skip pebbles she rose and followed him.

Nils having skipped pebbles till he was tired, was squatting by the water's edge, washing his hands; upon rising to leave the river, he was confronted by the woman.

The Boat of Longing

They stood face to face . . . Nils, his hat way back on his head and his hands dripping with water; the woman with her hands under her clean, threadbare apron.

She spoke first, in a voice so soft that it fell like a benediction upon his ears, filling him with a sense of peace, just as do the notes of a beautiful song; it was in the pure low dialect of Nordland.

"Aren't you from Nordland?" she began. Her pronunciation and inflection were as genuine as though the two of them had been standing on the beach in Norway.

With just as genuine open-heartedness Nils answered:

"Yes, I am. You are too, I hear."

Her haggard features distended, rounding out into a great childlike look; tears came into her eyes.

"Didn't I know it! I could tell by the tune you were whistling; to think I should hear that song again after eighteen years. And with you skipping those pebbles I knew I couldn't be mistaken. I had to follow and listen, I simply couldn't help it. You're the first Nordlænding I've met over here."

The expression on her face and the tone of her voice compelled Nils to turn away and dry his eyes. While his face was still averted, he answered,

"Reminds me of home here."

"That so?" she came back eagerly. "It really isn't bad right here by the river, is it? But in this country no one seems to care about such things," she added, as if to inform him.

"What sort of people live here?"

"Very kind people, for the most part."

Her answer made him laugh. "I was wondering where they came from."

"Oh, I understood you all right," she smiled. "They're Bohemians, mostly. They call this Bohemian Flats. But there are quite a few Scandinavians, too. A Swedish family

In Foreign Waters

in that little house over there; and one from Trondhjem on the street to the east of us. And they say there are a couple of other Norwegian families, though I haven't learned to know them yet."

"What do these people do?"

"Well, some do this, some that. . . . But you really must come in, so I can talk to you. My feet have sort o' played out on me lately," she added, as if by way of excuse for her invitation.

Nils went with her.

The room she ushered him into was a veritable doll parlour. The ceiling, distressingly low, almost touched his head. All the objects seemed to be scaled to proportion: a cot did service for both bed and sofa; the stove was of the small oil-burner variety, such as young women frequently have in their rooms; the table was diminutive; and the chairs looked as though they were never intended for grown ups. But the room was as tidy and attractive as human hands well could make it.

Upon the walls hung many small pictures. Also a violin. Which struck Nils as being strange. He fell to looking at the instrument, curious to know the owner.

"Who plays that?" he enquired, pointing.

"That? Oh, that was Johan's violin."

— A memory was here being kept sacred; Nils asked no further questions.

"Karl Brakstad drops in occasionally and plays me a tune on it. He's the Trondhjemmer I mentioned. . . . Maybe you play?"

"Well—not to speak of."

"No, that's hardly to be expected; very few can. But Brakstad is really pretty fair—at times."

Nils vouchsafed no reply.

"From what part of Nordland do you come?" he asked.
"Ravnøy."

The Boat of Longing

"In Helgeland?"

"Yes. What about you?"

"From Dŏnna."

"Dŏnna in Helgeland?"

"Yes."

"Did you ever!" she exclaimed, striking her hands together in amazement. An even deeper music and warmth came into her voice. "Then we two are neighbours, so to speak, from the old country!" Tears came into her eyes.

"So we are! How long have you been in America?"

"Just eighteen years in September since I came. When did you come?"

"The fifteenth of June this summer."

The reply touched her instantly.

"Then you have just come from there!" she cried.

"Oh no, I shouldn't say that exactly. It seems long since to me. . . . I suppose you've earned a good deal, when you've been here so many years?" laughed Nils.

She laughed, too. "I'd hardly say that; but it's a fine country for anyone who can work."

Day wore on and Nils stayed. It was so pleasant to sit here by the little window and look at the cliffside and at the river flowing by on its long journey to the sea.

They spoke of many things; but most about Nordland. The information he could give and the happenings he could relate fell like precious rain on thirsty earth. If he showed signs of leaving, she would instantly think up new questions to ask him, and spin new conversations. She enquired about persons and conditions, about the mountains, calling them by name, about the sea, and whether it were still as dangerous to fare upon it as in days gone by. And about the gull.

— Did it still cry strangely on summer nights?

— And were the early fall nights when the herring commenced arriving and seining was about to begin as beautiful

In Foreign Waters

as ever? Such wizardry could hardly be equalled anywhere in the world, could it?

When it came dinner time, she would not hear of his going; no, now he must sit still right where he was. Surely he would do an old woman who had had no news of Nordland this many a year that much kindness!

She drew the little table out on the middle of the floor; and when she had decked it, she bade Nils sit down to it. To Nils it was a meal of rare delicacies. There was flatbread, and savoury cured meat, and the teaser *gammelost*—yes, even smoked herring. And tea! Only on festive occasions like Christmas that Mother Anna had served tea.

The conversation continued quietly and intimately, as between two bosom pals who have been reunited after a prolonged separation. It seemed to Nils that he had lived in that room many, many years.

"What is your work?" asked Nils.

"I go around and take care of sick people—mostly such as can't afford a trained nurse. I'm supposed to be a sort of midwife, on call at any time."

— Had she learned in Norway?

— Well, was that likely? Oh no. But here one had to try his hand at whatever he could find. And precious little difference it made in the end. She now had all the work she could possibly do.

But she had little interest in discussing that subject, it seemed. What she wanted was to have him tell about Nordland, and then yet more about Nordland.

— Did they still have those queer happenings there?— Well!— And did one hear as much about it now as in the old days?— Strange about all that uncanniness in Nordland. There could scarcely be another place in Norway where there was so much of it, could there?— Had he ever heard about the mysterious boat—for there really was something

The Boat of Longing

mysterious about it—which so many had seen sailing along the coast of summer nights?

A great depression settled over Nils instantly, in which he became so transfixed as to find speech difficult. He felt a desire to cry, and was unable to answer more than *yes* and *no* to her questions.

His taciturnity disrupted the conversation. She cleared the table; which done, she took a seat on the sofa.

The sun had now got so far to the westward that most of the kettle lay in a shadow; it had already begun to grow dark down there. Within the little room it was half-dusk. But high on the rocks at the top of the cliff a golden light still gleamed. Like the last look of an eye before it closes.

Nils gazed at the colour-play. It was speaking to him. He felt he must answer. Rising, he went to the wall and took the violin. He was a long time in tuning it, seeming unable to get the pure tone which his ear was seeking.

Then he sat down. Country dance followed country dance; between times, a snatch of ballad, or a hymn tune. Now and then a little of what he himself had dreamed.

. . . She listened, rapt. Her hands were folded. No word escaped her. Her eyes swam. Nils could feel how completely she was being carried along. That enabled him to put all the more earnestness into his playing.

When he finally stopped, she begged him, in a voice so low as to be hardly audible:

"You must play the song you were whistling today." And to put him in mind of it she began humming it softly.

Nils played the melody for her a couple of times, glided from it into a more sombre one, was presently off on a madcap one. And then, like the onrush of a great, cold wave, the melody about the sea overwhelmed him, just as it had done up there on Værőy Mountain last Easter Day. While he played, his eyes lay fixed on the sunband glorifying the rocks. Of that, too, the melody sang to him. Only for him

114

In Foreign Waters

to follow now! And Nils went on and on, borne along by the sunbelt into the infinite and supernal, the little parlour lost to his sight. Before him, in the sublime, lay a wide-stretching sea, drifting in golden calm. Out against the sky-line, sped a boat under bellying sails. . . . Foam broke white around its prow. From aboard came music . . . with laughter in it . . . and crying. It laid itself upon the sun-kissed waters and came rocking toward him.

. . . The longing to be aboard seized him, filling him with nameless anguish. . . . He gave a swift, sharp stroke on the fifth, and laid the violin down. The room shrieked.

. . . He rose and returned the instrument to its place on the wall; his face was very pale and his hands trembled.

She, too, rose from her place on the sofa, drying her eyes.

"That I must say was music. I haven't heard such playing since Johan went away. Nineteen years last spring since that day now!"

Her gratitude made Nils feel better. Her good will stole into his spirits and calmed him. He wanted to go now.

"You must tell me the name of the last one," she begged. "It could scarcely be either danced or sung!"

Nils looked down, embarrassed. "It is called 'The Boat of Longing.'"

He had already gained the door, hat in hand. But she would not let him go.

"Won't you come again? Come next Sunday; come early!" she beseeched him.

"It's easy to find the way back to so pleasant a place. . . . Oh, that's right," and now he laughed heartily, "I suppose I should have enquired the name! People certainly do have queer manners in America!"

She laughed, too. "Never mind about that. It's Kristine Dahl, if you want to know it. . . . I could really wish to call you Johan, though it's hardly to be expected you would have that name."

The Boat of Longing

"No," replied Nils, laughing again. "My name is just plain Nils—Nils Vaag. But I should like to come again, for all that."

VI

When Nils ascended the stairs, it was with the sound of the melody still ringing clearly in his ears. Contrary to his experience a few hours back, the surroundings now made no impression on him; he wasn't aware of them. "Merciful God," he cried, "guide my life, so that I may in some measure do what I now feel."

And the kettle bottom from which he emerged lay behind him in deepening twilight. Up on its rim day was still bright, the oncreep of dusk-time only barely discernible there. The heavens had the purest colourings; the first delicate flush of the west sky was stretching forth to meet the night blue of the east.

Seven Corners was teeming with life; everyone must be out. Throngs of merrymakers rushed by on every trolley; those returning from Minnehaha Falls were packed to the gates. Most of it was youth.

Nils made his way up Fourth Street, scarcely seeing those who passed him.

He approached the corner where he lived. Already from a distance he discerned a light in his room. So the Poet was home? This evening he was insensitive to the street; he strode briskly along in the grip of the melody.

A woman stood on the corner of "Babel." She appeared to be waiting for some one.

Nils made toward the door, when the sound of a voice arrested him:

"Hello there! Why turn in so early?"

But so generally was the question directed that it might have been meant for him, and then again for some one else;

In Foreign Waters

seeing no other person about, however, he concluded it must be meant for him; though he wasn't altogether certain, either, for she didn't turn toward him—only talked into the air, as it were.

When he paused to give the woman a look, whom did he see but Marie Gundersen, the companion of Dagny Hals? And because they had spoken to each other a few times in passing, he now returned her greeting.

She was so beautifully dressed this evening. A veil softened her somewhat coarse features and gave them a certain comeliness; and the evening glow was playing upon the visible portion of her luxuriant brown hair, giving it a deepened richness. Nils came more wide awake and gazed at her in wonder. Why, she looked as lovely as the finest lady on Nicollet. No poverty about Marie, you might be sure! . . . The odour of perfume came floating upon the air, inlaying his mood with memories of fair, far-off places, and transfusing the present with brightness.

That he had stopped embarrassed him; a poor newcomer like himself was out of place in such fine company.

When he turned to go, she accosted him again:

"Been out for a good time today? You might be a little more civil to folks living in the same house with you."

Still she had not turned toward him. She spoke to him; yet not exactly to him, either. Her whole demeanour was strangely impersonal; for all that she addressed him from only four or five feet away, she might have been standing on the far side of the street.

Nils felt bashful, and uncertain what he should do. He couldn't very well walk off and leave her, when she had spoken to him; but proper words for one so stylish wouldn't come.

— Yes, his day had been very pleasant; best Sunday he had had since he came to America.

— Was that so? Well, that was nice.

The Boat of Longing

Nils thought he detected a note of sadness in the words. "Come on, take me out, so I can have a good time, too!"

This sounded downright pathetic. Nils was moved. Forgetting his bashfulness in the brightness of his spirits, he went straight over to her, reached out his hand, and said, in his heartiest manner:

"Well, if you aren't too proud to walk with a newcomer, I'll certainly go with you. Where would you want to go?"

Privately he was saying: "She must be feeling very downhearted, and is wanting to go to some friends, most likely. . . . She'd like me to take her; which I certainly can do. I should think I could find the way home again. . . . Not so easy for a woman to go alone to places evenings in a big city."

Her reply astonished him:

"How much money have you got?" she asked, as if jesting.

"All I own is in my pocket," he came back, ingenuously. "I haven't earned more than I can easily carry with me wherever I go."

"That'll probably be too much." She laughed in the same enigmatical manner. "What, say, do you figure you can afford to kill if we two should go out for a—well, for a little party?"

"For a what?"

"Oh, you're dense! All newcomers are. We can have supper uptown, see? I'm starved; haven't had a bite to eat all day. Had a headache. We could see a show afterward. Say, don't you want to take me?"

Nils stood there not knowing what course to steer.

"Sure, well—sure, of course!" Never before in his life had so fine a lady shown him so much attention, and he caught himself in time, realizing that it wouldn't do to refuse here.

"All right, we go then!" The voice sounded tired again. And Nils thought, "She must be very unhappy."

In Foreign Waters

With a sudden impulsiveness she thrust her arm into his, and Nils, to his amazement, found himself walking. He inhaled deeply of the rich fragrance enveloping him. Beside her he felt so insignificant and shabby that he could have sunk through the pavement; and still he was strangely elated. It sang within him. "The folks at home should see me now," he exulted, inwardly.

"What kind of work do you do?" she asked as they walked along.

Nils was ashamed to admit it. But it seemed not to shock Marie in the least; which heartened him.

"Making much?"

Nils told her that, too.

"That all?"

"That's all!" He himself could clearly see that it was too bad it wasn't more. Happily it would be different as soon as he had learned English and could go out and command the work he wanted, he asserted with confidence.

"You must quit such work and get something better."

Nils thought her uncommonly kind; the extent of her solicitude moved him.

"What could I find, do you think?" he asked, confidentially.

— Could he read and write?

— Well, yes, he had thought so.

— Was he good at figuring?

— Yes, he thought he was that, too, moderately at least.

— Then why didn't he try getting into a store as a clerk? Nothing but business here; only thing that counted in this country. How would he like that?— She was now speaking almost naturally.

Not receiving any answer, she reiterated:

"If you want to be anybody in America, you've got to learn business, see?"

— Was that so beautiful, then?

The Boat of Longing

— Beautiful?

— Yes? Any future in it? Nils asked, searchingly.

Slackening her gait, she looked straight into his strong, honest face. It was so kind and handsome. The eyes under the veil grew smaller.

"What do you want to become?"

"I want to learn to play the violin better than anyone else! . . . I promised Mother when I left that I would make something of myself before I returned!"

"Do you mean to say that you are going back to Norway?" A note in the voice puzzled him, but his mind was so full that he forgot it instantly.

"Yes. Mother and Father are there," he answered, simply. He thought he felt a tug at his arm. . . . They'd soon be in the more fashionable part of the city now; it probably embarrassed her to be walking thus arm in arm with him . . . "I'll have to get some better work soon," he continued. "Mother is aging; so is Father. They'll be lonesome this winter, I guess, being there all alone—though I was away last winter, too."

Again he sensed a tug at his arm, a more distinct one this time. He thrust his arm farther out, so as to permit her to free her own. But she seemed not to be desiring that, either.

"Worst of it is," he continued, gloomily, " 'tisn't only myself I have to look after; I've got to get Per Hansen into different work."

"Him? That fool? Say, you aren't related to him, are you?"

"No, but he's starting wrong, and his parents in Norway are expecting him to come back when he's made good, you see. And I've—well, I've promised to look after him."

"You have? Well, you'll have some job!" Marie laughed as though Nils had told her a good joke.

Her laughter nettled him. Because she was better acquainted than he and could talk English so well, he had

In Foreign Waters

confided some of his worries to her, hoping for advice; and here she was laughing at him!

They began gliding into the Nicollet throng, where confidential talk became difficult. He had, as a matter of fact, no time for it, either, being too intent upon the gay, beautiful stream and upon steering her clear of automobiles whenever they crossed a street.

She now announced their destination. Never having heard of the place, Nils asked where it was; whereupon she took the lead. They turned off first into one side street, following it for a spell, and then into another. After a few blocks she stopped in front of an entrance which lay in the half-dark.

"We're going in here!"

"We can't get supper here, can we? The place seems to be dark and there's nobody around."

"Come on!" she said, hugging his arm more firmly and piloting him down a long, shadowy corridor to a door in the far end. Here she rappèd. A finely dressed servant appeared and admitted them to a second corridor, better lit. Presently they found themselves at another door.

"Don't talk now, but follow me," she commanded.

She opened the door and drew him in. For a moment Nils stood utterly bewildered, the glare of light into which he was thus unexpectedly thrust blinding him completely. He gasped at what he saw. Before him, in a vast saloon, stretched a sea of tables, thronged with elegantly dressed diners, eating, drinking, talking, and laughing. Shuttling briskly in and out among them were other finely dressed gentlemen bearing trays filled with all sorts of delicacies. These princely-looking persons must be more than just ordinary servants, concluded Nils. High under the mammoth chandeliers the cigar smoke hung in milky-blue clouds. Mirrored walls gave a look of endlessness to the room. But best of all, thought Nils, was that great fairyland of happy human beings; he caught the spirit instantly and smiled along with all the others.

A swallow-tailed one came hastening toward them, bowed deeply, and enquired obsequiously, as though he were addressing the prince and princess, if he might usher them to a place.

But Marie disdained to waste even a look on him. "Where's Ben?" she asked, curtly, as one who commands.

"Ben?"

"Yes. Number Eighteen? We want him!"

Nils's eyes went large with happiness and wonder. If she didn't walk right into this place and command as though she had been accustomed to it all her life! Could this actually be the Marie who lived in that squalid little room in "Babel"?

Marie looked at him and laughed; she too must have caught the mood.

At that moment a superfine gentleman stepped up to them. Nils observed that he wore a large silvery button on his lapel, bearing the number 18 in black letters.

"Hello there, Mary!" he greeted her in a suppressed voice, half facetiously and half professionally. She answered his greeting in kind, and added, jokingly:

"My brother. Just arrived from the old country. Now get us a nice, quiet corner where we can see well; and a bottle of fizz! And get a move on yourself!"

The fine gentleman bestowed a lame nod upon Nils; then fixed his look tenderly on Marie, saying in Norwegian, "Don't you know what day this is? We keep all the Commandments here! *Fizz* did you say?"

He beckoned them to follow, and led the way in among the tables and beautiful people to a yet larger room, also thronged with happy guests. In a corner he found a table just large enough for two. From here they could observe the whole room floating in light and gayety. Nils gazed en-

In Foreign Waters

tranced. He folded his hands; into his face came the same sort of transfixed expression as had come into the face of Kristine Dahl when he played the song for her.

"I've never seen a sight more beautiful! Nor so much happiness!" he cried, in ecstasy.

"Do you like it?" she asked, carelessly teasing.

This he did not answer; but he set upon her two great, honest, childlike eyes so full of gratitude that she was discomfited by it.

"What's the name of this place?"

"The name? Oh, never mind! Just speak to me when you want to come back. How long have you been in America?"

"A little over five months."

"Lots for you to learn yet!"

Before Nils could reply the fine gentleman returned with a bucket of ice, from which protruded the slender neck of a bottle. The bottle was sealed with gold! The gentleman removed it from the ice; the cork came with a cloop. Thereupon he poured into sparkling goblets a liquid resembling crystal spring water with pearls in it; the pearls stole to the top, swam about, and gathered around the edges.

Marie lifted her goblet and clicked it against his.

"Welcome to America! And good luck to our first party!"

Nils let his goblet stand, and asked, innocently:

"Is this strong stuff?"

"Don't be silly!" she said, witheringly. "It's only fizz."

Nils noted the enjoyment with which she drank her glass. So he followed her example.

Marie seized the bottle and poured each another glassful.

"Two eyes, two glasses! Here's to the right. Say, what are you winking at me with your left for?" She laughed loudly. "Don't you feel yourself getting happy now?" she asked.

"Happy? I should say so! I can see suns all over!" Nils laughed like a youngster.

123

The Boat of Longing

"Well," she said, "this is what you call 'Oh, be joyful'; whenever you get the blues, drink some of it."

Nils didn't understand her. But just then she changed the subject.

"What would you like to eat?" she asked; she herself was studying the menu. "What would taste extra good to you, friend?"

"Fish!" laughed Nils.

"You said it! What kind?"

"Boiled halibut!"

"Is that very good?"

"The best in the sea!"

"Make it boiled halibut then," she ordered, shoving the card aside; "and let's have one on the goodness of it," she added as she refilled the glasses.

After some time the fine gentleman returned with a delicious meal, which he placed before them and served. They felt like plutocrats, with millions in their pockets.

Marie talked quietly and pleasantly. But whenever Nils looked at her he encountered a pair of strangely luminous eyes. "It's just that she's feeling so happy now," he concluded; and the thought of her having thrown off all the gloom and sadness of the earlier evening augmented his own happiness.

It was an hour before they had finished their meal. Then the fine gentleman reappeared, and brought with him a little brass plate on which lay a piece of paper. Nils wondered what it might be, for he could see no writing on it.

Marie rose immediately, saying to Nils:

"We'll go now." To the one with the brass plate she said, carelessly:

"See you later, Ben."

Nils looked at the man; and again he was perplexed. The expression on the man's face was that of one who had got some unsavoury morsel in his mouth; and the smile on his lips was far from amiable, Nils thought.

When they had reached the door, Nils stopped, terrified: "Sha'n't we pay?"

"No," laughed Marie, "I get everything free here! We have to hurry now!"

VII

They were back in the street once more. By this time dark had set in, though to Nils it did not appear so, for all lay in a flood of light. The street lamps were suns shedding a noonday brilliance upon himself and her and everyone.

Nils felt an ungovernable desire to sing. . . . It seemed almost a sin for him to be withholding so much joy and not let it mingle with all the rest. . . . If only he had had his violin now, how wouldn't he have played! For he could hear tones, see them; Marie and he were walking to them. . . . He carried his hat in his hand, swinging it rakishly.

But as they now made their way through the streets, Marie did not, as before, thrust her arm into his; instead, she took him by the hand, as though they were two children, and she his sister. . . . A nice little hand; soft as silk. . . . Nils clasped it, fondled it, stroked it with his fingers, stowed it away within his own large one.

. . . And happiness sat even more luminous in people's faces; and there was more sunlight in their eyes than he had ever seen there. . . .

He noticed that they were on Hennepin, certain landmarks in the various streets helping him to keep his bearings. Here was the West Hotel. Otto Hansen had taken him and Per Syv into it on their first Sunday in America. Otto had on that occasion shown them all through the place and had comported himself in so elegant and lordly a manner that Nils in his great innocence had asked if he owned this

125

The Boat of Longing

building. He had to tell Marie about this amusing experience of his first Sunday; and then both of them laughed like children at some ripping fairy story.

Bearing down Hennepin, they came presently to a building having a projecting entry studded with lights. "New Palace Theatre" Nils spelled out in illuminated letters. Well, did you ever! That people could make letters out of light, too! He must remember to tell about it next time he wrote home. . . . A shadow swept over the lights at the thought.

"We'll go in here," said Marie, stopping at the entrance. "Your turn to pay now. Be fifty cents for the two of us. We're a little late already."

The place was filled when they entered. Nils heard Marie whisper to the usher about a good place up in front. She was a marvel. . . . Always knew just what to do! And so kind-hearted! . . . He must tell about her, too, when he wrote. In only two hours she had shown him more of beauty than he had experienced in all his months in America together.

The half-dark of the theatre made it difficult to distinguish much within; an ocean of swaying heads was about all he could make out.

Nils stood as if rooted to the floor: A woman came running out of the wall ahead of him, her hair all dishevelled, unspeakable terror stamped on every line of her face. Hot in pursuit of her came a great thumping fellow with an evil countenance. He caught her, grinned malignantly, dashed her to the ground, bound her hands behind her back, gagged her, then bore her away up a steep hillside. In the next instant there appeared on the road he had just abandoned a troop of horsemen riding at breakneck speed. Then suddenly the wall went black; in another second it came back, and the man was seen far up the heights with the bound woman.

Marie sought his hand again, and they were ushered to a

126

In Foreign Waters

place far forward. Removing her hat, she placed it on his knee, her hand in under.

Nils was aware only of the pictures, following every motion so intently as to become oblivious of all else. When the man gained the top of the cliff he tied the woman to the trunk of a dead tree which leaned over the yawning abyss. There she hung, swaying. Nils was on the point of rushing to her rescue.

The picture ending, he let a long jerky breath escape, like one just awakening from a nightmare.

The lights came on, and he began to look about. He thought it so pleasant to be here among all these people; he was actually in a real theatre now. But the audience sat listless and dull, seemed not the least interested. Queer that it should be so. And there was no joy in their faces! Marie didn't appear to be looking on, even; she merely sat there, indifferent, chewing gum.

"Isn't this wonderful?" he turned toward her, full of ecstasy.

"Fudge! Just a cheap movie, that's all. You've seen a movie before, haven't you?"

— No, he hadn't.

"Say, what have you been doing these five months? You must have gone some places!"

Nils could now clearly see what a fool he had been since he came to America. Obviously, it wouldn't do to be so saving of every penny and only go drifting along with the current on Nicollet for an hour every noon. Embarrassing to be so green about such common everyday affairs as these. That they were affairs of everyday was plainly enough written on the countenances; they all looked bored and indifferent; not the slightest trace in them of the bright happiness which made faces so comely.

Nils passed from wonder to wonder that evening. In a moment a man in black dashed out and fell at once to performing the most incredible tricks. Finally Nils had to conclude that the fellow simply didn't have a bone in his body. Only rubber. He bounced about with the resilience of a ball and ended by sitting on his own head. Nils thought it plain uncanny to watch him. But the masterliness of this climaxing feat seemed potent to break the lethargy of the audience, slightly at least, for several laughed and applauded.

Marie looked mildly enthusiastic:

"Not much wrong with that fellow's back!" and she went on chewing gum.

Again the room went dark.

Directly in front of where they sat yawned a pit illuminated by unseen lights. It began to play down in the pit, from all manner of instruments, several of which Nils had never heard before. And so many violins! He sat scarcely able to breathe. . . . Soft and delicately airy this music. Out of it escaped now and then more frolicsome tones, full of rollicking laughter, which did not die wholly away. Never before had he heard such tones; hadn't even dreamed they could be. And though rippling so lightly, they straightway insinuated themselves into his mood . . . lay there calling to him. And didn't he—yes, didn't he feel an awareness far, far within his innermost being which was growing more living . . . which responded . . . which stepped boldly forth and suffused him with a strange warmth? . . . Didn't he feel it? . . . He lifted the hat from his knee, observed the hand resting there, but took no thought of it. For now he had become completely occupied with a face down in the pit, that of an elderly man playing a violin. The face was spectacled, and leaned well forward over the score, on which account it got an intense light upon itself. Never had Nils seen so weary a face. It looked even more spent than had that of his father the rain-night he bade him farewell on the heath, in the west-wind storm.

"Surely a soul knowing pain," mumbled Nils.

In Foreign Waters

The curtain went up, diverting his attention. Shafts of coloured light—green, blue, yellow—sped across the stage. The rest of the house lay in darkness. A being came floating out into the fickle aura and began dancing hither and thither with its shifting movement. From the violins rippled lighter tones; but venturing ever up against the sportive, they became inflamed. Nils's eyes were riveted; took in the whole scene at a glance. He wanted to look down and could not, didn't have the power to. His eyelids pasted themselves to his brows. Shame surged hot through him. His cheeks burned. He heard his heart pound. Feeling Marie's eyes upon him, he went still hotter.

With a desperate wrench he pulled himself together, straightened his position sharply, swept her hand aside so unceremoniously that the hat fell down. He bent over to pick it up; and so got his eyes off the dancing one.

He returned to the tired face. There it was as before, leaning forward over the score, too weary even to glance up at the rim of the pit. How such tones could be got to issue from that violin was more than Nils could understand. He stayed by the face until he heard a loud clapping of hands. Whereby he guessed that the unclothed one had made her exit and that he could look up once more.

"How did you like her?" asked Marie, unabashed.

"That was not nice!" he answered, sick at heart. "It spoiled the evening for me. If it weren't for those violins, I'd like to go home now."

Marie veered directly upon him, and again she tried to do what she had several times attempted in the course of the evening: namely, to penetrate that face. And she met as before a fine, open countenance, strong, free, and nobly chiselled. But over its purity a veil had now spread itself, the stuff whereof she did not know.

Once more the stage went dark, and pat a whole wall of words sprouted. A music firm was advertising a new song

The Boat of Longing

hit. The words were beautiful; they told of a child in prayer
at bedtime entrusting itself to the care of Jesus, of its fold-
ing its hands and going to sleep. A throaty male voice came
out of the dark and sang the words. In the melody lay a
peculiarly mournful strain; the composer must have felt it
a sad misfortune that the child should have thus fallen
asleep. But the song was beautiful despite the voice.

And now a strange thing happened: the moment the song
ended, the whole audience fell to applauding, even more
enthusiastically than for the sable trickster who awhile back
had sat on his head. Nils was at a loss to fathom it; one
might as well have set up a Crown of Thorns on a saloon
bar. It would have been just as fitting.

He was back with the tired face above the violin. The
man was not playing now, but the accompaniment continued
to come from a piano down in the pit. The arms lay folded
upon the score, the head resting upon them. To Nils it
seemed that there was more of life in the figure now that
it rested than there had been when it played those jolly
tunes.

Again the curtain went up, and a pair of plump females
in bathing-suits bounced in. They could hardly be called
bathing-suits, either, being too low above the waist as that
garb goes. No other clothing encumbered them. After putting on boxing-gloves, they staged an exhibition bout. They
slugged each other with rights and lefts, and landed blows
promiscuously. By and by the one fell in a heap, feigning
a knock-out. People cheered wildly and howled with
laughter.

Nils sat smileless. Marie fell to studying his face again.
The clean-cut features now wore a frank expression of disgust. Could you beat it! Here he sat in the midst of all this
merriment as sober as an undertaker. The tinder leaped to
her eyes and her eyelids began to blink rapidly.

In Foreign Waters

"We might as well go!" she snapped.

"Yes, let's!" he begged, wearily.

They rose and started up the aisle.

"Hello there!" came a voice from the rear row. It was Per Syv, sitting with his arm about Dagny Hals; the pair were apparently in the best of spirits.

Nils breathed deeply of the street air, like one coming to the surface after having been long under water.

When they reached Nicollet, Marie made as if to go down the street.

"Aren't we going home?" asked Nils.

"You can. I'm going down to pay for our supper."

With a sardonic laugh she disappeared in the crowd and the darkness.

VIII

Nils stood there on the corner, his glances roving restlessly. In reality they saw nothing. Then he glided into the Nicollet upstream and began drifting with it till it thinned out farther up; at that point he crossed over to Hennepin, and again struck off down the street.

The evening was truly beautiful, though Nils was not noticing it; nor was he regardful of the lights, which awhile ago had looked like suns. No, it was only human faces that he saw.

It came into his mind that old sea folk frequently feel ill against a storm, that some will even know of disasters before they happen, and will suffer from it. . . . Peering into the sky, he saw stars blinking far, far up; but there wasn't a cloud in sight; nor other bad weather token. Still he could feel it in his body.

He passed the West Hotel once more and came to the New Palace Theatre just as a great throng was pouring out of it; dammed back stood another waiting its turn to ooze in. He made his way through it and continued down the street. Could he reach the river by following it? Perhaps, if he kept on long enough. . . . The river! Yes, the river! It had run so swift and strong this morning. And it went toward the sea. Yes, it went toward the sea!

A crowd had gathered on the corner opposite the St. James Hotel. All were men. They lined the curbings; leaned against the wall; occupied the street. There must have been several hundred.

Just off the sidewalk, on a large box, stood a man, talking; his voice was husky from much overstraining in the open air.

Nils, curious, slipped into the crowd to listen. But the words he understood were very few. His English was too little; besides, the man was very hoarse.

Of those he did catch, he noticed that one kept recurring. Getting hold of it at length, he pronounced it over and over to himself until he was sure he could remember it. He never forgot it thereafter. It was the word *injustice*. What its meaning might be he did not know, but he stowed it away for future enlightenment.

Dusk lay over the crowd. Through it he again fell to studying faces. Plain that no joy dwelt here! But something inscrutable. The features were so heavy; the lines deeply cut. The pale light of the street lamps accentuated their sharpness, making them look more weather-worn than they actually were. . . . He thought of storms which he had seen threaten from cloudbanks west in the sea.

Injustice! Injustice! The word came again and again. So vehemently did the hoarse voice utter it that Nils could at last read the word in the faces, as plainly as if it had been written in an A B C book. . . . Was it possible these human beings had rowed against wind and storm all their lives? Did that explain their sinister, weathered look? . . .

He continued peering into faces as he walked down Wash-

ington Avenue. And not a single happy one did he see that
whole Sunday evening.

"At—last!" The words, which sounded like two pleased
grunts, came from the Poet, who was occupied over a sheet
of paper. "Comes, does he? And what desolate wastes, if one
may make bold to enquire, has our polar cub ranged today,
eh—what? How many tender seal pups has he torn asunder
and devoured?"

Quiet prevailed for a moment. The great head leaned low
over the paper. Nils could tell he was in good humour.
Which was to say that he had reached the first stage of
drunkenness; for he was always so jocular and full of
amusing notions in that stage. The one coming would be
worse; in it one would have to echo all he said, no matter
how absurd it might be. At that stage Nils could only wish
him so dead drunk that he'd fall asleep.

"If you're minded to absent yourself from these pavilions
come every Sabbath," he boomed, "I shall have to invite
some more peace-loving soul to live with me. I need company; that's why I took you under my protecting wings
when the Atlantic washed you up on these shores. What's
more, a polar bear needs to stay close to his lair when the
long night begins. Today you might have been privileged to
sit here within the castle and have drunk *dus*[1] with the
world's greatest spirits, and have nourished your impov-
erished soul. It would have profited you far more than
wearing out shoe leather along with the riff-raff on Washington Avenue."

The Poet laid his pen away and looked up for the first
time since Nils entered.

"Come now, confess your sins. Out with them!"

[1] A ceremony by whose performance two persons who would otherwise have to address each other in the formal form, agree to dispense
with it and to use thenceforth the familiar *du*—i.e., "thou."

The Boat of Longing

"Oh," faltered Nils, "I've been visiting a woman from Nordland, who lives here."

"There you are! Didn't I know it? The troll doesn't grow old before its tail curls. . . . But that aside, it isn't considered altogether good tone, even here in Minneapolis, for young cubs like you to be visiting women, no matter from what pole they derive. For such sport one must go farther east in Canaan; there it is said to be fashionable."

Nils looked down in silence.

"And she seemed fair to you, this lady from the Kingdom of Nordland?"

Nils, with a smile, confessed to a very pleasant day.

In a moment the Poet seemed to have forgotten his presence and sat deeply absorbed in the paper before him. He commenced writing.

Nils hung his coat and vest away first, then got out his own writing materials and joined him.

"Be so obliging as to journey over to the *Kingdom of Spirits* and summon hither Peder Christiansen Asbjörnsen, will you?" requested the voice above the paper.

Nils went, and after hunting among the books awhile, brought out the "Book of Wisdom," as the Poet called the fairy tales.

"And then will His Most Gracious Highness, The Prince of Nordland, also be so kind as to find the poem about Soria Moria Castle?"

Nils paged the book.

"Here's a fairy tale by that name; but no poem ——"

"That so?" The Poet looked up, his eyes now atwinkle. "The prince is not, then, of the opinion that a fairy tale may be a poem? You are indeed a dolt, my dear Nils, as truly as a native-born. But all stupidity bears its own punishment. For that reason this Nordland prince will now be so good as to seat himself there and study that poem!

In Foreign Waters

And in a few winks His Highness shall have an opportunity to recite his lesson."

"Do I memorize it?"

"*Ach,* how scant is your understanding! With barely a fifth of one small talent in that great tously head of yours, do you shuffle about. Who ever told you that to study was to memorize? It is the witling who stares vacantly and rattles off the words; the wise man, be it known, keeps his silence, and reflects whenever he finds aught upon his way. . . . Be at it now! By and by we'll confer."

In a mood halfway laughter, halfway tears Nils sat before the old crank, reading the fairy tale about Askeladden, fortune's favourite, who sallied forth into the world in quest of the princess and half the kingdom, and whose image had so often stood before him in his own longings.

As he read, he was more and more struck by the tale's content. Reaching the end, he returned to the beginning, only to be interrupted by the thunder of the Poet's fist upon the table, and the cry:

"There we've got the ending! By all the gentle gods of heaven, *there* it is! And the lines tread as neatly as milady's adorable feet in a beautiful waltz! Now you shall hear the poem that that fairy tale contains!"

He began to read immediately, piecing lines together now from one sheet of paper, now from another. The tale glowed under the fervour and pride in his voice:

"THE BALLAD OF SORIA MORIA
"Askeladden he sat on the hearth,
　　Stirring the ashes cold,
And he was aware of a castle garth
　　Hid in a haze that rolled
Over the keep and the barbican
　　In a broad twist of gold.

"He stood up by the kitchen fire;
　　His smile was lost and wise.

135

The Boat of Longing

He could not lie in his bed at nights,
  Nor in the morning rise,
But the singing splendour of Soria Moria
  Was ever before his eyes.

"He has filled his wallet with meat and bread
  He has whistled a foolish tune,
And is off for the land that is east of the sun
  And way to the west of the moon.

———

"He went by the crags and the brooding fens,
  And deep in the blackthorn wood
He broke his bread with the fox and bear
  Out of his brotherhood.

"He came by night on a wailing wolf,
  Gaunt as a wolf might be,
And he shared his meat with the raving beast
  Out of his charity.
And for his honesty, the wolf
  Dealt by him honestly.

"But terror whispered along the moors
  And straightly seized him, when
He heard the pant of the Mountain Troll
  Ranging for Christian men.

"Out of the murk came a groping hand
  And a foul hairy wrist,
But nimble-footed he leaped away
  From the hard hit of the fist,
For charity made his wallet light
  And saved him in the mist.

"Now Askeladden has trod the miles
  To the end of his desire,
To the golden turrets of Soria Moria
  Floating in golden fire.

———

"There was never a bleat of goat or sheep,
  Nor ever the song of a bird;
Alone in that glimmering solitude
  Only the stillness stirred.

136

In Foreign Waters

"Around the wall slept a dragon curled,
　　Sodden and glassy eyed;
Moss had cloven his brittle claws
　　And the grass grew in his hide;
And the lad crossed over him cannily
　　And cannily let him bide.

"He passed the slumbering golden bird
　　On a linden tree of gold,
And bravely thrust on the dusty doors
　　And gained the castle hold.

"Far through the long length of the hall
　　Like a swart crag of the shore
A Trollman twisted his vasty limbs,
　　And each enormous snore
Made the beams quake and you could feel
　　The shiver in the floor.

"A princess combed at his matty poll
　　And his thick shoulder-hair.
Lovelier than all of the Lady of Troy
　　Even her fingers were,
But her tears fell like the diamond rain
　　When all the sky is fair.

" 'What Christian man dare heartily
　　Enter the Big Troll's den?
For here is sleeping the bloodiest
　　Foe of all Christian men.'
'I come at the beckoning of the coals,'
　　Said Askeladden then.

" 'Take down the broadsword from the wall
　　And drink that flask of wine,
And gather your strength to swing the sword
　　For your sake and mine!'

"Now the troll rose and gaped his jaws
　　Like a cave of the rotting dead;
The lad has struck him below the beard
　　And smitten away his head,

The Boat of Longing

And it sprung a yard from the spouting neck
To a wide sea of red.

"There was a murmur around the sky,
  The silence snapped and broke,
The little birds cleared their throats to sing,
  And all the land awoke.

"Now Askeladden has taken the land
  Unto his governing,
He has wooed the Princess of Soria Moria
  And wed her with a ring,
But of the array of that wedding day
  No man of words may sing.

"For the proud line of the wedding march
  Was a whole kingdom long,
And men in the thirteen realms about
  Might hear the wedding song.

"And if you will win to Soria Moria
  Across horizons blue,
You may ask of the folk of Soria Moria
  If all these things be true."

The reading ended, the Poet looked up. His whole figure
was trembling. Tears of emotion and whisky gleamed in his
eyes; his eyes frankly sought Nils's commendation.

But Nils, lost in thought, did not find speech immediately; he only sat staring into the story: The lad in the
fairy tale became the lad of the poem; and the lad of the
poem, himself.

"I'll never win there!" he cried.

"No," responded the Poet, sulkily as a naughty child,
"that's long been plain!"

Thereupon he staggered across to the cupboard, poured
himself first one glassful and drained it; then another. The
bottle he carried back with him, placing it on the table
within reach. Then, slowly and with unpleasantly careful

In Foreign Waters

deliberation, he began destroying the poem, tearing it into tiny shreds. All the while he growled like a wild animal which is being molested.

A changed aspect began creeping over the figure, transforming him into something unspeakably repulsive and evil. Overwhelmed by a sense of being completely forsaken, Nils leaned over the table, dropped his head on his arms and commenced to cry. Like a terrific sea it surged forward—the loneliness, the anxiety, the awful hopelessness, the evil he had seen and felt in and about him. All came together, rising with greedy gasp as from the bowels of the ocean and sweeping him down to a deep knowing no bottom. He let himself go, surrendered completely . . . felt himself sinking lower and lower. . . . He thought it chilly in the depths. . . . But it also grew calmer there . . . only now and then could he feel the gentle rocking from some great billow overhead.

The Poet sat observing Nils through narrow, pursy eyes, looking extremely queer. Twice he reached out his hand for the bottle, but withdrew it halfway. As his astonishment mounted, his features softened.

"Are you drunk, boy?"

"No."

"Sick?"

"No."

Followed a long silence.

"Been fighting?"

"No."

Again silence. The crying had begun to subside.

"Been robbed?"

"No."

That exhausted the possibilities. He reached for the bottle. Again he let it stand. A thought dawned within him—fair as a room newly tidied and prinked with sunlight.

"Was it . . . hm . . . was it the poem?"

The Boat of Longing

"Yes," owned Nils, with difficulty; "comes closest to being that, I guess."

"Not a bad one, you know!" warmed the Poet. "Not bad. Beauty there."

Rising, he took to pacing the floor in devious courses. Now and then he blew his nose with a thunderous blast; this occurred every time emotion threatened to undo him. And as he now reeled about, the experience full upon him of having had a grown person sit crying like a baby over one of his poems, the blasts began to fall thick and fast. Emotion at length completely unmanning him, he seated himself on the edge of the bed and gave in. "That was beautiful, you know. Beautiful!"

Nils sat helpless, not knowing how he should try to calm him; he was moreover alarmed, for the great figure shook violently under the emotional surgings.

"What is the meaning of the word *injustice*, Weismann?" he finally asked, hoping to sidetrack his thoughts. But the Poet seemed not to hear; Nils therefore repeated the question.

"Injustice?" The Poet blew his nose with a deafening crack as he reiterated the word. *"Injustice?* That's what I've suffered from my people. There you've got the meaning of the word!"

Hereupon his thoughts glided in onto other tracks, giving further outlets for his feelings.

"For I tell you I've travelled the way of crucifixion among my people. Year in and year out I have gone among them, giving them of the beauty which my soul saw. And no one cared about it. Not one! . . . But now I'm through! So help me God, I am through!"

The Poet straightened. The massive features hardened. The eyes gleamed narrow.

"Can you imagine a person," he continued, "who walks

In Foreign Waters

about among fellow beings and is not seen by them? He meets one, stops and talks to him. He whom he addresses passes by in care-free complacency. He has not heard him, not seen him!

. . . "The lone one moves on. He encounters thousands, hails them, calls with might and main—only to find that not one among the thousand is even aware of his presence!

. . . "Or can you picture to yourself a man standing in front of a well-filled church showing people the fairest fabric that his soul has woven? Every strand in its making is the gift of God to a suppliant soul. Painstakingly he had laboured in order that he might gladden the hearts of men. And then there is not one in the whole crowded church who sees his treasure! Can you imagine the pain which that man feels as he passes the full pews? There is mortal bitterness in it, I tell you!

. . . "Or can you imagine a person sound of mind and altogether normal locked up in a madhouse because people think him insane? There he must remain year after year. All the time he has but one object; namely, to demonstrate his sanity. He gets up when morning comes, dresses, eats, does his appointed work. Throughout the day he makes every move with the minutest care, in order that his fellows may see how rational he is. Nevertheless, the watchmen suspect him. That man, they say—pointing to him as soon as he turns his back—is a dangerous fellow. Yes, very dangerous! And incurable! Never yet have we been able to make him see that he is crazy. Such cannot be cured, they say! How do you think this man feels after ten or fifteen years?"

"That must be awful!" cried Nils jumping up, completely carried away by the picture.

"No," glowered the Poet, "it's not that, either. It is only—*injustice*!"

The Boat of Longing

With that he got up, lumbered over to the table, seized the bottle, and gulped whisky till it almost choked him.

That night Nils slept uneasily.

IX

Next morning he was awakened by a rumpus up above. The Swede, who had to be off early to the saloon, was scolding the wife because breakfast wasn't ready; and she was blubbering and hushing a couple of the children who were crying.

The coloured children in the rear of the court had also commenced their racket, a controversy raging over the ownership of a football; two angry voices each loudly claimed it. Further penetrating his half-wakefulness came the sound of Otto's voice informing Per in tones none too gentle that he'd better bestir himself lest both of them be late.

Though Nils could be lazy if he liked on Monday mornings, they being easier for him than the others, he was now so wide awake that it was useless for him to try getting more sleep; he therefore got up.

Over in his bed slept the Poet, fully dressed.

On top of the book pile stood a letter in a position so conspicuous as to show Nils that it had been put there in order to attract his attention when he should have got into his clothes. Taking the hint, he walked over to it; and then he discovered that it was addressed to himself in the Poet's handwriting. This amused him. . . . So he had written more poetry, had he? . . . Nils had read many of his productions in that way.

He took a chair near the stove . . . he might as well read the verses now, while he waited for his coffee to boil. And there wasn't much likelihood of his being caught, either, for the Poet wouldn't be awakening till noon. . . . He broke the envelope.

In Foreign Waters

This time, however, it was not poetry. It was a letter. And it read thus:

DEAR COMRADE!

I call you that because I find you so true a friend; know in return that David could scarcely have thought more of Jonathan than I do of you. Only David had many friends, or could have had for the wanting; whereas I have but you. You are assuredly a gift. This I find it easier to say when you are asleep. Now I sit here looking at you in your corner. You seem so innocent; and I can talk to you unhindered, without any interruptions from your *yes'es* and *but's*.

There you turned. Are you dreaming, I wonder? It's sure to be of Nordland, if you are. Is it the ocean you see? and the melancholy gull?

Sleep on, lad! Sleep while you may; before the evil nights come, when you will say, I take no pleasure in it. Sleep, I say!

. . . What? Did you turn again?

. . . You think your comrade a swine, no doubt. And so he is. It's the whisky, you see; and life among the insane. The knowledge of their being strapped to their beds, and the sound of their shrieks have been inexpressibly hard to bear, you know. Especially of fall nights with the wind singing strangely about the corners of the house. Even cheap whisky becomes a godsend then. Only this fault to be found with it that it surrounds the heart with so much fat. And once that organ is wholly encased, says my friend the doctor, then all is over. Well, God be praised for that!

. . . Perhaps I've been made a swine in order to save you from destruction. . . . It may be. I do not know.

. . . But yours is so gentle a heart. Take good care of it. From it that life proceeds. Be a child always, and you will gain entrance to the kingdom of heaven. If you outgrow the child in yourself, the portal will be closed. Remember that now!

. . . The set of your mind too is fine. And it is still pure, although not clear. Fogs obscure, so that it sees but imperfectly; you would do well to keep the window panes clean!

. . . You wonder if you will ever attain your goal, I understand. That isn't new. All sober-minded people have done that before you. Precisely here that all the vague and unclear in you manifests itself. . . . "Shall I make it?" you ask. Of course you won't; not the goal you now have set. You may struggle a

143

few years, think yourself nearing it; having come close, you will find it paltry, of no consequence. And then you will feel more beggarly by far than you do now.

. . . What is the goal you now see? Does it stand out distinctly? Is it riches? "No," you answer; "not riches, exactly. Only enough to give me security." The measure of which varies with the individual. With you it is perhaps not so large yet. But—you do want *enough*. Hence money is a goal. Therein you are exactly like all the others. Thus far there has not been one Norwegian, setting foot on American soil, who has not seen gold. Therefore we'll say: you want gold, just a comfortable amount of it!

. . . And then you desire good clothes, and all else that is fair to look at. My dear boy, don't contradict me here! My day of watching life pass on this globe has been three times the length of yours. And the minds of men I have learned to read like an open book. Why, it is all I have had to do.

. . . Moreover, you want the esteem of mankind. That's obvious! People must speak well of you; shall say that which is of good report when the talk concerns you. And you prefer it to have a little admiration as well, since you are yourself a fine, good person.

. . . Yes, and you want the love of some young, rich, and beautiful woman—she whom you now see in the castle behind the evening star. Youth she must have, and beauty. Riches you may perhaps do without, reckoning to provide them yourself if need be. This woman shall be good to you, embrace you; she shall be your queen! You see her now.

. . . And you want a castle to put her in. That castle must be fully as fair as a palace; there together shall the two of you live in splendour till the end of your days. Thus lies life before you, gleaming in sunshine. You see it all so plainly now.

. . . And having managed to acquire it all, you will some fine day visit Norway: you feel it imperative to show the folks over there what a devilishly smart fellow you turned out to be; besides, you gave the old haunts your solemn promise that you would come back. Perhaps you will get that far; perhaps not. Most people do not. I did not. But you are so fine a lad and your heart is so brave that we shall assume that you will!

. . . Granted you reach Norway. The day you sail up the fjord is a beautiful one. Waves splash about the boat and nod you a welcome! Men celebrate in your honour. Flags float on high. Words of praise are spoken. And your heart swells and grows big within you; you are at your goal! And all is exceeding good. It may also happen, as it has so often happened to others, that there will be those who, when your back is turned, will smile credulous, enquiring by what knavery that fellow has succeeded in amassing gold among those barbarians yonder. But such contemptible pettiness we shall pass over. For it is now far into the night, and I am drunk, and your faith in mankind is still strong.

. . . And so you come back, fêted and much esteemed—rich in flocks, great and small. Of gold you have sufficient to feel reasonably secure. Your children have turned out well. All is good. Yes, all is very good!

But, and this is what I want to add before I go to bed (it's late and I'm drunk), then along comes the Old Fellow with the Scythe. He is so lean, and grudgy by nature. I always see him as a gaunt, lantern-jawed merchant; never as one of your sleek kind, for they are, as a rule, jovial, and like to chat with folks. It is possible to dicker with them and strike a bargain and have a fairly pleasant time meanwhile. . . . But he who comes to you now is, as I said, of the skinny kind. Such fellows are usually in a hurry; have barely time for each transaction. The Lean One will then say to you—curtly and dryly and business-like—"Fool, out with your soul! Out with your soul!" . . . Then it's another jig you'll be dancing. And one Nils the Nordlænding, that fine, handsome fellow of whom people spoke so well, will be scurrying around from cellar to garret, hunting in nook and cranny for what he cannot find. There is no trace of soul. Actually pitiful to see how he strives. Below in the cellar, or mayhap in the dark garret above, among heaps of trash and rubbish, he finds a miserable little dried-up pouch of skin which he seems to recognize as having seen before. With it he hastens to the Lean One. But the Lean One minds neither him nor his pouch. He stands there, telephone in hand—the telephone is always at his right hand! He calls headquarters and orders: "Come get the cadaver! It is now ready!" . . . Then there is no more.— Thus sped that "pillar of church and society," greatly lamented! *Punktum!*

. . . And this was you, blessed comrade of mine.— Now you turned again. You sleep uneasily tonight!

. . . But that was not the lad about whom I read to you in the fairy tale. Don't ever think it! What did he see in the

The Boat of Longing

embers of the grate? Gold? Fame? The good life together with an excellent woman? Oh no! Before him rose visions of a far different order. That lad saw his own potentialities, that's what he saw! God's deep intention with him. And the eventuality of his finally reaching the castle and winning the princess after incredible difficulties is merely the folk mind's poetic way of expressing an ethical truth. Simply stated, it means that he gained his own soul, his own Self. That's the most which any human being can win! Of such the Lean One will have to keep hands off; God's own good angels will come for them!

. . . Did that lad win gold? And fame? And the pleasant life? Far from it. He encountered wild beasts and trolls, not people. To the wild beasts he showed kindness. From the trolls he stole away. Finally he reached his destination. Not a soul accompanied him on his perilous adventure. No one saw him. There was no waving of flags; no speech-making. How indeed should the rabble have accomplished that? It lay leagues behind him, wholly content where it was. And why should it not be content? When it had its fields and merchandise, its wives and mistresses, its herds big and small, its Fords, and its movies? Still he did not lack company, that lad!

. . . But now I am going to bed, for I'm fearfully drunk and it's far into the night. You are sleeping more quietly, I see. If you are a true comrade, stay away from me tomorrow—I'm due for a headache, and then I'm quarrelsome and nasty at biting.

. . . I append a few lines for your comfort and encouragement:

"To a Silent Bird

"What are you doing
In this thin rain,
Dreaming old memories
Over again?
In the wet oaks here,
And conifers
Not a leaf flutters,
No twig stirs.

"All the wise singers
Have found new skies,
Where like loud trumpets
The mornings rise.

146

In Foreign Waters

This is a fearful place
  When bleak winds call,
The last crow shivers,
    The last leaves fall.

"Wisps of darkness
  Twine in the bare
Branches, and creeping
  Evils glare,
The quick grim shadows
  That cold nights bring,
But you sit silently
  Listening."

P.S. I hear sounds in Mike and Maria's room. A kettle is being flung on the stove; and a shoe drags heavily across the floor bumps. The woman isn't quite awake yet, I reckon.

K. H. W.

x

It rained throughout the ensuing week; otherwise it passed much as had those preceding it.

Nils, however, left off his customary noonday trips to Nicollet and took to reading instead. His old zest for it returned. Resolving to read the entire collection of fairy tales, he attacked those first. Frequently they would lead him into a blind alley, requiring that he call upon the Poet for guidance. Having made his way out, he would move on to greater heights, where he would find new worlds beckoning to him, gleaming and bright; he had never seen the like! And if by chance he found his way out unaided, he was like the lad of the fairy tale who, sallying forth to outwit the princess whom nobody could silence, exulted as he went along: "I have found something! I have found something!" Each truth discovered gave him joy.

Every noon he kept after Annie to help him with his English. Sure he'd take her to the movies some evening;

he might even take her to a show, though that he wouldn't promise for certain. He was for that matter almost ready to go the limit in promises just to get her help. He wanted to learn the language; simply must learn it! Life here required it, both the part which was worth having and that which might be passed by; until he could command the language, he must of necessity stand outside, be an alien. He likened himself to a baby sitting on the border of a great meadow and looking at a game in progress upon it, unable to participate because unable to walk. The game went merrily. There was song and sunshine and flowers; there was youth and joy and all that was alluring. He must get into it; Annie must be his nurse girl and teach him to walk.

Every evening that week he waited for Per Syv, so that he might speak with him. The subject never varied: "We've got to hunt better jobs, you and I; the way it's going now, we'll never get anywhere, never get to be decent folk. It will take different work for both of us. You scarcely earn enough to keep you in board; and I'm not doing a great deal better; never be any steamship to take us back to Norway at this rate!"

Per really had to throw curious eyes upon him. Just where had he got that gas? Did he think to begin bossing him around, too? Still he listened, for Per always listened.

— Well, had he any suggestions?

— No; but they'd have to hunt up other jobs. Others had found them. Why couldn't they?

— But others had money.

— Couldn't they, too, lay by a little? Though as far as that was concerned, there were plenty of people who had come to America just as penniless as they.

— Yes, if only they could think of some kind that paid better and wasn't too hard.

But, happening to be on a merry pin, Per Syv would

In Foreign Waters

protest and pass it off, for there was that about Nils's insistence which irritated him.

— It would be better after a while, most likely. Just wait. They had only just landed, hadn't they? They couldn't expect anyone to stand and throw the gold in their faces, could they? Look at Otto, now; next spring he'd be starting in business for himself!

— Was Otto going into business for himself?

— Certainly he was! He was going to run a saloon for Charley Swanström and have a share in it. "Then I can tend bar for Otto; he's promised me that. Soon's I've learned a little more, I'll be earning three times as much as I do now."

"But you'll never get to be a doctor that way," Nils reminded him.

"The hell with being a doctor!" blew Per, haughtily. "Think I want to be anything as dirty as that? Say, you should have heard the two university students who came into the saloon for a glass of beer the other day. They were talking about Dr. Cushman. Know what they said? That he butchered people like flies, and got money for it to boot. Yessir, from one to five hundred dollars. And then they laughed and sat there chuckling as though it did their hearts good. Got the stiffs, they said, to dig around in. Now isn't that beastly? No, thanks, I'll not be a doctor!"

"All right—be whatever you like; but as for me, I'm quitting my kind of work. And unless you do, you'll never get anywhere, either. There's better employment in America, you know that as well as I."

"Better? What's wrong with this, I'd like to know? As long as people want drink, there's got to be some one to sell it to 'em, hasn't there?"

"Oh yes," said Nils, glumly, "all the while there are murderers, there must be some one to hang them, I suppose."

Thus it ended between them one evening. But Nils was

not daunted; the next found him again at the saloon, waiting for Per, ready to renew the attack.

That week he wrote two letters home. In each he mentioned Per, saying that both of them were in good health and were working every day, but that both were on the lookout for better-paying jobs.

Sunday morning Nils was early on his way to the queer woman by the river. The weather was raw and sloppy. Occasional snowflakes drifted through the air. They fluttered, fell, and vanished in slush.

The river ran turgid and black after the prolonged rain. Nils had to go down, none the less, to pay his respects and skip a couple of pebbles. Today, as before, the sight of the water excited him. He felt his chest swell and his breath come more easily. . . . Almost more pleasant down here in the kettle bottom now than it had been last Sunday.

Aloft, from the direction of the bridge, came shouts and loud whoops. But the mist hung so thick that he could not easily distinguish the boys; only in between times, when he stood still and looked hard, that he could discern their shadowy gliding forms. Apparently they were having great sport.

Up on the river bank a prodigiously fat woman went gathering bits of driftwood into a sack. Nils could not remember ever having seen a human being so much like a barrel. She had a large black kerchief on her head, and a pair of blue, striped overalls around her neck. A little girl with flaxen hair ran about, helping her gather, exclaiming in Norwegian every time she found a chip, "Granny! here, Granny!" Whereupon the barrel would trundle round to it and thrust it into her sack. . . . So there were more Norwegians down here?

The yellow house still squatted on its haunches, staring at the water, but appearing in this day's greyness even flatter than before. Today, however, it seemed also to squat more securely.

In Foreign Waters

Kristine Dahl must have seen him, for she met him in the doorway. Once more he was struck by the childlike goodness of her. To look into her face was like being welcomed home after a long journey.

"Been waiting for you all morning," she greeted him, "worrying that you wouldn't get here in time so we could talk. You see—Mrs. Brakstad is expecting today; and, being I've promised, I'll have to be there, though I warned her not to send too early. I told her about having found you— well, did you ever, if I'm not saying *du* to you! But it seems as if I must today!

"Goodness, how rattle-headed I am! Let's see, what was I going to ask you? Oh yes—have you had breakfast? Oh? Well, then, I'll have a bite for dinner that'll taste good to a Nordlænding. I only hope that woman waits so I can get it prepared decently. You see there were so many things I forgot to enquire about the last time you were here."

Nils chose the chair by the window, where he had sat the previous Sunday. Again the distinct feeling overcame him that here he was a different being; it was as though he were sitting in the neighbour's house at home; all strangeness, demanding alertness of senses, had vanished. All he needed to do was surrender to the peace and security of the place.

Meanwhile she moved about, talking steadily as she busied herself with this and that. The rich music of her voice filled the room like the purl of water upon ocean strands on still nights. One who begins to listen to it quickly finds that he loses awareness of all else. And it made one feel so good to sit here looking at her face and conversing with her.— The forehead loomed large; myriads of wrinkles cut it, lying, standing, creeping, running in every direction. But the eyes shed a glorifying light, so that the face, despite its wrinkles reminded one of sunshine breaking through a thin veil of cloud. Softening the whole yet more was the slow, easy cadence of her speech.

The Boat of Longing

"The moment you were gone I thought of so much that we might have talked about; seems like I never have my wits about me. And they clean deserted me when you played so strangely. You're an expert, you are. Who taught you?— You don't say!"

— He wasn't by any chance acquainted in Heröyen, was he?

— No, he didn't happen to be: he knew of persons and places there only by hearsay.

Even that made her happy.

— And were the menfolk still going to Lofoten? And did as many lose their lives up there as before? . . . "Yes, yes, likely so," she sighed heavily, seating herself.

— And did the eider duck come up on shore and lay eggs under people's porches the same as it used to?— Yes, wasn't it fine in Nordland?

— And were they still holding fairs at Björn?

— Did he know who was the minister at Heröyen now?— Well, she could hardly expect that.

Then with greater animation:

— Had he seen the hole in the Torgehat? Well, did you ever! Had he seen that, too? Yes, wasn't it odd?

And so she was brought in upon the myth about Hestmanden, who stood there north in the sea, raging with thwarted love for his neighbour, the Maid of Leköy. Unable to make the haughty damsel listen to his wooing, he had in a fit of anger, seized one of the Tom Needles and hurled it at her. And the needle had gone straight through the Torgehat, leaving a hole which could be seen to this day. . . . She glided into the myth, telling it with quiet feeling.

Nils had not heard exactly that version of it, but thought it impolite to correct her. So to her he merely wondered if there might be any truth to the story.

This almost offended her:

152

In Foreign Waters

— Truth to it? The hole must have got there some way! Human hands hadn't cut it. Nor was there another like it in the world. God had scarcely made it; for it only weakened the mountain. . . . And besides Tom had but two needles, when he should have had three—as anyone could see by looking at Tom Akselen; plain enough that Akselen was the remainder of the third peak!

"I'll tell you," she went on, as though confiding a secret to him, "there was much that was strange in Nordland, and a lot that never got told in books, though the world's going blind with conceit in its own wisdom. I know what I experienced the summer Johan died!"

— Was Johan her husband?

She did not answer immediately; instead she went to the stove and began pottering with a skillet.

"No," came the answer after a bit, and as from a distance, "he wasn't that, either, exactly. We didn't get that far, Johan and I . . . though I'm convinced that before God we two are man and wife as truly as if we had stood at His altar. I've never looked at another man since he was lost. That guilt I do not have on my soul."

"Did he die?"

"Yes, he went down in that storm on Veröy Sea in 'ninety-three."

"Huh!" Nils could only shake his head.

Too gripped by the memory to speak further, she began decking the table; at intervals she went to the window to peer up the street.

Nils took the violin from its peg. He felt he could have cried with her; but he commenced playing all the lively tunes he knew, hoping they might distract her from the sad memories.

She listened in silence. The music seemed to cheer her.

Into the spirit of mirth which he now strove to express came a few of the tones he had heard last Sunday evening.

The Boat of Longing

Coquettishly they came, offering themselves. He tried to take them along, and found it not difficult, for with the mood created by the look of his listener's face and the memory of what he had seen at the time of his last bending over this violin, the tones seemed to glide in of themselves. That he was succeeding made him happy.

But then she approached him, a troubled look on her face. "No," she said, shaking her head, "you'd better not attempt that dance tune, or whatever it is. That sounds too frivolous. It's Johan's violin you're playing. No, no, don't stop! Play all you like!" she pleaded, seeing that he intended to put the instrument away. "That wasn't my meaning; for Johan and I were both fond of music. But," and her voice lowered into a strange secretiveness, "there's something very unusual about that violin!"

"Oh?"

"Yes, you see ——"

"In what way?"

"Yes, Johan gave it to me after he was dead!"

"After he was dead?" Nils stared fixedly at her.

"It happened like this, you see. After Johan died, Jens Kalsa from Hesta bought the violin of Johan's father. You have heard of Jens, I suppose. He was the greatest fiddler in the countryside in those days. Everyone knew him. I used to hear him often both in Björn and elsewhere. Well, there was to have been a big dance at Hesta the summer after Johan was lost, and Jens was to have played. He was to have used Johan's violin. But the dance never came off. For when Jens had tuned the instrument and was ready to start, some one came and snatched it away from him!"

"Did they see anything?"

"See anything? Hardly! Jens felt a hand on his arm just as he lifted the bow. It was that of a strong man, you may believe, whosesoever it was! Jens Kalsa took it seriously

that he had two men row him to Ravnöy late that night.
And he brought me the violin!"

"Did he know that you and Johan were engaged?"

"How could he? No one knew that!"

"And still they found the way?"

"You may well marvel! The likes of those men's exhaustion after that trip, I've never seen; you would have thought they had raced with death. Jens's face was as white as that cloth when he came into the room. At the sight of me he stared very strangely. Finally, he stammered, 'Do you know this?' Then he took the violin out of the case and handed it to me.

"Let me show you something very odd," she said, coming to Nils and turning the instrument in his hand. "Look here, on the back. See that cross in the grain of the wood when you hold it this way? Can you see it? You will hardly have found that in any other violin, I believe.

"I took the violin from Jens and looked at it. Not that I needed to, for I recognized it immediately; but I did it just the same. 'Perhaps I do know this one,' I answered. 'Well, then you'd better take charge of it,' he said, and sank down on a chair. After that he was sick abed for a month.

"Since then I've had the violin. What to do with it after me, I don't know. You see, only good hands must have it, hands that won't shame it." She looked at Nils beseechingly.

"I might as well tell you, since I've thought about it all week, that I've wondered if you wouldn't take it? You'd have to promise, though, to find some good person to take it after you again. Don't you think you could do me that kindness?"

Nils had cast his eyes down.

"I already have one," he said, bashfully, "and I think of so many kinds of tunes that perhaps Johan ——"

A terrible din upon the door interrupted the conversation. A small boy thrust his head in timidly; and then, con-

The Boat of Longing

fronted thus unexpectedly by the presence of two persons when he had been dead certain there'd be only one, he completely forgot what he had come to say, and only stood there sucking his thumb.

Kristine Dahl rose abruptly and went toward him.

"What is it, Tommy? Is your mother sick?"

It took the boy a few moments to recover the use of his tongue. After a little, however, he managed to deliver himself:

"Mommy said for me to tell you she was getting sick now." He was as grave as an undertaker.

"All right, my boy; tell your mother to send you back as soon as she feels she must have me; tell her I've got company now. Here's a piece of candy for you. Can you remember what I said?" she asked, helping him gently through the door.

"I'll have to get on with my dinner," she said as soon as the boy was out of sight.

"But don't you have to go?" asked Nils, concerned.

"No hurry about it; it's only three or four houses away. You don't understand such matters," she added, maternally. "Sit down and play and I'll finish the dinner."

She busied herself while he played. Every now and then she came toward him with a question; but she did not mention the violin again.

Presently the delicious odour of fish began filling the room. Kristine Dahl moved to and fro in housewifely fashion, now decking the table, now occupied at the stove.

At length the meal was ready. There steamed a platter of fresh boiled redsnapper; and a tureen of fish soup. But before she invited him to come to the table she brought out a bottle and two glasses.

When they were seated she asked the blessing. Then she poured red wine into the glasses and drank a *skoal* with him. That done, she put the bottle away without offering him any more.

Nils had not felt such coziness within a house since he left home; and he grew more talkative concerning himself than he had hitherto been.

"What kind of winter employment do you think an ignorant newcomer could get so he could earn a few shillings?" he asked.

"Well, that's a little hard to say, offhand. Usually not much to be had in town during the winter months. But why don't you try the woods for the winter? And then come back here in the spring? You'd have to give up your room, of course; but you could leave your trunk with me."

"The woods, you say?"

"Yes, cutting timber. They say it's hard work; but the pay is good. And you'll save what you earn."

"How could I get it?"

"Go to an employment office. They're sure to be hiring men for the camps right now."

The dense fog which had been enveloping Nils for the last couple of months began to lift. Here apparently lay a way out that would be easy to follow.

He began telling her of some of his cares, including Per Syv.

She listened to him wonderingly.

"Yes, promises are easily made. I can see it's been difficult for you. But since you've undertaken to look after him, you must do it, of course. By all means get him out of the city; the sooner the better."

XI

They had finished their meal, but continued to talk.

Nils wondered if she were not going soon. Since no sign

The Boat of Longing

of departure came from her, he rose and reached for his hat, not wanting to detain her.

But she wouldn't hear of his leaving. Why need he hurry? "You haven't played the song for me yet, you know."

"What song?"

"The one you whistled last Sunday. The one I knew you by!"

"Which one was that?"

"Don't you remember? It begins like this:

"Hearts when young are always hungry;
Love they want and much they need.

You played it the last time you were here."

"Are you so fond of that?"

"I'd have to be, wouldn't I, since it brought me Johan?"

"That song?"

"Yes. It would hardly have come to aught between us except for it. Johan was very bashful, you see; and I, poor thing, wasn't much better. Besides, some one else nearly came between us!"

"And that song could bring it about?" exclaimed Nils in quiet amazement.

"It actually did!"

She slipped into the past, far back, her voice soft and melodious.

"We had liked each other since childhood, Johan and I, ever since I was about ten and he about thirteen, I should think. He was three years older than I. But he wasn't the kind to speak up, or even to venture so much as a hint. No, he wasn't like that. He was queer that way. And still there wasn't any need that he should. It wasn't hard to tell how he felt, especially at times when he looked at me. He had such kind eyes—Johan. They were just like the sea on a moon-night in autumn.

158

In Foreign Waters

"Besides, he was unspeakably kind to me, though he was that to everyone.

"After we were confirmed we didn't meet very often. He prepared for confirmation a year ahead of me. He wasn't so quick at books. I really think I could beat him in that. Then he came to be gone a good deal, as the young folks are up there. In summer there was the herring-fishing; in winter, Lofoten; and in spring, Finmarken. Betweentimes he was at home and then we saw each other.

"One Christmas I got a pretty silk kerchief in the mail. I didn't need to be told who it came from—I knew right away, even though there was no name or anything on it. Christmas Day I wore it to church. After services Johan came up to shake hands, and then he pretended he'd never seen it before and remarked that it was mighty stylish I had become—God bless him, where he sleeps! He knew better, all right. But his saying it made me so happy that I could have put my arms around him right before the whole congregation. Queer, I tell you, when the heart begins running over like that!

"Then don't you suppose matters turned out so badly the next summer that one of the lads from Ravnöy began following me! I don't understand to this day what he ever could have seen in me. But he was stark mad; every move I made he was at my side; I couldn't stir of an evening without his being right there. And yet, do you suppose I could bring myself to refuse him straight out, even though I didn't care for him that way? It seemed as if I hadn't the heart, I felt that sorry for him. He was such a fine lad; besides, I knew only too well what it meant to be so unreasonably fond of a person. The Good Lord didn't give us all the same strength—no, that He didn't. But likely He has His purposes in that, too.

"The worst of it was that people began talking about us. You know how they are. The young crowd nearly teased us to death. And then Johan changed; I could feel it. He wouldn't look at me. And when I did catch his eyes, they had such a peculiar look in them. Merciful God, how I suffered those days!

"Then one summer evening—a Sunday it was, I remember it well—several of us young folks were out for a stroll. Goodness! what summer nights! It nearly makes me cry to think of them! All evening the lad had stuck by my side. Then finally I managed to break away, and Johan and I fell into company. How, I do not know, but, anyway, it happened. At first he was very quiet. And talk didn't come easy for me, either, exactly.

"We started up the hill together. There was a fine view from the top, of the islands and skerries, and of the sea. So we sat down. Johan stretched himself full-length in the heather, his hands under his head; and I sat by his side not knowing what to say. After a while he began humming a tune. 'Is that a new song?' I asked. 'No, not very, I guess; but I learned it in Lofoten last winter,' he answered. 'Can't you sing it for me?' I asked, that being all I could say. And he did. And that's the one you whistled. By the time he was through, I sat crying like a child that's been punished! I just couldn't help it.

"When I finally got so I could speak again, I said to Johan that in case he really wanted me there'd be only one answer for me to give. Yes, I spoke straight out. For how could I do otherwise? If there was any sin in that, then I must long since have atoned for it.

"That evening, then, we became engaged. Mercy! what happiness for two poor souls! Neither of us could say very much. We just sat gazing at the sun. That night it seemed to be playing for us alone."

She drifted so far away into the memories that the words ceased coming.

In Foreign Waters

But so intently had Nils followed her that the moment she stopped he asked:

"And it was the next winter that he was lost?"

"Yes, the following winter! Something had to happen, I suppose. Such happiness was too great for human beings."

"And then you went away?"

"Yes, the next fall."

"You knew you wouldn't be happy at home after that?"

"No, not that altogether," she said slowly—"not altogether. It was probably restlessness most of it. For a long time that summer I thought I saw the Boat. Every night it happened. But when the heart is so heavy with sorrow as mine then was, the eyes will often see much that is strange!"

"Do you mean that you saw it yourself?" asked Nils, tense.

"Yes."

"Often?"

"Oh yes. I usually saw several in a company."

"Was there more than one?" cried Nils.

"Yes; you see, I was so depressed that I couldn't sleep at night, and then I would see them. And they were always leaving. Always putting to sea. Finally, I went with them."

Nils's eyes were riveted on her as though he were locked in a spell. He wanted to speak, but could not. A far-away look had come into her eyes. Her face was drawn. The wrinkles stood out sharply.

"Dear me," she said, with a heavy sigh, "Mrs. Brakstad is wanting me now. It's time for me to go, I guess. But you stay right here!"

She sighed again, said a hurried good-bye, and left.

III. Adrift

I

THE month of May came with balmy weather and the strong scent of spring in the air. Even in northernmost Minnesota the season was well on its way.

The snow was gone; only on north slopes, in among the impenetrably dense undergrowth of timber-shadowed windfalls, one could detect a dirty grey whiteness.

The leafwood stretched and strained, and shot wee glistening sprouts from every tiny twig. It was alive from root to crown.

And the evergreen wood—pines and firs and balsams—sweating in the warm May sun, exuded a fragrance which spread itself far over the landscape and gave it a pungency all its own.

All nature was being filled with life. The brooklet gurgled and sang, the partridge cackled and flapped its wings, the roe ventured out upon the forest path, gazed surprised and unafraid at the approaching wanderer, then sniffed up at the sun and disappeared at a bound within the thicket.

Only the soughing of the forest which did not change. Neither balmy weather and sun, nor warm winds, availed to stifle its moan. Day and night it sang its song. And strangest of all in the tensest stillness its lament was ever the deepest.

Often of quiet evenings Nils had stood wondering if he could not capture its tones. He had tried it, too, in the shanty on Sunday afternoons, for he had brought his violin along. But the courage to let himself go had failed him with so many listeners sitting about, and he had made no prog-

Adrift

ress. Still he was determined to continue the attempt whenever the opportunity should come.

Life in the logging-camp had been strenuous that winter; in the beginning so strenuous that neither Nils nor Per had thought he could endure it. The quest for other employment looming too formidable an alternative, however, for two newcomers unacquainted with the language, they had stayed. After a time they had become inured to it and to the jibes of the veterans as well.

For Nils it had been especially difficult before he became accustomed to it. During the first couple of weeks he had worked like a slave; then finding that he was standing it, he had fought out another two weeks, after which he had felt more sure of himself. Thereafter he had grown to like it. And today, yes, today, as he sat there aboard the dinkey, which drumbled along whenever it got ready and stood still at the sight of a cow switching its tail in a new clearing, he felt regret at the thought of leaving this great empire of solitude.

But spring was singing to him, and he listened. Before him lay life, open, in dream and mist. His longing to know what it might be holding for him made him happy to be moving, eager to meet it.

He had been able to lay by all of one hundred ninety dollars this winter, which, together with his previous savings, gave him a good two hundred and sixty; it was not altogether unlikely that he felt himself rich as he now sat there upon the hard seat, enjoying the leafy woods through which they were passing.

For Per Syv, on the contrary, all had gone easier at the outset. As long as the experience was new, it had delighted him. Later, losing its glamour, it had become tedious and boring; but since it was Per's nature to let each day's trouble take care of itself, he had managed capitally none

The Boat of Longing

the less. His work had been that of a cookee; Nils's, that of a sawyer.

Today Per Syv sat with one hundred fifty dollars in his pocket—the biggest sum he had ever owned. Consequently, he felt extravagantly prosperous. Summer was just ahead! And Minneapolis! Where, indeed, were many pleasant attractions. All the drink money could buy! Though Per would, for that matter, really have no need of buying, since he would be selling, and it was customary that such fellows get enough for personal use. Then, too, the place was full of pretty girls always on the lookout for a jolly time! Truly, life had never looked more enchanting than it did today, thought Per.

The dinkey had switched in on a siding and was endeavouring to hook up a string of flat cars loaded with logs.

"Be fun to stay up here awhile now," remarked Nils. "It's going to be beautiful in the woods this summer. And there should be some fine fishing on Wild Horse."

"No, thank you," blew Per, "no more savagery and tyranny for me! I'm off for the city, the gay old city with the jolly wenches, as Brother Carlson called them the other day. Enough of torture and torment now for a while!"

"Oh, we shouldn't complain! Feel your steam-hammer fists, boy! And your face is as brown as an Indian's. Maybe you think the girls on Seven Corners won't gaze after you," teased Nils. "And now you can write home and tell the folks you've got so much money you don't know what to do with it all. Do you realize how much one hundred fifty dollars is in Norwegian money? Get that done first thing! I've always mentioned you and sent your greetings. Now you can do me a service."

"Would you like me to write about us fooling you into eating mustard instead of jam, too?"

"Sure, go ahead, for all I care! But then you've also got to tell about the night you went to Wild Horse Lake and

Adrift

stuck the leaven in the water so we'd be sure to have enough when we began cutting farther west! How about it, was the ice very thick where you cut through?"

"Thick? Man, I'll swear it was a fathom! Worst of it was that I had to make the hole so wide, you see, because it got to be so deep. Finally, I stood down in the hole chopping!"

Both laughed at the memory. But Per had not laughed the night of the episode; it had been four miles from the camp to the lake, with three feet of snow on the ground and walking none too easy.

They continued to recount the winter's experiences; but the mildness of the spring day moderated even the worst of them and enabled them to laugh at them all. They were now on their way southward—Minneapolis-bound, both of them. Borne along by the train, they felt as though they were approaching home.

Per Syv, in too topping spirits to sit still for many minutes at a time, flitted about from place to place, occupying now one seat, now another. He seemed to fear he might miss something; besides, he felt the urge to share his fine spirits with the other passengers. So he spoke to everyone whom he thought enjoyed talking.

But Nils sat still. In him, also, the mood was very bright. Yet he was not the Nils who a few months back had made his way north; his experiences in the wilderness, the hard labour and all, had matured him greatly and clarified much that had hitherto been vague in him, giving it more distinct form.

Here, on the threshold of new fairy-tale adventures, his thoughts played with many strange fancies. Most of them concerned the future. If God had a special intention with him, as the Poet had put it, it must lie along the path of music—quite definitely he had begun to feel it. For his deepest cravings led him that way.

The Boat of Longing

The overpowering need in his soul was for the beautiful, the actual existence of which he never questioned. But would the road he had chosen lead him thither? Was the beautiful really to be found among men? Yes, that it was!

And the happiness he had so often dreamed about . . . the bright, shining happiness! Where, then, was it? Surely, it too was among men. Where else would one seek it? . . . And since the kingdom of beauty was little likely to be crowded, he could probably slip into it off and on. But— would it then be the dwelling-place of happiness? He was measuring with himself as the yardstick; and it stood clearly before him that those moments when beauty had affected him most poignantly, were precisely those in which happiness had been most strengthless.

Reckon or reason as he would, he could not find that happiness and beauty went hand in hand. And yet the two must accompany each other. They simply must! If only one could follow the two pathways long enough, they must ultimately be found to join. Right at the junction signpost is where he would like to start; from there the road must lead straight to the Golden Gate!

Nils's awareness of the foliage and evergreen woods had vanished; his vision had glided out into the infinite. Over his face lay the old expression of discontent and longing, an expression peculiarly characteristic, and capable of suddenly printing many years into his frank, open countenance.

Yes—the Golden Gate!

Among the camp crew that winter had been an old Stril,[1] a man of quiet, reserved ways to whom Nils had taken a fancy. The two had often of a bright Sunday afternoon struck out on some rutty logging road for a woodland tramp together and been gone till supper-time. On these occasions the Stril had opened up and related at length. He had been in all lands and ports; had fared the seven seas. At the age

[1] A person from a coast district near Bergen.

Adrift

of sixty, twelve years ago, he was mustered out in the city of San Francisco, to become thenceforth a landsman. But his restlessness had not abated, and he had wandered constantly ever since. To him the Atlantic and the Pacific seaboards signified more than two crooked lines on a map; they signified cities and states, people and many tongues. He had fished in the Gulf of Mexico as well as off the coast of British Columbia. Only one place left now which he must see, he had confided to Nils, and that was Alaska. And after he had quizzed Nils about Nordland, he had concluded that the two must resemble each other. Then, eager to know all about the place so that he might make comparisons, he had asked all sorts of questions about Nordland: about the colour of the sea, the contour and depth of the fjords; about sea vegetation, mollusks, and bird life; about currents and seasonal changes.

"And where will you go after you've seen Alaska?" Nils had asked.

"Then I think I'll be through with these parts and can steer my course westward."

"Westward?"

"Yes, on the sunset, where the Golden Gate opens into new lands. My hour is nearing."

"And are you through here now?"

"Through?" the Stril had ejaculated, with a characteristic inflection. "I've been that these forty years."

"And have you met many who were happy on all your wanderings? Where, say, did you meet the happiest ones?"

The question had provoked a quiet, good-humoured chuckle. "That's easily answered. I remember it very well. It was sixty-two years ago; and the persons were five boys minnow-fishing on a bay, rocking about in a four-oared boat in the glittering summer sun. Guess I ought to remember that all right! The lines they used were of thread their mothers had spun; their hooks were of old brass wire; they had gathered snails for bait. And they were so ragged that their tatters beat each other to death. But *they were happy!*"

Nils had laughed at the answer and remarked that they must have been Strils, those five.

But the old man had not laughed. For a while he had walked along silent and preoccupied.

"No," had come the tardy reply, "neither Strils, Nord-lændings, nor any other earthly sort; nothing but five boys fooling away the hours out there on the bay, fishing with tackle they had stolen or had made themselves."

Because of the man's grave mien, Nils had not wished to question him further, and they had trudged side by side wordless upon the logging road. Dazzling white snow had blinked on every hand. Now and then the loud report of cold bursting in some giant fir had boomed hollowly and heavily through the great solitude.

After a little the Stril had come back to the question.

"You were asking about the happy people: Well, they don't live on our planet, you see; we'll just have to wait, my boy! On this one human beings are not human beings. They are seamen and farmers and miners and lumberjacks; they are tramps and preachers and professors; they are this and that and the other. And happiness departed from them when they left off being human beings and became this other; for then strife began. And strife may harden, but it cannot give happiness—except to the professional murderer. And scarcely to him!"

Disliking to accept such a view, Nils had begun to dispute the Stril.

"You cannot deny the existence of happiness, man," he had remonstrated. "There must be happiness. It can't be otherwise!"

"There must, you say? Now that's a foolish argument. The world is full of things which are and which ought not to be; as again, there is much which ought to be and which

Adrift

simply is not to be found. What do you make of that?"
The Stril had gesticulated vehemently to these arguments as
he strode along.

"It's a foolish argument . . . and that's the truth of it!
There should be somewhere near enough for all, but is
there? The world ought by this time to have progressed
sufficiently in wisdom so that no one owned more t,an he
could take care of, as long as others have so little that they
can scarce keep body and soul together. But has it? We
stand exactly where we did in the days of the Flood. There
should be no murderers. But aren't there, perhaps? There
should be no cheap whisky for the poor man, nor sweet
wine for the rich. And yet there is. There should not be
war and wholesale murder, but there are, just the same.
And take now this beautiful landscape through which we
are passing; it could produce bread for thousands of hungry
mouths, but here it lies, undiscovered and unproductive,
while scarcely one hundred and fifty miles away lie Sodoms
and Gomorrahs wherein 'human beings are huddled together
like lice in a cold pelt and haven't a foot of green earth
whereon to amuse themselves. Never you talk of *must* or
must not!"

To which outburst Nils, calling to mind the life he had
lived together with Mother Anna and Jo by the Sea, had
countered in quiet sincerity:

"Yes, but I know there are happy people to be found."

"That you can well make me believe!" The Stril had
begun sucking an icicle out of his mustache, wherefore an
interval before he continued:

"Certainly they are to be found! We lay in Calcutta
unloading cargo once, when the captain dragged a troupe
of actresses on board for the crew one night. A damnable
low-down skunk, that's what he was! His ship was unsea-
worthy. The food so bad that it became a byword; every
mother's son of us was discontented, and not a day passed

169

The Boat of Longing

but what we talked of deserting. Can you guess what he did?
Yes, to pacify us, he arranged a glad evening—the beast!
The mate poured the grog, which *was plenty*! Then the
captain came in with the troupe—five wenches in all. Hardly
a one of them could have been past twenty. All were dressed
in flaming colours. Well, they sang for us, and did their
tricks; they yodled, they danced; they drank grog with us.
It can certainly be testified that they were a gay lot of birds,
those five. Finally, they flew straight into our arms and
kissed us."

At this point the Stril had stopped to dispose of another
icicle.

"Well, afterward, the ship's carpenter told us that all five
were insane, and that their malady broke out in just that
kind of joy. One had only to watch out so they didn't become too wild; for then they would bite. Laws, yes, they'd
bite! Ever hear, boy, of people as happy as that? And their
manager, who evidently had bought them from the various
asylums, made big money by taking them around to the
boats, when these came to port after long voyages. No beings in creation so starved for joy as sailors are after a
voyage. Guess I'm the one to know that, having tried it these
livelong years!"

The winter sun had long since set, only a dull saffron
glow remaining to show whence it had gone.— Once more,
the scene stood vividly before Nils; he even remembered
the chill he had experienced that night, and how he had beat
his arms to throw it off.

"You're not freezing, are you—you a Nordlænding?" the
Stril had asked.

"No, I'm only a little stiff," Nils had answered.

But ever since that afternoon the vision of the Golden
Gate had been playing in his mind. Evenings, when he stood
alone out under the stars, listening to the soughing of the
forest, and waiting to catch the tone which would fit it best,

it would come bobbing up and make him glow with warmth. Thus it was that the Golden Gate became the embodiment of all that he had dreamed about the happy and the beautiful. Thenceforth it was to him the Soria Moria Castle toward which he, from now on, would journey.

He was indeed a remarkable fellow, that Stril, reflected Nils, as he now rolled along through the alley of woods. Late in April, when mild weather and thaw had begun to change the season in earnest, he had dropped out of sight.

He had gone to the office and asked for his wages. However he had managed it before his time was up, no one knew, for he had hired out till the 1st of May. Nils was the only soul to whom he had confided a word about leaving.

He had called Nils out of the shanty after supper one night.

"I'd like to have a word with you," he had said, adding, when they came outside : "I'm going now."

"Where are you going?"

"I'm leaving, you understand."

"Are you leaving?"

"Yes, I'm leaving."

"Have you gotten your pay?"

"Yes."

"And where are you bound for?"

"West. Alaska first of all."

Nils had tried to dissuade him; he mustn't leave now— alone, with black night coming on!

To which the Stril had only given a laugh. "An old sea dog who has kept the middle watch as often as I can get along all right. I just wanted to say good-bye, that was all."

Nils had commenced walking with him. "But, my good man, you can't start out tonight!" he had remonstrated.

"Oh yes."

"To Alaska?"

"Certainly."

"Have you any acquaintances there?"

"Not that I know of."

"But you have relatives in this country, haven't you?"

"That I couldn't tell you."

Nils had continued to walk beside him. It was as though he could not tear himself away.

The air upon the woodland road had smelled suspiciously of spring. Tepid gusts of south wind had come sweeping through, and now and then driven a few raindrops before itself, which it had filched out of the darkness.

The fir trees round the camp, spared to give shelter against wind and driving snow, had sighed and moaned; they had been like a great breast breathing sorrow and gloom out into the night.

"And when you have done with Alaska, where will you go?"

"Huh—then I'll set my course straight on the Golden Gate! For I reckon by that time my bark will have seen its day. Besides, it's sure to take me at least two years out there. Alaska is big, you see. And should the old hulk still be seaworthy, it'll not be a great run across the strait to Siberia. But I don't suppose I'll ever get that far, though it, too, is a place I've not seen."

"Time for me to turn back, I guess."

"Yes, I suppose you must. For you have much ahead of you yet!"

And then, with a clasp of hands, they had gone in opposite directions: the Stril into the south wind and darkness, Nils toward camp. Before he had got back the rain had begun to pour.

II

It was sunset time. The passenger train was ready to pull out of Cass Lake on its journey southward.

Adrift

A man came running up the track alongside the coaches, just in time to swing himself on board the steps of the smoker as the train started. He had no baggage.

He was slightly above medium stature, and appeared to be about thirty years old. His brown flannel shirt was offset by an expensive-looking tie; and his suit, of the best-quality material, fitted his fine figure to perfection. His darkly tanned skin testified to constant exposure to the out-of-doors.

The moment he stepped inside the door, he shoved his hat back on his head, took to mopping his face with a large silk handkerchief, and said in a jovial voice:

"Holy smokes! what a race. I'll swear I've left chunks of me all down the street." He came forward into the coach a couple of steps. "Must've mowed down at least one dozen women. If I don't land in the lockup now, I'll certainly give a thank offering to some female saint!"

He was not talking to anyone in particular. When he got well past the first four or five seats, he stopped, wiped his face again, and looked around at those who were seated.

"Any decent soul here got a match to give away?"

Not even now did he direct the question to anyone in particular.

Nils and Per, occupying a double seat, sat facing each other. Beside Per sat a young travelling salesman, who was getting off a station or two farther down the line. But Nils had, as yet, the whole seat to himself.

Per's eyes had been riveted on the stranger from the moment he entered the coach; and no sooner had he asked for a match than Per had one ready to give him.

"Thanks! I'll sit here, if there's no objection," he said in the same jolly voice, dropping down beside Nils. One could easily be attracted to the large, somewhat rough-hewn face, for it was radiant and likable. The eyes twinkled with life. Only Nils, catching their basic look, did not take to him. Per, on the contrary, was immediately impressed, thought

The Boat of Longing

this the finest fellow he had ever clapped eyes on and wanted to talk to him straight off.— The chances for that, however, turned out to be pretty slim, for the man's own line was so breezy that Per could scarcely wedge in a word.

"You fellows just blown in from the woods, have you?" he burst out, the moment he had lit his cigar and got himself settled. "Whose camp do you come from? That so? Well, I guess I ought to know who those fellows are! Live right up here, both of 'em, George Huestis in Grand Rapids, Mc-Guire in Duluth. Believe me there's a pair have made a nice little pot; no need of them dirtying their hands any more. But small thanks to them for that—they came into this country in the good old days when a man could go out and grab up whole townships of the finest timberland in the world for a bottle of old rye and a box of cigars."

— Was he acquainted with the men they'd been working for this winter? Per had enquired, timidly.

— If he knew them! Should say he did! He had scaled for McGuire for three years, when McGuire was going his biggest up near International Falls.

Nils sat studying the man closely from the side. . . . Was it possible that this man had been a scaler? Those he had known this winter hadn't looked like that!

"Have *you* ever worked in the woods?" flashed Per, astounded.

"Who hasn't, up here? Hardly a job round a logging-camp that I haven't had. Got my start as a bull cook when I was fourteen, and was bullied and laughed at and chased like a dog right and left. You bet I know a little about life in the woods!"

"So you've worked with the cook, have you?" laughed Per, enthusiastic.

Nils gravely suspected the man was lying.

"That's what I'm telling you!" answered the stranger. "And I've been cook, and loader, and sawyer, and teamster;

174

only job I haven't tried a hand at is blacksmithing. The last three years I worked in the woods I was boss for Huestis." The stranger began to chuckle quietly and good-humouredly at the experience which his memory seemed to be recalling.

"And I won't forget those first years so very soon, either. Had my hands more than full, I can tell you!"

"Was it a big camp?" asked Per.

"No, not very—a hundred men in all. 'Twasn't that. But I hadn't taken the job till just the last minute. Was a little afraid of it, see. Huestis wasn't the easiest cuss to get along with and I knew it. But he kept at me all summer, and then just when he was ready to start he came clear to Brainerd and made me an offer such as I couldn't turn down. Well, we set out. The hiring he'd already done. And that's where I'll tell you I got into a soup! What sort of crew do you suppose he'd collected? I'll be dog-goned if they weren't Irish and Italians, every mother's son of them—about half and half of each!"

The stranger paused effectively, glancing at Per and Nils; the salesman, however, he ignored.

"What are you fellows?"

"Oh, we're Norwegian," Per enlightened him after a moment's hesitation.

"Norwegian—eh? Thought maybe you were Swedish. Well, I know the Norwegians pretty well. Kind, peaceful people, they are. And good workers. No nonsense about them in any way—excepting when they get whisky, but then they're the devils. Lord help the boss who's got a lot of them on his hands! You see," he leaned forward and confided directly to Per, "the Norwegians aren't like the rest. They don't club together against the other fellows—they tear loose at each other!"

"What's your nationality?" asked Per.

"I?— Now that's a question! My grandfather was a horse thief, they say. So what can you expect of me? Aside from

that, I'm Canadian, French, and Dutch, and as to what
more's in me I haven't been informed and haven't bothered
to find out. But thank God I'm neither Irish nor Italian!"
The stranger laughed good-naturedly.

"As I was saying, they were the only two sorts I had in
my crew that winter. And—well, sir, I'm here to tell you
it was a circus from morning till night. There was a fight,
sure's the day. Never an evening that some one didn't need
to be sewed up. I used to lie awake in my bunk nights, so
scared of what might happen next day that my hair stood
on end. We ate up the provisions, but got hardly any work
done, and after a couple of weeks of continual warfare we
had a dozen cripples on our hands. Some start, I'll tell you!"

"What did you do?" asked Per, eagerly, leaning forward
in order to hear better.

"Well, what would you think?" The stranger paused, settled his elbow on his knee so that his forefinger pointed in
the air. "What would you have done under the circumstances?" he asked, confidentially.

Per felt greatly flattered that the stranger took so much
notice of him. After pondering a moment, he vouchsafed
the solution of shorter rations—of starving them awhile.

"You're crazy, man!" the stranger punched Per on the
thigh. "Say, give me another match!" He drew a cigar-case
full of cigars out of his pocket and passed it round. All,
except Nils, took one and lighted up. Nils did not smoke.

Gradually, as Per succeeded in getting his cigar to burn,
the feeling of security and well-being mounted in him, and
he immediately attacked the problem again to see if possibly
he might find some happier solution.

"But couldn't you have separated them? Put the Irish in
a camp by themselves, and the Italians by themselves?" he
ventured again.

"That would never have done. Thought of it, all right,
but I saw at once that it wouldn't work. 'Twould have meant

Adrift

setting up two entirely separate camps and increasing expenses."

"Couldn't you have beat 'em up, pounded the devil out of 'em?" remarked the young salesman.

"Ha, ha," laughed the stranger. "I'd like to have seen you try it! I might have, if I'd been like Samson in the days of his strength, before that beastly woman got hold of him."

"Would being very kind to them have helped any, do you think?" volunteered Nils, quietly wondering.

That brought a loud guffaw from the stranger:

"No, friend, you might just as well have tried kissing tigers! Or whistling at a cyclone!"

The salesman laughed. Per laughed, too—slightly embarrassed at his comrade's ingenuousness. . . . Nils ought to have known by this time that kindness wouldn't work with such folks!

After that Nils kept silent for a long time; but he listened to the story.

"Well, sir," the stranger continued, momentarily, blowing a succession of blue spirals into the air by way of beginning, "I was at my wit's end. And the more I cudgelled my brains the more stuck I was. Fists and knives were the order of the day. Some way out had to be found, that was certain! Well, I'll tell you what I did."

The stranger paused, like one who knows he has something particularly choice in reserve.

"Happened to know of my old friend Charley Carlström's being in camp ten miles west of us. Almost believe Charley was a Norwegian. However, that's no matter. He was boss for McGuire that winter.

"I got to thinking that Charley was a good deal older at the game than I, and that he might be able to give me a pointer or two on how to get out of a squeeze. So I drove over to see him one Sunday. I just thought to myself that if they wanted to kill each other off while I was gone, they'd

The Boat of Longing

have to go to it, that was all. Might as well have it over, the sooner the better. And with the Canadian border so close I could clear out, all right. Besides, it would be a damned sight cheaper for Huestis!

"Well, I got to Charley's safe enough. And he seemed glad to see me again, and mixed a stout punch straight off for the two of us. Knew what was needed after a long drive in the cold, that boy. This was in the days before these damn temperance people started ruining the country up here. They've got things right where they want 'em now," he added, gloomily, "and they've wrecked the place absolutely!

"Well, sir, I unloaded all my troubles on Charley. 'I can see you're in a fix, all right; sure looks bad for a start,' he said. 'I know that old fire-eater, George Huestis! Be the devil to pay when he finds out how things are going with you. You'll get yourself fired, old boy—that's what!' said Charley. 'Well, look here now, Charley,' says I, 'you don't need to tell me that—I can see that much myself. That's not what I drove ten miles through snow and over rough country to hear. The point is, Can you give me a tip as to how I can get out of this soup?' 'Hold on now, hold on!' says he. 'You didn't jump into this world ahead of time, either. But let's have another bracer, then our minds will work better.' So he poured another glassful.

" 'Can you talk Finnish?' he asked me, after a while. 'Finnish?' says I. 'Are you crazy, Charley?' 'No,' says he, 'not exactly. But it is possible I may be having so much sense that I seem crazy to you. I'll tell you,' he said, 'I've got a Finlander in camp that I probably could lend you for a couple of weeks, providing you'd pay me decently for it. But being you're so ignorant you can't talk people's languages, it isn't likely he can save the situation for you. That Finlander would handle twelve of your best men easily; in a pinch he could even manage another half dozen, particularly

Adrift

if you could talk to him,' said Charley. 'Take long to learn Finnish?' I asked."

Per and the salesman wept with laughter; even Nils had to turn his head and smile.

The stranger leisurely relit his cigar.

"You laugh, boys, but I'll tell you that when a man's desperate he's apt to get a lot of senseless ideas. And that's what I was.

"Well, can you guess what Charley answered? He was a damned tease, that fellow! 'Yes,' says he, 'for the likes of you, Tom Brown, 'twould take years. You might even have to go to Finland.' Charley filled the glasses again, and I sat there and couldn't say a word; couldn't even touch the glass. 'Maybe I'd better show you this Finlander of mine,' says he. So he got up and went out, and was gone a long time.

"Finally he came back with a man. And I knew immediately it must be the Finlander. He wasn't very tall, that's certain; but, man alive! what a chest and a back! You'd have sworn that back was a barn wall—no exaggeration! 'This is Makki!' said Charley to me in English. Then he turned round and spoke to the man in a lingo that I didn't understand one syllable of. And the words ran out of his mouth as fast as logs when a boom's open. Charley was a smart fellow, you bet! Too bad he had to come to such an end!"

"Did he come to such a bad end?" asked Per, sympathetically.

"Bad? All depends on what you call bad!"

"Did he die?"

"He did, my boy. Some Irishmen hanged him one night up in the north woods near Bemidji. That was five years ago the 1st of April." The stranger smoked on in silence; he sat looking at Per. "Does that seem so terrible to you?

The Boat of Longing

A lot of stuff happened in the woods in those days, I can tell you. Now there's nothing—it's as tame as singing in the Salvation Army."

"Jesus Christ!" breathed Per, quietly and visibly moved.

"Well, how did it turn out? Did you get the Finlander?" enquired the salesman. "I'm getting off pretty quick, and I'd like to hear the end of the story." He rose and began assembling his baggage; the train had already whistled for his station.

"Yes," answered the stranger, with no show of haste, "I succeeded in borrowing him of Charley for two weeks. And that was the kindest turn any human being has ever done me, even if I did have to fork up a twenty-dollar bill to Charley and pay the Finlander to boot. But what did I care about that! Certainly worth it for such friendly service. Anyway, I got most of it charged to 'necessary expense,' figuring old George Huestis could stand it better than I."

"And you got him along, did you?" the salesman reminded him.

"You bet I did. I got him along all right. 'If things get desperate,' said Charley after we were in the sleigh, 'all you need to do is to give him a schnapps, or maybe two. Outside of that you'll have to make your own plans! Only—don't give him *more* than two. You'll have a berserker on your hands if you do!' Don't know to this day what Charley meant by that word, but I've remembered it ever since. I could understand it was something I ought to look out for!"

He got no farther in his relation before the train came to a stop. The salesman had to leave; expressing his regret that he didn't get the end of the story, he laughed and went.

The stranger rose, too, and slid into the stream of departing passengers. He left his hat in the seat.

"Getting off here?" asked Per, alarmed.

"Just for a little airing."

Adrift

III

The lights were long since lit within the coach. Darkness had gathered outside.

— Must be a large city, this.— Nils was leaning out the open window and peering at the throng on the station platform. . . . A veritable church populace, he mused.

A flock of happy-looking girls in particular drew his notice. They strode about in couples, with their arms about each other—ever so many of them; up and down, back and forth, the whole length of the platform they walked. Their talk was subdued, and the subject apparently amusing. Nearly all were chewing gum. Now and then a bold remark would come floating out to them from a coach window; usually it fell unheeded, running like water off a duck's back; but occasionally it was caught up and would then cause a face to look toward the window, laughing; whereupon a low remark would follow, and a second laugh; after which the pair would move on. They looked so care free and gay in their spring apparel.

It did Nils's heart good to see them; he sat smiling broadly at the whole bevy. And smiles came back to him, enquiring at times; but all of them bright and cheery. These he took and hid away.

"The old Stril should have seen this!" he reflected. "Wonder what he would have said then? Of course happiness still exists!" When the train started up he thrust his head clean out the window to learn the name of the place. *Brainerd,* he spelled. . . . Wouldn't it be a fine place to spend a summer? . . .

Per, meanwhile, was flitting about. He had risen to follow the stranger, but, concluding that it might appear presumptuous, he had restrained himself and not at once left the coach. He had gone to the water-cooler instead, taken a

The Boat of Longing

drink, and spoken to a couple of workmen in the rear seat,
enquiring where they came from and where they were going.
Then he sauntered out, intending to look for the stranger.

A sea of light streamed at him through the doorway of
the adjoining coach; he looked into it and laughed. . . .
That coach was much finer than the smoker, and it was full
of people; every seat was occupied. Per could see from the
elegance of their dress that they were well-to-do.

He drew a step closer; ventured a couple more steps and
stood inside. He encountered eyes and questioning glances
everywhere. But the eyes did him no harm; simply lay back
against the cushions, passively observant. Here and there an
individual reclined, sleeping. Per mustered courage to walk
the entire length of the aisle.

"Well, now, if this isn't jolly," he mused when he discovered another platform and door, and another carful of
quality lolling in elegant ease. This time he strode in with
all the self-assurance of one whose chief occupation in life
had been that of walking through crowded passenger
coaches.

At the next door he went right in without stopping. Here
he found himself within a narrow corridor which led past a
curtained opening and round a corner. From behind the
curtain came voices. "A private room for the train crew,"
concluded Per, and stalked past. But when, at the head of
the sleeping-car, he saw a darky pull down a part of the
wall and make a bed upon it, his satisfaction reached the
pitch of a whistle. "Simply amazing how ingenious and
splendid everything was in America! If this didn't make that
measly cabin in Jörgensen's schooner look like two cents,
he'd like to know!"

The porter, noticing him, approached and enquired the
number of his berth; but then Per, taking fright, turned on
his heel and retreated in a hurry.

The train having begun to move again, he had to step

Adrift

briskly through the churches of half-sleepers. Back in his own coach once more, he found the stranger returned to his place and already lighting a cigar. With that, his spirits revived, and he sat down in the brightest of moods.

"Well," he began, "how did it go with you and the Finlander?"

The stranger puffed away in silence, studying Per with a protracted, thoughtful look. The brown of his face had now, in the light of the lamp, turned copperish; and sitting there leaning forward, with his feet on the opposite seat and his elbows on his knees, he loomed larger than he actually was. To Per he became altogether dynamic, the living embodiment of the urge and drive which makes the world go; the spirit symbolized in the fairy tale was in this man.

"Well, there are certain experiences not so pleasant to relate for the one who has had to go through them. That Sunday night is not one of the most enjoyable in my life, I can tell you."

"Was there a row?" asked Per, eagerly, upon the other's pause.

"A slight one, yes!" sighed the stranger. Then, pulling himself together:

"On my way home from Charley's that night I mapped out my whole campaign, laid out every detail of it—on the general assumption, of course, that I'd find them in fairly good health when I returned.

"And, as luck would have it, they weren't all dead, though there were two injured. Yessir—two! One was an Irishman, the other an Italian. The Irishman was in bed with a nasty cut in his side, and the Italian was wearing a beautiful shiner.

"Soon's I'd left in the morning, trouble had started. Two of the men had got into an argument over who was to empty the wash-basin—the one who had used it or the one who was going to. When the Irishman was through, he had said

183

to the Italian that if he wanted the basin, there it was—he was welcome. Well, the end of it was that the Irishman got a knifing and the Italian a thrashing, though not enough of one to prevent him from parading around all day and playing the hero among those brown devils.

"The moment I was back in camp I called two of my most dependable foremen into the office and enquired how matters stood. The one was whole-skinned, but the other had a number of cuts and bruises and was pretty sorry-looking. Both were terribly discouraged; one of them declared that if this was to continue another week we'd all be ready for jail or the graveyard. The fellow with the bruises thought it would take less time even than that. The way the situation was shaping itself now, we might expect mass action any time: another Flood, was the way he put it. All that had saved them today was the fact that they'd had no weapons on hand."

"Well, what had they done?" asked Per. He was terribly excited and had begun devouring the words again.

"That's exactly what I was coming to," answered the stranger, with added emphasis.

"After the morning's rumpus it had been fairly peaceful throughout the day (that is, comparatively speaking) and up until supper-time. But then it had ripped loose again. It happened this way, you see, that at dinner the Italians had felt themselves beaten by the Irish. Which they certainly had been. For what sort of scheme do you suppose those infernal sons of Erin had hatched up? Well, sir, before the dinner bell had even rung, they'd broken into the cook shanty and grabbed up every end seat in the place, so's to have first chance at the grub!"

"Couldn't the cook and cookee have stopped 'em?" exclaimed Per.

"Well, it's queer, you know, how everyone tries to save his own hide as long as he can."

Adrift

"But they should ——"

The stranger paid no attention to him.

"But the sons of the south had no such luck when they tried the same tactics in the evening. They found the foremen standing guard at the door, waiting for them. For the time being, the trouble blew over. But the air was loaded with dynamite. The Italians hadn't got even, and they were laying for a chance to settle the score.

"That was the situation I found when I got home that evening. The crew had just gone to bed for the night.

" 'Well,' says I to one of the foremen, 'you round up the other foremen'—I had just four—'and we'll hold a council of war.' I had Makki in my own room, back of the office. None of them had seen him yet.

"In a short while all five of us were together, and then I asked them to express their opinions frankly, without any hesitation. The verdict from the four was unanimous: The whole outfit might just as well pack up tomorrow and go home. No use trying; this simply would not go!

" 'All right, boys,' says I, 'since this is to be our last day, we'll plan a little picnic before we go to bed tonight! You say now who the wildest ones are, the chief trouble-makers and those who are readiest to pick a fight, regardless of nationality. Give me the names and I'll write them down.' And by the time we were through we had twenty-two on our list!

" 'Very well!' says I, 'we'll take a preliminary vote on the twenty-two. I want the twelve worst devils in this camp!' And we weren't long in agreeing on that.

" 'Now,' says I to my foremen, 'you make the preparations for action. Get your revolvers ready, a loaded one in the pocket of every one of you. But mind you, not a shot is to be fired, not even in self-defence, till I say the word. Remember that! Meet me here again in twelve minutes. Those of you who can remember any prayers better say

The Boat of Longing

them before you come back. And every one of you must have a lantern!'

"So off they started."

Seeming suddenly to have become conscious of other matters, the stranger broke off his narrative. "Well, now, this'll never do! I'll have to have a smoke. No chance here for a drink, I suppose."

Thereupon he produced two cigars, and offered Per the one.

"You'll have to furnish the matches. I'll provide the rest."

Per accepted the cigar and lit it. His eyes hung upon the stranger; the more he looked at this figure the more he became a part of all the romance he had dreamed about America. Here were power and ingenuity; here the easy elegance, the happy freedom from worry, and the devil-may-care indifference to both life and property. And here he sat, this man who belonged to the higher-ups, and conversed all night with a poor devil of a newcomer, and treated him to boot!

Per's eyes could not let go of the countenance. So intense was their imploring that the man continued.

"Like excitement?" he asked. "Well, one usually finds what one likes."

Per then mentioned his having on several occasions helped throw drunks out of a saloon on Cedar Avenue. But that was, of course, little in comparison with this!

"You don't say?" exclaimed the stranger, blowing a couple of rings into the air; "not a bad beginning, now, for a newcomer. Worked in a saloon, have you?"

— Yes. And his brother was now in the business for himself. Per intended working for him. He might even be starting tomorrow.

— That so? Didn't he think it might be wiser to look about first? Precious little future in the saloon business now. None whatever, as a matter of fact. At the present

Adrift

rate the prohibitionists would be having the country ruined in just a few months. "No, my friend, you should look for a more promising opening," counselled the stranger. "But, of course, that's up to you.

"Let's see, where did I leave off?"

Per reminded him that he had just sent the foremen out of the office and asked them to return in twelve minutes.

"Right you are! Well, as soon as they were gone I went to the door and beckoned Makki to come in. After motioning him to a place near the desk, I went to the safe and picked a bottle of the best whisky I had on hand—Simon-pure goods, that I could guarantee, since I'd bought it myself at Bill Dugan's in Duluth.

"Well, I handed Makki first one glassful. He sipped a sample of it, and then did away with the rest! 'Well,' thinks I, 'these are strong wares, to be sure, but I'd better not take any chances.' So I poured him another and motioned him to drink it. No hesitation this time—the stuff vanished in the wink of an eye. 'Well, now,' thinks I again, 'if Charley Carlström hasn't told me a whopper, this ought to suffice.' Calling it good, I took a swig myself, and locked the bottle in the safe again.

"These were the preliminaries, you understand. Then I took paper and pencil and went over to Makki. I spread the paper before him on the desk and began to draw! Yessir, by golly, I drew pictures for the Finlander!

"Here, I'll show you how I did it!" The stranger producing a letter from his pocket, laid it on his knee, back side up. "Yes, I drew a large room, with tiers of bunks along the walls. About like this, you know. Then I put a lumberjack in every bunk. In the middle of the floor I drew a circle, and placed twelve men around it—just about like this! Right in the middle of the circle I put a big hulk of a man. 'You, Makki!' I said to the Finlander, pointing first to the figure and then to him.

The Boat of Longing

"Yes, he understood that, all right!

"Well, thinks I, if it's not more difficult than this to talk Finnish, I probably won't need to be making that trip to Finland!

"But I soon discovered there was something Makki couldn't grasp. He was screwing up his face, and his eyes grew narrow and he began pointing to the figures and talking some devilish jargon that was Greek to me.

"I thought, however, I could guess what he meant. So I pulled off my coat and rolled up my shirt sleeves; pointed first to him, then to the figures around the circle, and hit at one of them—like this—and acted as if I was mad.

"And don't you suppose, when I looked at Makki, that I actually began to feel queer myself—in my knees and stomach? If I could have remembered a prayer just then, I'm sure I'd 've said it!

"A peculiar, uncanny brightness had got into his face, like waves, you know, coming and going. And his eyes beamed so unnaturally clear. Then he set up a low humming. About as though you'd hear a bumblebee buzzing round your head in summer!

"Well, it may be those foremen were a bit surprised to come back and find him there!

— " 'Where had I got him?' they wanted to know.

" 'Never you mind, boys,' says I. 'He came in while you were out. Guess we'll let him in on our picnic. And don't let's waste any time.'

"So off we marched to the sleeping shanty.

" 'Light every lamp along the bunks,' I shouted. 'And stack the tables and benches in front of the doors.' It didn't take but a jiffy before we had a free deck.

"And there's no telling but what we may have attracted a little attention, besides. Those who had gone to sleep were aroused by the racket, until, finally, we had a wide-awake,

Adrift

curious man gaping at us from every bunk. Which was, of course, part of the plan.

"Then I jumped up on a bench and made a sort of speech to the men!

" 'Boys,' says I, 'I'm very sorry to have to disturb you like this in the middle of the night, but a stranger dropped into camp tonight who won't listen to reason and leave in a quiet manner. So I'll have to ask your assistance.' I then read off the names of the five Irishmen on my list—there were five of them and seven of the others. 'Boys,' says I, 'will you be so kind as to step out here and teach this fellow what it means to come in here in the middle of the night and insult peaceable Christian folk! In case you five can't handle him, I've planned to have some of the others help you. But not until I see you can't manage it!'

"And then I read off, slowly, the names of the seven dark ones.

" 'Well,' says I to these, 'if you cold-blooded Irish can't handle the job, you seven sons of the south please step up and lend them a hand. Good, congenial brothers in the faith that you are, I know you'll do it!'

"Well, sir, you should have heard the howl those black devils set up as soon as I'd finished my speech. And God save my soul, the way those Irish swore! 'Twas like puncturing a hornets' nest. The equal of the number of pet names I got myself called on that occasion has never been uttered to any human being before or since, I can tell you! Evident enough what I had in store, if Makki didn't make good!

"Meantime Makki had pulled off his coat and rolled up his sleeves. This didn't look bad at all; still, I couldn't help wishing with all my heart that I'd given him at least one drink more!

"But can you guess what that Makki did? Well, sir, you know when those Irish had lined up in battle formation—

in a semicircle, with their faces toward the door—Makki steps up to me, points to them one by one, and says something for each. I thought I understood what he meant. I only nodded in a friendly way and said that would be all right. 'You just go ahead and settle these. You'll have the others later on—I'll not cheat you in any way. Don't you worry!'

"And there wasn't much time for any lengthy explanation, I can tell you.

"'Open that door!' roared Hank Manahan, glaring at me and then at Makki.

"'Oh, that's all right, Hank,' says I. 'You just tackle him! We'll have the door open by the time you're ready to use it!'

"Then they tore loose. But it wasn't as bad as I'd expected.

"Hank led the attack, so Makki settled him first. He laid him on the floor, pinned his arms across his breast and sat on him. He was tough on Hank, all right, but not worse than what he had coming. The dose couldn't be too big to suit me.

"And did those Italians ever rejoice to see Hank get his deserts! They sent up a whoop like an opera chorus.

"Well, the other Irish leaped to Hank's rescue, all landing on Makki at once. Just how Makki managed I can't tell, for the one thing about his method was that he worked fast. When I finally sensed it clearly, he was sitting on a heap of five half-naked bodies round which the arms and legs were going like windmills! But that didn't bother Makki. He sat there cool as you please, and seemed exceedingly well satisfied. It was a sight to cheer my depressed spirits, I'll tell you!

"And if I was glad, you should have heard those Italians! I thought they'd gone crazy, the way they yelled.

"I went out on the floor to Makki, tapped him on the

Adrift

shoulder, and told him he was a mighty good boy. Then I let him understand that that might do for those fellows. Well, he hated to get off the pile, but he did it.

" 'Now, boys,' says I to that crowd, 'go to bed! Tomorrow night you can have another chance. Perhaps you can do better then!' "

"Were they badly hurt?" interrupted Per.

"No, not so bad. Manahan's arm was broken, and the rest had a good many scratches. But otherwise none were seriously hurt."

"And were they quiet when they got up?"

"Oh yes. They had sense enough to have respect for a superior, all right.

"Well, that cleared the deck again.

" 'Come along, boys,' says I to the Italians. But now it looked as though they weren't at all keen for a fight.

" 'Quick now!' I commanded once more. 'I'm wanting to go to bed pretty soon, and we've got to turn this fellow out of here if we're to have any peace in this shanty tonight.'

"Well, they shuffled into the ring; but they looked pretty limp. They steered lamely round in a circle, sized Makki up from one angle and another, and made the show of a sally, but there was no action.

"Then Makki lunged, grabbed one of them, pulled him close, picked him off his feet, and, by golly, he heaved that son of the south straight into the bunk of one of the wounded Irish! When he had executed that act he leaned forward, plastered his hands on his knees and laughed at the other six.

"Give me another match, will you?" The stranger quickly lit his cigar, took a couple of hurried puffs, and continued almost in the same breath:

"And then's when it happened! A little black-haired devil not on the list suddenly came leaping out of his bunk with

The Boat of Longing

a knife in his hand and landed square on Makki's back—yessir, he bounced like a rubber ball! I shot forward to warn Makki, but I was too late. 'You're done for!' it sank within me when I saw the knife come down. And it certainly looked it. But what do you suppose that Finlander did? Unbelievable how fast he could work. Well, sir, he threw himself into a shaking, like a horse, you know, after a roll on the ground, and shook that fellow so hard that he missed his mark and went sprawling on the floor. All that Makki got out of it was a long scratch down his neck, which bled a little.

"Then Makki raged! Up to this time he had regarded it as play, but when he reached back on his neck and saw blood on his hands, he simply went wild. He seized that runt for a weapon and cleared the floor with him faster than I can tell it. The brown ones bolted for shelter, disappearing like rats. And when none were left to be seen, he whanged the man a blow on the head and knocked him cold on the floor."

"Jesus Christ! Did he kill him?" breathed Per, terrified.

"Didn't you just hear me say so? We buried him in the woods the next day!" he added, soberly. "And," he continued, immediately, "he wasn't the only one whose life was in danger that night. For now the Finlander was wild. He grabbed an upper bunk with one hand, gave it a jerk, and wrenched the whole business loose from the wall. With that for a weapon he strode through the shanty to our end. 'Now your time's come, Tom Brown,' thinks I. So I walked straight up to him. Yessir, straight up to him. And can you guess what I did? I'll bet you can't—for I can scarcely understand myself how I could think that fast. Well, sir, I began to whistle! And looking Makki square in the eye, I marched at him. Yessir! right at him.

"Well, however it happened, I don't know, but he dropped the bunk. And I stood right up to him and took hold of his

Adrift

arm. 'Open the door!' I said quietly to the foremen. And I got him into the open air. There I let him stand a few moments while I went back to the shanty.

" 'Well, boys,' says I, 'we've had a jolly good evening. And from now on, the first one of you to start the slightest rumpus will have to take on my new man. I hope you all understand me clearly. Every man will be on the job on the dot tomorrow. Hank Manahan can help the cook!' Then I ordered two of the Irish to get up and carry out the dead man and put him in the snow till we could bury him decently; and I called two of the Italians to get dressed and scrub the floor. 'You stay here,' I said to one of the foremen, 'and see to it that there's no further disturbance. If there's the slightest sign of it, report to my office at once.' Not a one there but heard what I said. And there was no more trouble that night. From then on I knew I was boss in that camp, so George Huestis could come along any old time that he pleased!"

IV

The crowd in the smoker had thinned considerably at the last three or four stations.

Night lay black outside; the light from the coach windows bored only a feeble tunnel into it.

Two stars accompanied the train . . . moved with it all night long . . . stood when it stood at a station . . . started up when it started. But they went in the opposite direction. Nevertheless, they were the same two stars that accompanied it all the time.

"Must surely be past midnight now," thought Nils, who had by this time moved across the aisle. Having wearied of the stranger's story, he had taken an empty seat there. The man's power to work up suspense was uncanny. His voice, manipulated according to the content of his story, rose and

The Boat of Longing

fell variously above the clank and roar of the cars, now lifting itself into shrill terror, now booming gruff and threatening, or again shunting into sharp derision. But deep in the man who used the voice lay a warm joyousness.

The many new words and phrases which the stranger employed had made it difficult for Nils to follow the story; it was only by straining to the utmost that he had been at all able to catch any of the meanings.

For Per it was easier. The advantage of his position helped him, for one thing, to hear better; and besides, the stranger sat talking directly into his face. Then, too, his proficiency in English was greater than Nils's. Nils had often been compelled to marvel at all Per knew.

Nils, tired and indifferent, wanted to sleep. He tried lying down in the seat as he had seen others do. Just back of him lay one thus cuddled up, snoring blissfully under his hat.

"In a couple of hours we'll be in Minneapolis," he comforted himself. . . . "Karl Weismann and Kristine Dahl will be there. . . . Wonder if they're still alive. . . . It's a long time since I left them."

Nils had debated whether he would want to share the room with the Poet again; but thus far every attempt to settle the question had ended by his not knowing just what to do. "Well, I'll see—I'll see when I get there. I'll talk it over with Kristine Dahl and get her opinion. But if there's decent lodging to be had by the river, I'd certainly prefer it. Although," he reflected, "it won't be easy to leave the Poet. There's not a kinder soul in the world, if it weren't for the whisky. . . . And then there's Annie; yes—Annie! I couldn't find a better helper in English; she can't be beat for being straightforward and specific. . . . She'll have grown a lot this winter."

The thought of Annie gave a pleasant warmth in the chill spring night.

Nils went on thinking. In the venture before him lay so

194

Adrift

much of the unknown, so much of potential fairy-tale experience. And beyond it rose the Beautiful, smiling to him. "Certainly—he'd come."

"Tomorrow," planned Nils, "after I've talked with the Poet, I'll go down to the river. On my way back I can stop at the Cedar Avenue studio, and if I have her violin along, it will be convenient to start in at once. I expect I'll have to take it if she offers it to me again. Yes, I expect so. And if it's true that an unseen hand once kept one person from using it sinfully, might it not very well be that the same hand would aid him who tried to express the beautiful? And it was a good violin!"

Nils was no longer very conscious of his weariness. His hat lay over his eyes, shading them from the light. Only a couple of hours now and Per and he would be in Minneapolis —the thought persisted in recurring. What ought they to do when they got there? They couldn't go to "Babel," not at that hour of the night. And it would be a long time to wait in the station; perhaps they wouldn't even be allowed to. A hotel might be best. If only they could find one that wouldn't be expensive.

Nils lay wishing the stranger would quit, so he could confer with Per. . . . They must be nearly there now. . . .

But there came no sign of stopping from across the way; the voice continued to rise and fall, fall and rise through the pounding of the train. Now and then Nils could also hear Per's voice intruding with a question or a remark. Whenever Per used a long word which he knew he could pronounce correctly, he would utter it very emphatically. Occasionally he would inject an oath. Per had taken to swearing a good deal when he spoke English. His oaths were at times so terrible that Nils shuddered at hearing them. There was one in particular to which he seemed to have taken a fancy—namely, "Jesus Christ!" Nils had spoken to him about it once during the winter; but Per had only re-

The Boat of Longing

torted in a very superior way that everyone said that in English. It belonged to English. In Norwegian it wasn't used. And Nils, knowing that his knowledge of English couldn't be compared with Per's, had had to yield and keep still, even though he was far from convinced.

— There, wasn't Per saying it again?

Countless thoughts plied his mind, racing hither and thither. One kept recurring—"soon they'd be in Minneapolis!"

Nils pushed his hat just far enough off one eye to allow him to see the edge of the lamp up in the ceiling. But whenever the train swayed strongly the lamp would disappear altogether, or else shoot way beyond his hat brim. This amused him. It reminded him of the times when on spring nights the sun had hung low upon the sea rim and he had lain in the stern, watching it.

The train rocked and roared; by spurts it sped madly on, like a boat zipping full press down a mountainous wave.

Nils closed his eyes; but from time to time he would open the one a wee bit, to see if the sun was still there. . . . It wouldn't be going way down tonight. . . .

The voices across the aisle mounted and fell with the swaying. . . . Was that a cormorant shrieking? No, the cormorant had no cry. . . . Must be the eider ducks paddling the billows and calling to the gulls. . . . Of course, 'twas the gull! There was one now, lifting wing and flying out! . . .

. . . Nils, in an open boat far out at sea, was pulling in halibut lines, was hauling up a monster halibut. A great swell fetched his boat from in under and lifted him clean to the sky. Instantly he slackened line. The boat glided down again. Nils hauled and hauled. Well, did you ever see the beat! If there wasn't another boat close by! And in it stood the stranger, likewise hauling in a halibut line, and shouting "Jesus Christ" to Per, who sat in front, rowing. . . . Now

Adrift

their lines got tangled—the stranger's and Nils's. Nils pulled for dear life, till the perspiration poured from him. He meant to have that fish. The stranger pulled equally hard; looked as though he wanted it, too. Just then another great sea rolled up, took the boat from in under and again sent it clean to the sky. . . . "Watch out or we'll lock! Slack your line!" shouted Nils. "We'll be dashed to smithers!"

"Min-ne-ap-o-lis! Minneapolis!" called the brakeman through the train. "Min-ne-ap-o-lis! Minneapolis!" Nils jumped up with such a start that his hat rolled way down the aisle.

Immediately a great noise and commotion began within the coach. Most of the passengers were getting off here. Nils, in a daze, stood there rubbing his eyes. Were they there already?

V

Per and Nils found themselves in the vast Great Northern Station, much bewildered. Even at this hour of the night the human current moving to and from trains ran very swift.

In the press of the crowd the stranger had lost them for a moment; but then his eye had caught sight of them again.

"Come along with me," he invited; "and I'll find you a place to sleep where you'll be as safe as at Mother's."

Per followed unhesitatingly; Nils somewhat reluctantly. Out on the sidewalk Nils paused. He had to look about and greet the place. The lights along Hennepin Avenue twinkled festively; they resembled two rows of pearls hung out on both sides of the street. Just a few steps below him ran the river; he knew its every bend as far as the Washington Bridge. He felt at home there on the sidewalk, was a part of the metropolis which now lay in peaceful morning sleep. Something within it was his; he belonged here!

The Boat of Longing

"We'll take the street car!" called the stranger from the car stop. Nils gained the place just in time. Per was displeased because he was so slow.

They rode up Hennepin—far up through the city.

"Here's just the place for homeless birds like you," said the stranger, as they walked into the Y. M. C. A. on Ninth Street. Per followed close on the heels of the stranger, wrote his name directly under his in the register, and in every way deported himself as though his only business in life had been to travel and register at big hotels. Nils wondered if it wouldn't be pretty expensive here, but took the pen, nevertheless, and signed his name under Per's.

That night Nils slept the sleep of youth. Before he went to bed he took a shower bath, scrubbing till he felt sure every trace of the woods was removed. Passing Per's room, he heard voices—the stranger's deep bass relating, and Per's eager one questioning. But he hurried by, only too happy to escape. And stretching himself upon his bed with a feeling of luxurious well-being, he fell immediately into a deep sleep, from which he did not awaken till, judged by the noises on the street, it was well into the day. He recollected a dream in which some one had rapped at his door and called his name; and he had come half awake of it, too, but, having concluded it to be only a dream, had rolled over and dozed off again. . . . Surely it had been a dream? . . .

Again he sought the shower and scrubbed from head to foot. Then he opened his valise, took out his best suit of clothes, brushed it, and tried to stretch out the wrinkles. He'd soon be having to buy a new one, he could see. This would hardly do for Sunday wear in the big city! Still, it wasn't looking so bad, either, now that he'd got it smoothed out a bit and had it all on. He certainly had seen them worse! Nils had dressed with great care.

On the way down he stopped at Per's door and rapped. No answer. Then he tried the stranger's door; no answer

Adrift

there, either. "Are they as sound asleep as all that?" Nils wondered. "Perhaps Per's gone already."

Upon enquiring at the office, he learned that Per had left a couple of hours ago. At the moment, however, he took no thought of it; altogether natural that Per would be anxious to see his brother. . . . What if that hadn't been a dream? . . . Perhaps it had been Per trying to rouse him before leaving. . . .

In reality, Nils was happy to be alone; the prospect of freedom to roam around as he pleased for the day and to enjoy himself in his own way gladdened him. He paid for his lodging and left.

If only he could find a good, quiet place to eat! He felt terribly hungry—'twas already half past ten, and all of twenty-four hours since he had tasted food. Had he but known the name of the place where Marie and he ate that Sunday evening, he would most certainly have gone straight there, for today he meant to celebrate. Yes, today he wanted to play the plutocrat! Time enough tomorrow to begin thinking about the future.

He continued up Hennepin; wasn't ready to cut over to Nicollet just yet. Far up he found a place which he thought might do. The restaurant was small, but quiet and pleasant. It was still too early for the noonday patrons to have begun arriving; when Nils entered there was only one individual there, an elderly man who sat well back in the rear and was reading a newspaper.

Nils chose a corner table near the window, where he could entertain himself by looking at the faces passing by, guessing which were happy and which were not.

A waiter coming, he ordered the best he could find on the bill of fare; it amounted to sixty cents' worth by the time he had got all he felt he must have.

Just as he was finishing his meal the greybearded man,

who had been watching him from over his paper, came sauntering through the restaurant. He paid his bill and then stopped in front of Nils.

"Fine day."

"I should say so."

"A workingman?"

"Yes."

"Looking for a job?"

"Well, maybe."

"Scandinavian, are you?"

"Yes."

"Norwegian or Swedish?"

"Norwegian."

"A newcomer?"

"Yes."

Whereupon the man began talking Norwegian.

"I just got here a little while ago and am looking for four reliable workmen. A fellow gambles a good deal on what he gets from the employment agencies, and for that reason I prefer picking my own men. Do you drink?"

"No," smiled Nils.

"Care to hire out for the summer and fall?"

Nils looked at the stranger. He had a fine face, browned by sun and wind. His iron-grey hair sat close upon his head.

"What kind of work?"

"Repairing railroad bridges."

"What do you pay?"

"Forty a month and expenses, travelling included. Cheapest way to get acquainted with America!" he laughed.

"Is it here in Minneapolis?"

The old man laughed again.

"No. It's between here and the Dakota line. We start out from Brainerd on Monday, leaving here Sunday night."

Nils looked down.

Adrift

"No, I don't think I can take it. I intended to stay here for the summer. Was it—was it Brainerd you said?"

"Suit yourself," said the old man. "Here's my card; you'll find me at that address between six and seven every evening. We're leaving Sunday night!" With that remark he went.

Nils stood looking at the card. "Lars Korsness" was all it contained, and the address. He thrust it into his pocket. . . . "So it's from Brainerd they start? . . . No—I think I'll stay home this summer." Thereupon he went to the cashier and paid his bill.

He sauntered out and over to Nicollet, arriving just in time for the noonday concourse. Today everyone, it seemed, looked happy. He felt happy himself.

He let the stream carry him downstreet, smiling so broadly and brightly at all the faces moving in the opposite direction that many turned to look at him. The windows he ignored today; the faces were more fun. And he kept going, his mood too bright for stopping; but at a place far down, the stream waxed so swift and full that he had to be careful; he'd be bumping his valise into some one if he didn't watch out.

Reaching Fourth Street finally, he swung in on it and followed it the rest of the way. The clock in the Court House tower pointed five minutes of twelve. . . . The Poet would probably be out now.

His heart beat audibly when he saw "Babel." Familiar sights greeted him, the north alley being, as usual, full of Negro children at play. They were barefooted already, though it was only the middle of May.

Nils stepped into the hallway of the Fourth Street entrance and rapped at the corner room. Getting no answer, he bent down to hunt for the key in its accustomed place under the threshold. It was there, all right. Thrusting it promptly into the lock, he turned it and walked in.

The Boat of Longing

A whiff of the room sufficed to assure him that the Poet still lived here; then, too, the place looked much as it had when he left last fall.

There stood the *Kingdom of Spirits*; and there in the middle of the floor the ponderous table with its usual welter of books, newspapers, and writing materials. The beds, too; his own stripped bare, by which he could tell that the Poet had not rented to anyone; he was expecting him, evidently. The discovery made him happy.

He walked over to the bed and set down his luggage. Unless the Poet had altered his habits, he might be expected to arrive about two o'clock.

Then he went to the table and looked for stationery; he'd better get that letter off while he waited. Several sheets of paper, filled with writing, lay spread out in a row in front of the Poet's chair; Nils knew the neat script well. Was all of it poetry? he wondered. He bent over a sheet to read.

"Grief of the Moon

"The moon had finished his supper. He said:
'My cheeks are gallant, and gold, and red.
  I'll gather a bunch of the liveliest stars
To twist in a wreath for my old bald head.'

"He hustled the clouds from his wallowing track,
He waggled his head till his cheeks went slack
  When he squinted under the lake and saw
How fine he looked when he squinted back!

"Oh, the pride of the moon was a sight to see,
As he rode the darkness vaingloriously,
  And leered down on the quivering earth.
'And the things that I've seen!' said the moon, said he.

"Then he peered and puttered till he saw soon
A white nymph dance to a faëry tune,
  Silver and slim as an icicle,
Under the lily leaf, under the moon.

Adrift

"He wobbled his head like a man who dreams;
He built her a bed of white moonbeams,
   Scarlet and gold on the still grey water,
And spangled it over with glows and gleams.

"But her laugh was cold as a diamond jewel:
'You'll pardon me if I do seem cruel,
   You're only an empty reflection made
Of yellow vapour and water gruel.'

" 'You're showy enough with your red and gold,
But your heart is cynical, thin, and old.'
   And he sunk his head in his scarf and muttered
'The night is weary, the clouds are cold.'

" 'I think I'll be getting on home. A kiss
From an average nymph I'll never miss.
   But I'm not the moon that I used to be;
It'll take me a month to get over this.'

"This is the tale of the old moon's grief.
Though the moon's sorrow is light, and brief
   Is the moon's madness; he looks no more
Under the shade of the lily leaf."

Nils read the stanzas through to the end. A melody offering itself, he began to hum it. Curious to know if all of it was poetry, he picked up another sheet and read:

"Nocturne

"Here on the rim of the moorland the homing tune
   Of the last bee wavers. Purple and grey
The endless heather out to the unborn moon
      Reaches away.

"This is the edge of quiet: the white dusk sings,
   Under the heather sprigs small breezes mutter,
The moor stirs in its sleep, the whispering wings
      Of bats flutter.

The Boat of Longing

"Let down your hair now, pillow your gold head,
　　Sing of tremendous lovers and their ways
In the bear's fastness and the deer's bed,
　　　In olden days.

"Here we will make our house with gloam of dreams,
　　Thatched with the mist of stars. Make haste and wind us,
Night, in your passionate darkness, till the gleams
　　　Of dawn find us."

Nils looked no farther. He sought the window, hot of cheek; began humming the first poem; returned to the table for a second look at the beginning words; went back to the window. Yes, that tune would fit, all right!

Of a sudden he became aware of a girl heading across the street. She took long strides, swinging her arms like a boy, and gave several sharp tosses of the head, disencumbering her shoulder of a thick braid of hair.

My land, if Annie wasn't coming! Nils drew back from the window a little, not wanting to be discovered. . . . She hadn't grown as much as he had expected; but her body looked firmer, seemed to have knit itself into greater comeliness.

He hurried out into the hallway and placed himself flat against the wall, so he couldn't be seen from the outside.

Annie came in dancing and humming, too engrossed to notice his presence until she came directly upon him. The sudden sight of him bewildered her completely, and for a moment she lost her speech.

"Why, Nils!" she cried, grabbing him by the wrists. "My, but you scared me!"

Nils stood there, chuckling giddily; he couldn't find words, either. What could he say to a face wherein childhood and womanhood contended?

She retained his hands.

"Were there many bears up in the woods?"

"Oh my, yes, Annie! Full of 'em!"

Adrift

"Didn't you get scared?" she exclaimed, fearfully.

"Oh no, that I didn't!" He freed his hands. "You see, I just took 'em like this and ripped 'em in two," he demonstrated solemnly.

"How terrible!"

"No, not so terrible. You see, they grew together again as fast as I'd thrown down the pieces," he explained, with the same serious mien.

"Now you lied!" Her eyes blazed a moment, then instantly gave way to laughter. "I'll get even with you! Going to live here again?"

"That depends—I don't know just yet."

"Depends on what?"

"On you, Annie!"

"On me?" She turned crimson. "There you're lying again!"

"No, that's the honest truth, Annie," laughed Nils; "because it depends on whether you'll be my teacher."

"Shucks!" snorted Annie, secretly disappointed. "Don't you know English yet?"

"Not very well," answered Nils, embarrassed at his stupidity.

"Well," she bargained, business-like as a grown-up, "if you'll take me to the movies a whole lot of times, I'll teach you English, because I'm a sophomore now and I've written a lot of compositions this winter and read a lot of books and everything, so I know all about it, I can tell you."

"Why certainly I'll take you to the movies! You teach me two evenings, and I'll take you to the movies the third," proposed Nils.

"All right!" Her eyes beamed at the proposal. "That'll be fun!"

Nils, regarding that matter as settled, began enquiring about the other tenants of "Babel."

— How was the Poet?

The Boat of Longing

— Him? Huh? More piggish than ever.

— What about Pinskys?

— They had moved. Two boys had that room now; they must be newcomers, 'cause they were working on a sewer near by.

Nils gave a laugh.

"What are you laughing at?" she snapped.

"Oh," he hedged, "it's just so nice to be standing here talking to you again."

The explanation must have been satisfactory, for she immediately became friendly again.

— Was Otto Hansen living here yet?

— Yes, he was here; not Miss Hals and Miss Gundersen, though.

— Had they moved?

— Oh yes. . . . Her voice suggested there was more to be said.

— What had become of them?

— The police had come after Miss Gundersen this winter, and then Miss Hals had moved away.

— Had the police come after her?

— Yes, they had taken her. She was put in jail.

— What had she done?

Annie shook her head and looked down.

"Dasn't tell you that," she said, in a veiled manner.

The happiness which had been upon Nils disappeared instantly, and a dense fog took its place; he felt as if he stood in darkness.

"Shall we begin studying tonight?" asked Annie.

"No—yes—no, let's leave it tonight," he mustered himself. "Do you think—do you think Marie Gundersen will have to stay there long?"

"Don't know. But I can ask my mother if you want me to."

"No, no, never mind; I was only asking."

"Well, what time shall we start, then?"

Adrift

"We'll see tomorrow night."

"All right. Tomorrow night for sure, now. I'll tell my mother. You come up to us, and I'll bring some books from school. Guess you aren't very smart," she added, teasingly, "when you haven't learned yet."

"I reckon you're right."

The sadness in his voice moved her.

She looked at him.

"Say, come on now, you old dunce!" she boomed in a gruff bass, the deviltry sparkling in her eyes. "Don't you know I didn't mean it? Not that way!"

"What didn't you mean?" Nils rested himself against the wall.

"There you go again! You're a mutt!" She grabbed both his hands and shook them impatiently. "But I've got to go now—I'm late already. Don't be so blue!"

She disappeared up the stairs, leaving Nils alone. He heard her voice above, talking in loud, high-pitched excitement, and knew that it was about him.

Returning to his room, he sat down to write home. But the letter, which he had expected to be so glowing, turned out to be very dull—the spell of dead commonplaceness lay over it all. He mentioned their having worked in the woods during the winter and having laid up a neat sum of money, stating the Norwegian equivalent of his own savings, but making no comment on Per's. They would be working in Minneapolis now for a time, so their address would be the same as last fall. Both were getting along well. He would, however, have no objection to being at home with Father right now, fishing as in the old days; though, of course, it would be out of the question for a while. Having struck out in the world for himself, he'd have to stay till he'd made good; though for that matter being a fisherman in Nordland was probably as fine as anything! So they mustn't be expecting him for a year or two yet. He'd likely be going to the woods again next winter.

Meanwhile, he continued, they must get some one to come and stay with them, preferably a young person who could be of cheer and comfort to them till he returned. But they must be sure not to look for him for a year or so. He would, however, write faithfully; the opportunity for it would be better this summer.

— The oyster-catcher had been back a long time now, he supposed. And the geese had come, too? But it was certainly too early for the saithe; it ought to be there along about the time the birches began sprouting in earnest. And it was now well into May, wasn't it? Had Father begun painting the boat yet? With a dry spell over there similar to the one over here, the weather would be fine for it. He must be sure to be careful when he went out alone on the open sea! He'd better take Mother along, then they'd both be safer; be more pleasant for them, too. Mother was an uncommonly good rower! They'd have to try and manage as well as they could till he got back. Might be a year yet, maybe longer. He must admit that he was feeling a little lonesome for the place right now! He hoped they were both well. And he sent his good wishes.

VI

The old man's emotion, when he entered and found Nils in his accustomed place at the table, was touching to see. Tears came into his eyes; these he tried at first to laugh away, but when that failed, he resorted to cursing the chill spring wind for being so severe on people. He coughed, he sneezed, he wiped his face; and at the same time he had to laugh, which only worsened matters.

Nils not daring to laugh, yet unable to restrain himself altogether, opened a book which lay handy; he thereby got an excuse for keeping his eyes on it while he talked. Off and on, however, he had to look up.

The months had left their traces on the Poet. The wisps of hair had grown thinner, and the slacker features had more of the cadaver's ghastly hue. The whole figure stooped more noticeably. It was only in the eyes that any of the life vigour remained; they might still be seen to glow when mood and spirit kindled.

Though the Poet did not expressly state it in so many words, Nils gathered that the old man had missed him; and the realization touched him. Now they were together again, the two of them—the old man staving about, blowing his nose and cursing, not daring to let go of his feelings; Nils seated, his eyes glued on a book, almost as badly off.

Finally the Poet regained mastery of himself sufficiently to begin talking. Once that was achieved, matters went more smoothly; it helped, likewise, that he could pace the floor and sneeze whenever emotion threatened to get the better of him.

— So—so the prodigal son had eventually found his way home again, had he? Had his fill of husks among the swine —eh? Well, here in the tents by the rivers of Babylon the door would always stand open to him. Here it was glorious to dwell; the joy of life had pitched its fair pavilion here— yessir, right here on the corner of Thirteenth Avenue South and Fourth Street!

— But how the devil had he got in? Yes, yes, that's right —he'd himself given the chamberlain the key this morning and requested him to give Nils admittance! "Now isn't it strange?" he halted, cocking his eye at Nils, the tears trickling down his cheeks, "I've carried that key in my pocket every day this winter and spring, but today a voice warned me to leave it! Solve me that riddle, boy! You weren't sending any messengers, were you—eh?"

Nils smiled and said that perhaps he had.

The Boat of Longing

"So you've been homesick, have you, my boy? You have now!" The Poet blew a thunderous blast, and stroked his eyes.

"Pure souls have such power; they can send messages over land and sea. And they'll get there, too! Well, boy, there's the bed waiting for your body; it must be tired after the strife. There's the *Kingdom of Spirits*, to which access is yours the livelong day. Yonder stands the stove, in case your inner man needs some further sustenance!" For each item the Poet described an arch with his arms and bowed like one making gracious promises to his subjects.

"From this trip, I take it, you've not returned with either princess or half the kingdom? Eh?

"No, it wasn't to be expected you'd find such treasures in the wilds of northern Minnesota among all the bears and wild beasts. Upon the fair highways of the spirit, you see, that such goods must be sought. You understand that, don't you, my boy? What the devil did you want to consort with hewers of wood and drawers of water for? You'll not become a man of renown that way—eh, now, what?"

Having grown more calm under the talk, he walked up to Nils, took his hand and looked him over, using him preciously now, as a mother would a child restored.

"You have fared hard, I see; damned hard among those wild beasts up there. I can tell it on you; now don't you bother denying it! But why did you depart from the hearths of your fathers where peace and safety dwell?"

"Yes, but I've fared uncommonly well this winter," insisted Nils, laughing, "and I mean to go back next winter."

"What's this you're trying to make me believe?" blazed the old man. "Have you fared well? Don't my own eyes tell me that you've slaved like a hound? But if you insist on making an end of yourself, why ——"

The Poet measured the floor with thoughtful strides, ending in front of the corner cupboard.

Adrift

"Ugh!" he shivered, "this chilly spring weather is tough on old fellows! We'll have to see if we can't overcome it a little." The last came somewhat shamefacedly; nevertheless, he opened the cupboard and drained a couple of glasses; which done, he brought both bottle and glass to the table.

"Haven't gotten the taste for such stuff, have you?" he asked, burlily.

Nils shook his head.

"Well—I'm glad of that; then I'm not having that sin on my conscience!" The Poet poured another glassful; but when he lifted it to his lips his hand trembled so violently that it spilled over.

A long pause followed. Nils addressed an envelope and sealed his letter; he'd better get it off at once.

The Poet, who hadn't recovered from his miff, sat watching him from the side.

"Some one here asking for you the other day," he announced, moodily.

"For me?" Nils glanced at him.

"If you'd inform me about your friendships, I could advise both you and your friends correctly. You should be careful with whom you pick up! Easy for a newcomer to be led astray and get to going wrong in a big city," he added, reprovingly.

"But who could be asking for me?" asked Nils, gravely, seeing that the old man was serious.

"A gentleman of the finest sort."

"Then you'd better tell me what the fine gentleman's name was. You remember it, I suppose?"

"No, that I do not," came the cross response; "but I imagine I can find it, since it seems so important."

He began rummaging about among the books and papers on the table.

"Ha!—there you are! 'Brakstad,' it says here. 'Brakstad' is, therefore, the name. And he hails from Trondhjem, if

The Boat of Longing

that interests you; his speech betrayed him; I didn't even trouble to enquire."

"What did he say?" asked Nils.

"Nothing, I tell you! The man was as mute as a mackerel. A characteristic, by the way, of the herr gentleman Trondhjemers; they're too crafty for speech."

"Long since he was here?"

The Poet scowled mistrustfully at the eager face before him.

"Why are you so agitated? You ought to be ashamed to sit here burning up with secrets you've kept away from an old man who'd gladly give his soul to save yours—so you ought!"

Nils could see that there would be no way of appeasing the old man except by telling him of his experiences down by the river; and so he told of his meeting Kristine Dahl, and about that part of her life history which she had confided.

The Poet's face brightened beautifully under the relation; when Nils had finished, it glowed like the sun.

"Look at that, now! Now there you gave me stuff for a jewel of a poem. Why in the world do you go keeping such treasures to yourself? There's your fairy princess in her castle. Well, she's needing you, I guess; so hurry up! Now that was beautiful, that was! That's what I call faithfulness!"

Nils rose and made ready to leave.

The Poet had seated himself at the table and begun stacking the written sheets. Then suddenly, without warning, he burst into a peal of laughter, and laughed so hard that his whole body shook. When Nils set dumbfounded eyes upon him, he saw that he was looking at a calling-card.

"What's that?"

The Poet dried his eyes, only to be seized with a second paroxysm.

Adrift

"At what time did you arrive today?"

Nils gave him the information; he simply could not understand what had come upon the old man.

"Heh-heh; heh-heh-heh! You came just a few moments too late to witness the most amusing experience I've had since I came to Minneapolis. It never rains but it pours—first they, then you! Now on that we must have a drink!"

The Poet drained the glass and began in the merriest of moods:

"Yes, you see, just before your weary feet began to set print upon the fair meadows adjacent to the rivers of Babylon, I, the unworthy, sitting here alone, brooding and in longing, was visited by two envoys—two superfine gentlemen. The one, by cracky! even had gloves and a cane! He swung the cane upon his arm and beat his porky thighs with the gloves. Which, of course, was all right; they were better suited to that purpose than to encase his gnarly paws." The Poet thrust his chin forward and let his head sink into his shoulders for a hearty chuckle.

"Can your young soul divine the mission of those two ambassadors to me? Heh-heh-heh! Don't you suppose they came for the one and only purpose of persuading me, a hard-shelled sinner, to join their church? Dandy apostles, I must say! Fit envoys to send to such fellows as you and me! And can you guess the burden of their witnessing? No, my son, how could you guess such riddles? Your honest soul is not sufficiently encrusted with hypocrisy. Yes, they said—they said their congregation was a—a—" the Poet cast about for the equivalent expression in Norwegian, but failing to find it, had to employ the English "a live-ly bunch!" The Poet hiccoughed it out. "Ever heard the likes of that for apostolic tidings?"

Nils had to laugh too, though he felt embarrassed.

"Were they Norwegian?" he asked.

"Naturally! As Norwegian as you or I, even though they

213

spoke mostly English. I'm almost positive the one was a
Sogning and the other a Stavangring. Yessir, I'd swear the
one was from Stavanger—the one with the gloves and cane
—though I'm not so certain about the Sogning. He may
have been a Vossing!

"And do you know what I answered them? No, my young
friend, you don't know that, either, since you didn't hear
me. Yes, I said, 'Have a drink, sirs! This spring air is raw
and chilly, and you need a little to hearten you on the way!' "

"Did they drink?"

"Did they!" exclaimed the old one, gleefully. "The Stavangring downed it without batting an eye, remarking that
he'd been bothered with a cold ever since Easter; yes, that's
what he said. But the Sogning made no apologies—he dived
straight to perdition, absolutely reckless! The Spirit worked
strongly in *him*, you can bet! You should have seen the eyes
he set on that bottle! I'll swear the content dwindled at least
two inches!"

Nils had gained the door. It was with a dreary smile that
he hurried away.

VII

No sun shone when Nils came out. A fog had settled
chillily over the streets; the wind was endeavouring to sweep
it away; but without success, for however much it swept,
more came to take its place; the source must have been endless. And it didn't come evenly, but bumped along like smoke,
rarefying enough at moments to enable Nils to see the Court
House tower, then again thickening so much that it cut off
the vision beyond two blocks.

Bracing himself, Nils walked resolutely into it. In reality
he liked such weather; it challenged whatever there was of
manly vigour within him, bidding it step forth and prove

Adrift

itself; and from unleashing the full measure of it he derived a sense of well-being.

When he stood on the rim of the kettle, ready to descend, he saw that the fog was less dense below. It drifted thinner, was more transparent; he could distinctly glimpse the river through it.

But the two, the fog and the river, drove oppositely, it seemed; it looked almost as though the two were contending for possession, the fog seizing all above the bridge, the river all beneath it.

Despite the fog's rarity, it choked the houses into the bottom; the one on the corner was sitting right on the cliff, its walls not even distinguishable from any point above the middle of the stairs. Its blanched, paint-worn patches reminded Nils, upon his closer approach, of an invalid face frozen with cold.

He neared the house cautiously, turned up the path, and rapped at the door. A soft voice answered; it belonged to a woman, but its owner could not have seen many summers, for it sounded too young.

Nils trembled; but then he ventured a second knock. Hurried steps came across the floor; the door opened and a black-haired, brown-eyed woman holding a black-haired, suckling infant appeared. She was but scantily clothed and walked unstockinged in her shoes.

"Does Kristine Dahl live here?" asked Nils bashfully.

The woman stared blankly, shook her head, and spoke a few words in an unintelligible tongue.

The pause grew so painful that he had to repeat his question; whereupon she nodded in a friendly way and motioned him to come in.

He followed; he simply must get inside for another look. He understood her invitation to sit down.

Because of being fuller, the room impressed him as being even smaller than it had seemed before; the woman had to

215

The Boat of Longing

tack her way across the little patch of floor in order to get to the bed, so she could lay the infant down. But an atmosphere of coziness prevailed now, too.

Nils let his gaze wander, taking in every article of furniture; but he saw none that was familiar. He sat like one who has just come home after a long journey, to find a house full of new faces.

Having put the baby down, the woman turned toward him and spoke. He could not understand her, and shook his head dejectedly.

She must have sensed that he was in dismay, for with a look at him and a word she fetched a bottle from the foot of the bed; and then, having found a clean cup, she poured him a drink and offered it to him with a smile.

Nils, seeing that it was not whisky, drained the cup and thanked her.

Then the woman left the house.

Soon she returned with an older woman, the colour of whose hair and eyes was much like her own and whose face had a kind look, but who bore no resemblance to her otherwise.

Nils rose in greeting, then enquired if she could tell him what had become of Kristine Dahl; he spoke the name slowly, taking pains to say it distinctly.

The elderly woman launched into a rapid fire in a strange tongue, her face heavy with dolour; Nils gathered more from her mien and tone of voice than he did from her words.

"Is she dead?" he asked.

"Yah, dead, killed!" sobbed the old one. The younger woman at her side wrung her hands and echoed the three words. Observing his dismay, she was quick to pull out the bottle again and pour him another cupful.

But Nils neither heard nor saw. Could not; for now he was standing there listening to the voice of Kristine Dahl relating softly and melodiously of the summer in Nordland

Adrift

when she and Johan had lived love's great ecstasy together. It seemed incredible to him that she herself was not here in this room. Once more he had to look about to make sure. But—she was gone. And the only discoverable trace of her presence was the nail on the wall where Johan's violin had hung; it stood out conspicuously against the painted background, because of the gold cord with which she had entwined it. The cord was still there! . . . Slowly his eyes travelled the room, coming back to the nail. . . . Distinctly he heard her voice requesting *Hearts when young are always hungry.*

Then he said good-bye and left.

He had no sooner gained the walk than the two women came running after him. The older one motioned to him that he must stop, and disappeared down the street. Presently she returned with a party of three—a stout, fair-haired woman with a baby in her arms and a small boy trotting at her side.

Nils recognized the boy; he was the one who had come to Kristine Dahl's that Sunday.

"Are you Nils Vaag?" asked the newcomer, in genuine Trondhjem dialect.

"Yes."

Mrs. Brakstad gave him a searching look while she shifted the child to her right arm. Her scrutiny seeming to have satisfied her, she continued, in a voice full of sadness,

"She's gone, the one you've come to see; she longed too much for you, I guess. Nobody but you and Johan, all the time. I don't think she thought of anyone else."

"Is she dead?"

"Oh yes, poor woman! Yes, she is dead. Two weeks now since they laid her away."

Nils stood staring at the sidewalk.

"How did it happen?"

217

The Boat of Longing

"She was killed at Seven Corners," came the reply, an edge of bitterness in it.

"Was she run over?"

"Yes. You see, she was stepping off the street car—without looking carefully enough, I suppose, and then her feet were poor, you know—and an automobile hit her. Struck her right in the back!"

"Did she live long?"

"Four days. She knew your address, so I sent Brakstad up after you one evening, but you hadn't come back from the woods yet. She cried then, poor woman, when she couldn't see you. Otherwise I've never seen a person more patient."

"Did she suffer much?"

"Oh yes, poor woman, she did! But then it didn't last long!"

"Did you have a doctor?"

"No, that we didn't; she wouldn't listen to it. She said this was the end; she had no sooner come to us than she said that. And we understood that she wished it to be so!"

Mrs. Brakstad, crying, shifted her burden once more. "Poor woman—she was such a good soul, too! She had her senses right up to the last day, but then she was out of her head. And it was only about Johan and the boat—yes, and about you—that she talked."

"About the Boat?"

"Yes, you see," she said, a smile breaking through the tears, "she imagined she saw a boat and was bound to go on board."

"Did she see it?"

"Well, she was out of her senses, you know. But she insisted she saw it coming for her, and she said we mustn't keep her. There was something peculiar about it, all the same," added Mrs. Brakstad, "for she was so happy."

"Was she so happy?"

Adrift

"Yes, don't you suppose she lay there smiling all the time?"

"She didn't suffer much, then?"

"Course, she suffered! But it seemed that what she was seeing made it easier for her to slip away. I've never seen a happier face."

"Where is she buried?"

Mrs. Brakstad moved the child to the other side; her face got a preoccupied and disconsolate look.

"No, that I couldn't tell you. You see, little Johan was so fussy I couldn't leave him, and Brakstad was working. But I think he knows the undertaker."

The little group stood there on the sidewalk.

The fog was beginning to lift now toward evening; there were glimpses of sun across on the university side.

Several curious onlookers had come out along the street. Most of them were women and children, with here and there a decrepit old gaffer; the latter sat in the doorways or leaned upon sticks.

Nils started to leave.

"No, you mustn't go yet; I've got something for you!"

"For me?"

"Yes, she insisted on that. Hold my baby"—she turned to the older woman—"while I fetch it."

The woman to whom she addressed the words took the child immediately and began hushing it.

"I'll be back right away," she said to Nils as she hurried off.

When she reappeared she carried a white bundle under her arm.

"There's the violin! She admonished us a hundred times, if she did it once, to get it into your hands. And here are a hundred dollars which she meant for you. She left nearly a thousand," explained Mrs. Brakstad. "The funeral and all cost two hundred and fifty; a hundred were to go to you;

The Boat of Longing

and our Tommy, that she'd taken such a liking to, got fifty;
and Brakstad and I were to have a hundred. The rest we
were to send to Norway to her half-brother; that's sent
already. Yes, God bless her! She was kind to everyone—
Kristine."

Mrs. Brakstad was crying; so were the two others. Tommy
hid his face in his mother's skirts and sobbed loudly.

A flock of children had gathered in the middle of the
street, the smallest of them gazing frightened, their fingers
in their mouths, wondering what it was all about; but they
came no nearer.

Nils removed the cloth from the violin and turned it over.
Yes, there was the cross in the grain of the wood; today it
could very easily be distinguished.

"No, keep the cloth around it!" remonstrated Mrs. Brakstad. "You can bring that back later."

Nils thrust the violin under his arm, said good-bye, and
hastened off.

At the top of the stairs he halted and faced about for a
look into the kettle. The flock of children had already dispersed into play. . . . And the house on the rock now
looked so dwarfish that its engulfment by the bank might
be expected at any moment.

VIII

He would walk Washington Avenue back, as far as Thirteenth; from there the way would lie straight ahead. He
clasped the white bundle tightly under his arm, his hand in
a firm hold upon the neck of the instrument.

Night was gaining.

Some distance up the street he came to a canopied wagon,
half off and half on the sidewalk; in front of it ran a bench.

Inside the stand a young Greek was braising busily away,

Adrift

humming merrily as he worked; the savoury odour of fried meat, onions, and seasoning wafted upon the air.

Wouldn't it be a treat to really eat one's fill of that food? thought Nils. Going over to the bench, he seated himself and placed the violin in his lap.

"Let me have some of that stuff you're making! It must be extra good!"

The Greek spared enough time to answer: "Yessir. Coffee too?" and went right on humming.

In a short while he handed Nils a hamburger sandwich and a cup of steaming coffee. "Twenty cents!" he hummed.

Nils paid him and ate. Well, now, this was unbeatable! Best he'd tasted in a long time!

"Better make me one more!" He turned to the Greek when he had disposed of the half.

"Yessir!" sang the other, braising and frying.

When he placed the second sandwich before Nils, he asked:

"Think that'll be enough?"

"Not so sure; better make me another while you're at it."

The Greek laughed and vouchsafed his customer a longer look.

"The old story," he burst out; "many meet the gods, but few have the sense to salute them! Comrade, you shall have a sandwich fit for a king!"

For the third time he fell to braising and frying. The song he started all over again. Nils learned the melody during the wait, whistling it to himself.

As he rose to leave, it occurred to him that he'd better stop at the saloon and confer with Per before he went home; he couldn't very well make any plans of his own till he knew what Per intended to do for the summer.

A bright idea began exciting his mind as he walked along. "I've unexpectedly been given a hundred dollars today, all because of the kind-heartedness of one person," he reflected.

The Boat of Longing

"And Per hasn't done quite so well in America as I have; I'll just give him half if he'll quit the saloon and find work that's more decent. Then both of us can put our money in the bank and commence saving in earnest; or we can exchange the fifty for Norwegian money and send it home. Wouldn't it be fun to see Ole Hansen when he got one hundred eighty crowns from his son!"

The longer Nils pursued the idea the better he liked it, and the more joyous he grew of mood. "Yes, that's exactly what I'll do," he decided as he stepped into the saloon. "I'll give Per fifty; when it comes right down to it, I haven't deserved them any more than he has, that's certain!"

It being long past working hours, a tight row of men lined the saloon bar; behind them pressed a crowd of others, waiting for a chance to slip in.

Otto Hansen and two other bartenders glided back and forth behind the counter, filling orders and rinsing glasses; the cash register clanged unceasingly. Liquor ran everywhere on top of the broad mahogany bar; now and then one of the bartenders would mop it up with a huge cloth. All three men were in their shirt sleeves, these rolled to the elbows, and were about as busy as mortals well could be.

Nils did not see Per, which puzzled him greatly. "He must've gone home and gone to bed," he concluded. Then, reflecting that he'd better wait and say how-do-you-do to Otto, as long as he was here anyway, he tarried a moment.

A couple of men up in front stepped out of the line, which gave him an opportunity to get next to the bar; he fixed his gaze on Otto till he caught his eye.

"Well, well! Hello there and welcome home!" exclaimed Otto, in a breezy and business-like way, as he approached with extended hand. "Just blow in from the woods? Pockets full of money—eh? Well, you've struck the right place, all right!" he laughed. "Have one on the house? What'll it be?" he offered expansively.

222

Adrift

Nils thanked him and declined.

"No? Well, well. Suit yourself—everyone to his own taste!" he smiled superciliously. "A cigar, then. Oh, that's right," he caught himself, "you're the Sunday-school kind; I forgot. Well, we have a fine line of temperance drinks of every sort. Not a saint we can't satisfy! This is a strictly up-to-date place, I can tell you, Nils. Yessir," he added, with great pride, "you'll have to go far to find the likes of it west of Chicago! How about it—want to come and clean for us again?" he asked, with the air of a proprietor.

Nils, who had cast his eyes down, replied that he couldn't answer him definitely offhand; he'd been thinking of different work for this year.

"Oh, if that's the case—" Otto had to be gone for a moment to wait on customers, and then came right back.

"Think it over, anyway, 'cause we're paying well. What do you say to two dollars a week? It's too much, of course, for that kind of work, but we'd like to get a reliable man, and we feel we can afford to pay!"

"Business pretty good?"

"Be a sin to complain; yes, mighty good! But you ought to let the firm treat the first time you're in!"

Again Nils thanked him and declined, just a little ill at ease in the presence of so much munificence. He'd just come in to meet Per, he said.

— Per?— Otto waited on a near-by customer.— He hadn't been there yet.

A sudden giddiness came over Nils; the floor began swaying beneath him, and the row of heads along the bar disappeared in a blur—they were there, they were gone. His hand closed round the neck of the violin so hard that the strings sounded. "Hasn't he been here?" he asked, mechanically.

"No, not yet."

Again Otto had to wait on customers; this was the busiest part of the day in the saloon; men passed in and out in a steady stream. The two assistants could not possibly manage it alone. But Otto was so brisk and efficient in his ways that the moment he took hold all seemed to clear off at once.

Nils slid his elbow off the bar, feeling that he must go. But when his feet wouldn't bear him, he raised his elbow to the counter once more.

Otto had returned and was talking to him.

"Been waiting for Per all spring. Terribly foolish of you to go up there in the wilderness and drag him along. What chances for young fellows up there? But I've a place for him now that's more like it," he confided to Nils.

Nils looked at him.

"He should be earning a couple of thousand a year at it easily—maybe more! Never seen such opportunities to get ahead as there are in Minneapolis right now—that is, of course, for those who want to! Well, what have you done with him?"

Nils began very circumstantially to relate all that had happened between the time of their arrival at the Y. M. C. A., and his own tardy rising, omitting no detail; but all the while he seemed to be talking to himself more than to Otto. When he had finished he said, "Can you understand it?"

"So he's sleeping there yet, is he?" asked Otto.

"Yes—but they said he'd got up," commenced Nils, wondering.

"Nonsense! Of course he's sleeping!" expostulated Otto, with sweeping superiority, half impatient with Nils for being such a simpleton. "He'd have come here if he'd been up; the boy couldn't have sunk into the street in broad daylight! 'Twon't be the first time he's slept through the day. What's the matter with you going to wake him up?" Once more Otto began waiting on customers.

It made Nils feel better to hear how Otto took the matter,

even though a voice within him protested that Per could not possibly be at the hotel—that was plain as day. The finality, however, with which Otto spoke and his lordliness drowned out the voice; moreover, the brother showed not the slightest concern.

Nils started townward with the violin under his arm. The sky had cleared; the street lamps shone so numerously and cheerily that they blotted out the stars, unless one looked sharply.

Nicollet was thronged with happy and beautiful pedestrians. Clinging fast to Otto's words, Nils slid into the stream . . . it was reasonable enough that Per couldn't have sunk into the earth!

The clerk at the desk was the same as the one of last night. But because he was occupied with a man, Nils waited till he was free before he walked forward.

Recognizing Nils, the clerk enquired if he wished a room. "N-n-o, not yet."

The clerk was a friendly-faced, middle-aged man, easy of approach. Nils confided to him that he had lost his comrade, the fellow who slept in 321 on seventh floor last night.

— Had he lost him?

— Yes.

— How could that be? Hadn't there been three of them? And hadn't the other two gone out together?— The man looked at Nils questioningly.

— Had the two gone out together?— Again Nils was affected as he had been in the saloon awhile back: the floor began to heave beneath him.— Did he say they had gone out together?

— Yes, the clerk remembered it distinctly, for the man in grey had seemed in a great hurry and had settled for the two of them.

— And was the other carrying a valise?

— He would have to think a moment. Yes—he believed

225

so. A black leather one with two straps, if he remembered rightly. Yes, that's what it was; it had stood on the desk while the man in grey paid the bill.

— And then they had left?— Nils's voice was toneless. His face looked blanched and almost comically old in the strong light of the desk lamp.— Had the clerk any idea what might have become of them?

— Well, where were they going?

"The young fellow intended to stay in Minneapolis," answered Nils. "We came from the woods last night, he and I. He had never seen the other man till yesterday!"

"Then you may be sure he's talked him into something."

"But where could they have gone?"

"That's hard to say," replied the clerk. "But unless I'm greatly mistaken, they're a long way off by now. I'm positive they were leaving on the morning train; otherwise they wouldn't have been in such a hurry. He wasn't your brother, was he?" he asked, solicitously.

"No—he was my friend. He ——"

Nils would have added more but couldn't. Swinging abruptly away, he walked out.

IX

For a long time he stood on the sidewalk, not knowing where to turn.

Finally he started off for the Great Northern Station. Here he entered.

The lights were lit within the vast waiting-room. Almost like getting into fairyland to step into this place, it was so large and so beautiful. Even the brilliance which lay over it had a dreamy look—that, too, accorded. And the decorations upon the one long wall hinted of fairy-tale adventures.

He commenced by taking a turn through the station, walking the entire length of it twice and searching every man's

Adrift

face there; then, after a further glance into the smoking-room, he took a seat near the front, where he could see all those passing to and from trains. "It was possible that they had been out around town today, intending to leave this evening," reflected Nils.

He laid the violin across his lap and folded his hands over it.

Along in the evening, as he sat thus hunting faces, it happened that one face separated itself from the rest and looked at him. That was, however, little to take notice of, for it was a bewildered face which looked at everything. Its owner was a little roly-poly woman of about forty, with five children in tow; the whole troop was luggage-laden.

She seemed to be having great difficulty in managing both bundles and children—the former because of their number, and the latter because of their unruliness.

The five linked hands, chain fashion; a small boy of about three years brought up the tail end, and a girl of about fourteen led at the other; the girl was at the same time sharing the burden of a heavy suitcase with her mother.

But on account of the mother's stopping every few steps to look for guidance, the whole fell into disorder frequently; the chain would either impede the progress of travellers who were in haste, or get tangled in legs and luggage going by, or wind itself around the mother so that she had to wait and let it unwind itself again.

Directly above where Nils sat they got into hopeless trouble. A fast mail was about to leave, and the descent of the passenger stream upon the woman threw her into a panic; her face showed such frantic bewilderment when Nils caught sight of it, that he immediately rose and went over to her.

"What's the matter with you, Imogene? Can't you look after them? Did you fall again, Le Roy? Haven't I told you time and again to stay by your brother? Goodness!—this trip'll be the death of me!"

The Boat of Longing

The woman spoke Norwegian. Nils quietly asked if he could be of any help to her.

Her excited face lighted like a desert traveller's at the sight of an oasis.

"Teddy, Le Roy, Kenneth," she called, joyfully, "go to the man there. He won't hurt you. Can't you hear he's Norwegian? Goodness! what a time I'm having with these kids!" This last came in the tone of complete exhaustion as she sank down upon the seat Nils indicated.

"Where are you going?" he asked, sympathetically.

"To Minot—Minot, North Dakota; must be the end of the world up there. Seems like we'll never get there, we've been travelling that long! Say, Imogene"—she spoke to the oldest girl—"you that can talk—set your stuff down and find out when the train leaves for Minot! I can't stir another step. Take Earl with you, so he won't get lost. Don't forget the time now, do you hear? The place is over there somewhere, I guess!"

The oldest, taking the next oldest by the hand, disappeared in the crowd.

"Whew! that was awful!" panted the woman. "I thought we'd never get here!"

"Where did you come from?"

"Clear from Chicago, mind you! But that wasn't the worst of it. I never saw anything so awful as getting from the Milwaukee depot and over here. That was a fright! Do you understand why they have to build depots so far apart? Teddy got so played out he couldn't stand up. I don't know what I should have done if that kind man hadn't come and carried him. I never knew there were so many kind people in the world till I started on this trip. My! almost everybody wanted to help! Now isn't that strange?" She removed her hat—which had slid pretty well askew—and began to smooth her hair.

Adrift

Imogene came darting out of the stream, holding her brother by the hand.

"You'd better go, Ma! We can't get through, and there's a mad man over there and Earl's scared. You go, and I'll watch Teddy and the stuff!"

Nils offered to go for them.

"The train leaves at half past eleven," he announced, upon returning, "and you won't have to change more than once."

Meantime the three-year-old Teddy had wandered about among the seats; this was as dandy a place in which to play as he had come across in many a day. He had at the same time discovered the package left by Nils in the seat. And it he must lift; feeling its lightness, he had to inspect it more closely. When Nils turned around, the boy stood with the violin in his hand; the cloth lay on the floor.

"Look, Mommy, look!" he cried in great glee. "A horse what c'n sing!" He had come to touch the strings so they sounded.

Nils sprang forward in instant alarm.

But Teddy would by no means relinquish his find; he had found the horse, and it was his. He only set up a howl and clutched the instrument more wildly with his arms.

Beside himself with fear for the violin, Nils caught up the youngster, sat down with him, and tried wheedling him to terms:

"Well, just listen to that now!" he said, stroking the strings with his thumb.

Instantly the tearful pout vanished and a pure radiance took its place.

"More, more!" he cried, his eyes gleaming; but he kept his grip on the instrument.

"You let me borrow it now!" coaxed Nils, his face vivid with excitement, "then you'll hear something awfully pretty!"

The Boat of Longing

Teddy's chubby face widened with joy and grew still more cherubic.

"More, more," he cooed.

Taking the violin gently away from the child, Nils gave the strings a few sharp twangs

"Hear that? Horsie's mad now; wants to bite! Ugh!"

Teddy stared at him sceptically and snuggled closer.

The other children drew near, stood around in a half moon.

Nils tuned the strings and took hold of the bow, without any intention of playing. But then the melody which the Greek had hummed so cheerily happened forward, and he had to see if he could play it.

— Well, this was indeed strange! The melody seemed to come of itself. Gladness intoxicating him, he forgot his surroundings; presently he was putting more intensity into the tones, and they in turn became more joyous. Nils could not understand it himself, but took fuller and fuller strokes with his bow, till the tones gamboled away in riotous jubilance.

Passers-by, curious, stopped to watch the group a moment and to listen before going on. Those occupying the nearest seats looked his way and smiled.

Having played the melody twice so that he was sure he knew it, Nils commenced to wrap up the instrument again; but the woman restrained him.

"Teddy ought to sleep now," she said. "It's long past his time, and I think he would, if you'd play a little more; I can see it on his eyes. Nobody will care, will they? People are all so kind here; it was certainly strange that that man would carry the boy all the way over here!"

Nils felt he ought to help the woman. Taking careful hold of Teddy, he placed him so that his head rested against the arm of the seat. Then he began to play—very softly in order not to attract attention.

Adrift

All the faces racing by glanced at him. They were now very vague and shadowy; that they stopped and looked at him, smiled or grinned, did not greatly astonish him; only natural that they would have to wonder when they heard all that he bore within him.

Aside from this, the many faces did not concern him; they belonged to a world gliding by. His mother and he were on a little skerry far out in the open sea; the deep had washed them up there. Around them the great ocean rolled ceaselessly between skylines. . . . He thought of their fate when the tide should begin to make. Would they again be swallowed up by the sea? . . .

— The passing faces dislimned; grew more and more unreal.

— Off and on he lifted his eyes to the lofty mountain on the wall.

— Now he himself sat on top of the peak, letting his thoughts rain like showers upon the human stream passing below in its endless trek upon eternity.

— For there was no end!

— Down on the lowland, near the base of the mountain, he discerned a few travellers. They were Indians on horse, peering under shaded eyes across an open water. . . . Nils looked at them and laughed. What a stupid mistake! It shouldn't have been horses and Indians at all, but a venerable, long-bearded billy goat squinting up at the strong spring sun in front of an elfin cote. Nor should there have been any water . . . no, not just there!

— A kindly smile from a passer-by made him happy; but he wondered that all didn't smile; for he was sitting here showing them the untold treasures of beauty.

— And the tones grew and became richer. . . . He glided into the strangely intricate and manifold world of his dreams about the "Boat of Longing."

The Boat of Longing

— So easy, too, to play this violin. Was that because a dead man's hand protected it?

— The tones waxed stronger and stronger. The effort to tame them made him flush of face. And now came the voice of the great forest moaning in lonely places, laying itself into them. . . . Difficult to hold back that strain! . . .

— Well, did you ever! There the Boat was appearing! And the tones already pregnant of the forest soughing took into the white sails and filled them to bulging! . . . On and on sped the Boat, over dull brown sea toward the coast of fairyland yonder, now rising faintly above the far-off skyline. If only the Boat would make port!

— Nils gave the tones freer rein. . . .

An unshaved face glistening with silvery stubble bent over his shoulder from behind.

"Your fiddle sounds right smart, lad, but this is no concert-hall! Better put it up!"

Nils came to with a start. The tones scattered; about him was darkness and void.

"I was only playing a tune for a tired child," he stammered, rising halfway in his seat.

"All right!" laughed the attendant and walked away.

Nils gazed like one who has awakened in a strange place. People came and people went; and all looked at him. The group which had clustered about him continued to stand after he stopped playing.

He felt embarrassed and cast his eyes down; the glad courageousness of a moment ago had deserted him.

But the tiny head slept at his side, its mouth gaping awry because the cheek was pressed against the arm of the seat. And all the other children, except Imogene, were sleeping. Nils wrapped the cloth about the violin and laid it away. Then he quietly lifted Teddy into his lap.

"Yes," said the mother, smiling tenderly from the seat across, "you must handle that baby with care. He's worth

Adrift

more'n all the rest put together, Teddy boy is. It's him that's going to be President some day! He shouldn't 've been called Teddy, by rights, you know. He should 've been *Ola.* But then it got to be this other, anyway. There's a lot that happens queer in this world," she sighed.

Nils not having yet come wholly down from the heights whereon he had sat, encountered her remark as though it had been some amusing object he detected by the roadside. Picking it up, he smiled at it and asked:

"And how did it happen?"

The woman was calmer now. " 'Twas his father wanted it that way. You see, his own name was Theodore, and he simply couldn't bear these Norwegian names. Now we've come to America, we'll be Americans, he always said. And I agreed with him in that. But he wasn't the one should have been the father of that child, though, nor of the others, either, for that matter. It was Ola should have been that, by rights!" she nodded joyfully.

"Is the father dead?"

"Yes, he died this last winter. A mercy, too, that he got to go; when a man can't work in America, he hasn't much to live for—I've found that out, I can tell you!"

"I guess that's so," agreed Nils.

She continued without heeding what he said:

"We're on our way to Ola now! And if he's as kind as I think he is, he'll take me, I'm sure, even if I have had five children by another. Say, Imogene, take that seat over there, then you can sleep a little, too; this man'll help us on the train, I'm sure. And you might as well move over here," she turned to Nils, "so it'll be easier to talk. We'll have to try and pass the time somehow."

The girl obeyed reluctantly; but Nils kept his place.

"Is Ola living in Minot?" he asked.

"Yes, his home's there, you see; he's got a house and stock and a farm and everything there. He's done well in

The Boat of Longing

America, Ola has! His wife died a year ago, so he advertised in *Skandinaven* this spring for a housekeeper; that's how I got the address. I answered right away and asked him if he'd give me the chance. 'I can keep house, all right,' I said. You see, I just about had to," she explained; "for what is a woman like me to do, sole alone with five children in a place like Chicago?"

"You knew him in Norway, then?"

"Ola?"

"Yes?"

"Certainly. We were engaged. I could hardly have written him otherwise. But he left first, you see, and then this other fellow began running after me all the time, wanting me to marry him. And I, big fool, didn't have the sense to say no. It's terrible how foolish a person can be! When I had the pick, I took the leavings. Then we set off for America, too. After that I heard no more from Ola, as you can imagine. But don't you think it's queer that I should happen to see this 'ad' just when I needed him most? It's the greatest miracle ever happened to me, I know."

"And you're on your way to him now?"

"Yes, now I'm on my way. He lives on a farm west of Minot. He sent me the money and everything. But"—she hesitated a moment—then added in a lowered voice, "the worst of it is I haven't told him all that I should have." She scrutinized Nils's sad, honest face, obviously wondering if she dared trust it unreservedly.

"Sit down over here; then we can talk better. You needn't be scared; I'm respectable enough."

Nils took Teddy and complied.

"That's better—makes it easier. No—you see—I—I didn't dare tell it all."

" 'Twould be a little difficult, I should think."

"Yes, because you see I was afraid he wouldn't have me if he knew. And I had to have him, that was all there was

234

to it. So I didn't tell him—I didn't tell him I had more than three," she whispered.

"You told him you only had three?"

"Do you think that was so awful?" she asked, reproachfully. "When I simply couldn't see how I could get along down there? And it wasn't so very far from the truth. Imogene's fourteen, going on fifteen, so she really didn't need to be counted; you can see that! And if Earl, who's going on twelve, gets enough to eat, he'll soon be able to take care of himself. So when you consider it all, it really leaves only three!" she triumphed. "What would you have done, now, if it had happened to you?"

"If I had been you?"

She nudged him and laughed.

"As if that had been possible! I meant, of course, if you'd been Ola."

"Oh!" pondered Nils.

"Yes; and then I'd have come to you with that understanding? Would you have turned me away?"

"Just for the sake of the two?"

"Exactly!" she cried, excited.

"No," admitted Nils thoughtfully, "I don't see that two more or less would have cut any figure."

"Exactly; two certainly can't make so much difference that he'll turn me away on that account!" she beamed.

"And as you say, they will soon be grown up."

"That's it! A man I talked with on the train thought the very same thing; he said three or five didn't cut any ice as long as there were any at all. Yes, that's what he said. I think he must have been a kind man. Strange with true love, you know," she added, more quietly; "I'd have taken Ola if he'd had a dozen. I'm going to tell him so, too— that is, if it's necessary, of course!"

Nils was dead tired; last night's sleep had not been sufficient for him, and it was already past eleven o'clock. Added to that, he had had a trying day, had received jolt after jolt, and his mind was spent and weary. He was, therefore, not in the mood to discuss the subject with her at any length; his position, moreover, was disadvantageous for seeing those who went to the trains. It was only those coming that he could see, and in them he had no interest.

He rose. By way of excusing himself, he enquired if she had procured her ticket.

"Ticket? Now you said it! Here I've been jabbering and fooling away my time till I've forgotten all about the tickets! Keep an eye on these youngsters, will you, while I go and get them? I'll have to be more careful, that I can see, and not act so brainless when I get to Ola's; he wants everybody to be just so, I can tell you!" She nodded energetically as she trotted off.

Presently the train came.

"Goodness! If you hadn't had sense enough to watch the time we'd have got left here now! Though I won't take all the blame; it was really your fault, some of it; if you hadn't been sitting here, I wouldn't have forgot the way I did."

Nils did not vouchsafe a reply. Picking up Teddy in one arm, and thrusting his violin under the other, he accompanied her to the train and helped her on board. She showered blessings in profusion upon him when he left.

x

Returning to the waiting-room, Nils took the seat he had first occupied.

"Now that homeless bird is once more on the wing," he remarked, mentally. "Wonder if there are many such in America. . . . I suppose so." . . .

Melancholy began pressing more heavily upon him.

. . . "Here I sit . . . alone . . . brooding," ran his thought. "I, who left against Father's will. Against Mother's,

Adrift

too. Scarcely a thing they've opposed as much. . . . Now Father sits there alone in his boat, with no one to help him; never in the world would he hire a man. The sea may be teeming with saithe and herring, but Father gets none of it, having no helper in the boat; the only son he had deserted him; how then can he have anyone with him? I scarcely dare think of such sin!" . . . The vein of self-accusation continued. "And there'll be no one to keep Father and Mother company in the cottage of evenings, now that I'm gone. And that's when it's so beautiful there, especially by the window overlooking the sea. Father sits grave and silent. Mother speaks to him, but she gets no answer; then she too grows silent. She goes to the window and gazes to sea; tries speaking again, but no answer comes; so she remains there, gazing. And it's I who am to blame. . . . The saithe will have come by now, with the evenings so long and light. . . . But Father doesn't trouble; his boat's at the pier . . . lies there unpainted though the season's far gone." . . .

Gloom closed thickly around him.

. . . "And Kristine Dahl has boarded the Boat of Longing, never to return. Will she meet her Johan, I wonder?

. . . "And Per is gone—the only one whom I could really call comrade! . . . Perhaps I shall never find him again. And his father—what shall I say to him? How can I ever return, now that Per has disappeared? I can't, that's all." . . .

An icy coldness shook him; perspiration broke out upon his forehead; his whole body grew limp. Unconsciously he wiped his face.

He pulled himself together with a violent effort, diverted his eyes to the mountain on the wall, and began to wonder what lay back of the mountain. It was a very large mountain, a towering one. . . . There was, of course, a landscape beyond? It couldn't possibly mark the end of the earth? . . .

— There was one picture which had at times stood vividly

before him this year; he did not know when nor how it had come; but it was there.

Now it came again. And tonight it was not a picture at all, but a reality he could put his hands on and feel. His immediate surroundings withdrew farther and farther into the background; disappeared at length altogether, and he lived only in the picture.

— Somewhere lay a valley. Its place he did not know; but tonight it happened to be here. He was up there on the mountain-top, and had to go into the valley. No help for it, he must. So he began the descent.

— Below him, a deep chasm; it seemed without bottom; ever and ever downward he bore, perpetually downward. But so broad and far-reaching was the valley that it formed a whole world.

— Its boundaries, declivous mountains which walled it in.

— And he must go down!

— On the uppermost heights, nothing save black slippery slopes of rock; but lower in the steep hillsides, thick, dark forest . . . soughing, always and eternally soughing . . . and marching in continuous procession to the ends of the earth.

— Way there was not. Bootless to search. Not even so much as a trail. In a place untrod by human foot, how could there be?

— And no ray of sunlight fell on the hillsides!

— But a pallid dusk lay over this desolate world. In, through, and blending with it coursed a livid nebulousness, impalpable, having colour only. The great forest's tops looked so queer in the drifting empurpled dimness.

— Here human voice had never broken. Only the trackless forest's deep rush, which in its most audible rhythms sounded like the thud of heavy footfalls shuffling along.

— It might happen that a moisture would lay itself into

Adrift

the half-light, and then the fearful thunder of landslips would crack the silence. . . .

An experience Nils once had lived through now rushed forcefully on him; momently, it had superimposed itself upon the picture and become one with it:

It was an occurrence of last spring, on the Stril's last Sunday in camp. He had gone with the Stril to Wild Horse Lake. A wind had been blowing from the south and it had mizzled. The ice was gone. The loon had just arrived; it rode yonder on the lake, crying plaintively against rain.

An old boat had lain moored at the water's edge; Nils had found line and bait in a log cabin near by, and, fisherman that he was, had not been able to restrain himself; he had felt compelled to try his luck. The Stril, however, had been in a grouchy humour, few of words and out of sorts, and had not wanted to go.

Nils had therefore set out alone; the pickerel had struck, and Nils had rowed farther and farther.

The fisherman's zeal in him had waxed so strong that before he was aware he had found himself in the middle of the lake. Presently, cold gusts had begun to whiffle out of the south; the clouds had sailed lower; the rain had spit larger; the wind had stiffened; darkness and night had begun to gather.

Nils had then realized his rashness. He had hastened to pull up his line, had seized the oars and begun to row hard against the wind; needing to race with time, he had rowed for all he was worth, and so had broken an oarlock.

He had not known what to do. He could not get back by boat; he would have to let the wind have its way and drive him to the north end of the lake. Darkness was falling, the rain beating down, the wind mounting; the waves rolling toward him across the murky waters were growing whiter and angrier. Along the shore and back a way, trunks of charred white birches had thrust themselves terrified out of the gloom and the heightening storm.

When the storm had begun to look bad, the Stril had grown anxious; Nils had drifted farther and farther away, and had at last disappeared altogether. The Stril had then gone down to the shore and, cupping his hands, had begun hallooing. Somewhere out of the darkness a loon had kept answering; at times it had been impossible to distinguish between the human call and the cry of the bird.

Nils had at last gained shore on the opposite side. But that trip back to the starting-point turned out to be the most perilous he had ever attempted. Compelled to follow the shore in order not to get lost, he had had to cross swamps and break his way through wild thickets. The swamps had been crusted with slushy snow, with ice underneath; every now and then he had plunged in up to his thigh. At intervals a cry had punctured the darkness—long drawn out and wailing. He had thought it must be the Stril; a loon could not possibly complain so loud; but he had not been certain.

By the time he had got back, the Stril was gone.

When Nils had reached camp that night he had been soaked to the skin and so worn out that he had been ready to drop before he could get out of his clothes.

— That night on Wild Horse Lake Nils had seen the colour which now lay over the valley. It was just before the rain had begun falling in earnest, and evening had turned into night. For then a grey-blue opaqueness had hung over all, through which the white-stemmed birches and the frothing waves had shone with an ingenerate wanness.

— Nils sat leaning heavily forward; he was no longer looking at the mountain-top; he was completely engrossed in the mind picture. He wondered if there might not be a sea at the bottom of this valley, a sea with moiling waters across which squalls raced black? . . . Impossible that these steep hillsides could continue downward indefinitely! . . .

Adrift

— He could feel slush underneath. His foot slid on a slippery wetness—it must be slush; all of a sudden he had to fling his arms about the trunk of a tree in order to keep himself from dashing headlong down the abyss.

— The thought sent a chill through him. He seized the arm of the seat; should he lose foothold here, he'd be gone for good! . . . Far down in the depths lurked all that was evil, all that engendered sorrow and despair, all that made the blood turn cold—all that the Divine Creator never had blessed. . . .

— He leaned still farther forward, thinking he glimpsed objects below. What were they? Luminous orbs? Well, sir, if they weren't! And light streamed so beneficently round about them! "Did you ever!" The sight amazed him. . . . "What in this country could possibly have light in it?" . . . He let himself glide faster and faster from trunk to trunk, down toward the lights.

— But then he saw what it was. It was the eyes of Ole Hansen! Yes, it was the eyes of Ole Hansen floating up the hillside.

— Nils could have shrieked with terror. He cast himself in dread upon the ground; began to crawl on his hands and knees, attempting to escape by a long circuitous route; not for all the world did he dare encounter those eyes of Ole Hansen's tonight! And in the anguish of his soul he prayed God to help him, so that the eyes could not find him.

— Well, he escaped from the eyes at long last; when he stole a glance backward he could no longer see them. . . . "Thanks be! If only Ole Hansen will be careful now, so he won't get lost in these hills!" Nils was at a loss to comprehend how the decrepit old fellow could make his way through such a wilderness.

— He rose to his feet and continued downward.

— But as he now walked, he thought the hills less steep;

241

and the steel-grey dusk seemed lighter below; a feeble yellowish glimmer had begun shifting through it.

— "Now you'll be seeing," thought Nils, and quickened his pace. "It's getting brighter and it's easier to walk."

— And he walked and walked. The grey-blue grew fainter, the dull yellow deepened; till at last only the latter prevailed.

— Then he was standing on a beach. Before him spread a sound crinkled over with little lazy waves. He could see across. On the opposite side stretched a tawny strand; its colour did not amaze him, for he knew what it was that gleamed so ghastly yonder. It was bones . . . bleached bones—that was all! . . . If only he'd had a boat at hand, he could have slipped over; there'd be acquaintances, he'd wager, among the skeletons on that wan yellow coast!

— He jumped to his feet with a start.

"Don't happen to have a match, do you, Mister?"

The questioner had laid his hand on Nils's shoulder in order to be friendly and thus assure himself of a match.

"What?" asked Nils. "Want to use matches in this place?"

The man stood with his hand outstretched. Nils gazed at it blankly; then came to his senses sufficiently to realize his whereabouts.

It was broad day; the light from the chandeliers had been turned out. But the human stream coursed as before, thin at times, but broad and swift whenever a fast train was about to leave.

Nils made his way to the street. Hunger pressed him and he went into a little restaurant.

Then he returned to the station and began pacing back and forth in front of it, keeping it up for a long time; when he grew too tired, he rested, only to resume his walking after the interval.

After a time he went into the station and sat down; here he remained until six o'clock in the evening. Then he took

Adrift

a business card out of his pocket, the one the bridge con-
tractor had given him, and studied it awhile; later he went
out to seek the man. . . . From that day on, Nils never
entered the Great Northern Station in Minneapolis without
feeling that he had come home; it was as though he had
lived many years of his life in that place.

On Sunday night he left the station in the company of
Lars Korsness; and thereafter he spent two years wandering
up and down the Great Northern Railway, from bridge to
bridge, and city to city. Happening to get into a city of a
Saturday night, he would immediately seek out the city's
busiest corner; and there he would stand searching and
searching, like a lone gull perched watchful on some bold
headland round which the ocean current runs swift.

Those really becoming aware of the face were involuntarily made to wonder at its sad and weary look, especially
since it seemed so young.

"That person must surely have committed some dreadful
wrong!" they thought, and hurried past. "Such ought not
to be permitted at large; strange the police don't lock
them up."

—Other than that, people bestowed little thought upon
the face or upon him who owned it, being too busy about
their own affairs to remember much else.

IV. Hearts That Ache

I

IT WAS lonely in the cottage at Vaag after Nils had left.
If Jo by the Sea had been silent before, he worsened
now; and it availed little for Mother Anna alone to
talk; the sound of her voice and the reply she never got
only increased the emptiness.

"We've fair weather today," she might venture. "Don't
you think, Jo, we'd better row out?"

And they would; but Jo had no zest. . . . Womenfolk
wouldn't do in a boat; a man wasn't served by them in the
long run! . . . Finally, Jo's excuses for staying at home
increasing with the months, their trips to sea as good as
ceased altogether.

It was only Ole Hansen who brought them cheer. He
began paying visits to Vaag to learn if there might be news
from Nils. His protracted stays would enliven the cottage,
for he was fond of talking and possessed much of that
brightness of spirit which had been given his son.

Days bringing letters from Nils came to be festal ones.
Generally, it was Ole Hansen who brought them. After a
time his appearance got to be as regular as the boat's arrival
from the south, whether there was any letter or not: it was
as unfailing as the sun. And when the day came that he
could bring two America letters, one for Jo and one for
himself, he felt so spry that he could nicely have thrown
his stick.

"Now isn't it exactly what I've been saying all my life,"
he cried, "that the likes of our two boys, your Nils and my
Per, are not to be found? There they are over in America,

going about like gentlemen already, and laying up a fortune. Some fine day we'll see them right here in this cottage with us, just like any two lords, their pockets bursting with money. Then all you and I'll have to do is sit down to our pipes and take life easy, Jo. No trick for anyone having such sons!"

Both Jo and Mother Anna liked very well to have Ole come, regardless of letters; it gladdened old Jo because it gave Mother Anna some one to talk to; and Mother Anna rejoiced because she noticed how the visits cheered Jo.

When, therefore, spring approached the following year, Mother Anna hinted to Jo that he ought to make Ole his partner in the summer fishing. "After all, menfolk in a boat are menfolk, Jo; and Ole is both quick and strong with his arms. He's sure to serve you much better than I."

At first Jo wouldn't listen; but then Mother Anna kept at him so long that finally he spoke to Ole one day.

It was as happy a proposal as he could have made. "It's exactly what's been on my mind," exclaimed Ole, "only I haven't had the courage to mention it to such an able fisher as you. I'll go right home now and put provisions in my chest, and then I'll come; the wife can manage the place for the summer."

No, Jo would not hear of that. "Food you sha'n't bring," he protested; "folk in Vaag aren't as needy as that. Keep and gear I'll provide, and you shall have a third of the profits, though that's not a great matter; I'll gladly give you more; Mother and I have enough for us two. Take Nils's oilskins, they're here; and we've plenty of tackle. All that's necessary is for us to get started." Jo by the Sea was so happy that his heart leaped within him.

Thus it came about that it was not Ole Hansen who brought the letter which told of the boys' return from the woods and of how much money Nils had saved up, but Mother Anna herself.

The Boat of Longing

When she reached a place up in the path where she would be out of sight of the store, she sat down on a heather-covered knoll to read the letter. She grew perplexed as she read, for there was that in the lines which made her wonder; it was what the boy left out that disturbed her. "But likely he's tired," she reflected; "he's worked hard all winter and had a long journey home; perhaps he hasn't had sleep enough, either—young people need a great deal, as I should know!" Then, reading about all the money he had laid by, she forgot the other, and, rising hastily from the knoll, hurried home; Jo and Ole must hear this at once! . . . "Bless my soul," her heart warmed with motherly pride, "if the boy keeps on like that for two or three years, he'll soon have more money than we, and still be in his youth. America must be a wonderful country!"

She quickened her steps in order to reach the cottage before the men's return from the sea, so that she might surprise them with some favourite dish; and by the time they put in to shore she was sitting on a stone down by the pier, waiting for them.

"Was there a letter?" called Ole.

"Guess now," she smiled, secretively.

Ole and Jo exchanged glances; both smiled.

"Today I think we'll guess *no*!" answered Ole, obliquely. "You came back so soon that I suppose there couldn't have been any." He now stood with his knees on the forethwart, pulling off his oilskins.

"What do you say, Jo?" she asked.

"Well, why predict the weather on such a sunshiny day?" questioned Jo. "Got the coffee ready for us, have you, Mother?"

That made Ole chuckle. "Aye, aye, 'tis a clear day, so it is; heh-heh-heh!"

Mother Anna had to laugh with him, despite the laugh's

Hearts That Ache

being on her; even Jo had to smile, the merriment grew so contagious down on the beach.

"Well, here we have further tokens," remarked Jo, slyly when they sat down to the table and he saw what Mother Anna placed before them.

"Will you listen to that, now!" retorted Mother Anna, affecting to be offended. "As though I didn't always prepare good food, even when there is no America letter!"

While the menfolk sat enjoying their supper, Mother Anna read them the letter. But because of the happiness of her who read, its undertone did not make itself heard; mother-pride quelled it.

When she reached the part which told of the money Nils had laid by, Ole Hansen laid his spoon right down and stared at her open-mouthed.

"Does it say—does it actually say thirteen hundred and fifty crowns? You must be reading wrong, Mother Anna; it must be three hundred and fifty. Which certainly isn't bad, either! Don't you think so too, Jo?"

Then Mother Anna was offended at Ole Hansen.

"Go along with you, Ole Hansen! Don't you suppose I can read? Think Nils would have said it if it hadn't been true? He's much too honest a boy for that, as I should know!"

"N-n-n-n-no," stammered Ole, apologetically. "Go right on reading, Mother Anna; don't you take notice of an old man's nonsense, who's so happy he's daft! We can all see plainly that it says what you say. It's just unbelievable that our boys can have done so well the first year. What won't they do when they've learned the language and really get started! I can't for the life of me see why we're so foolish as to go chasing about on the sea wearing out your gear, Jo!— Be somewhat there about Per, too, I expect?"

Then Ole Hansen held his peace long enough for Mother Anna to go on with her reading.

247

The Boat of Longing

"And our Per, now, has not done less well than Nils, I am sure," Ole went on as soon as she had finished the letter. "Per had a brother there to begin with; it ought to be easier for him to get ahead than for Nils. And he's no dunce, Per isn't, once he makes up his mind to a thing! Don't you think so too, Jo?"

Mother Anna gave Ole a look, but made no remark.

"Any more coffee, Mother?" asked Jo. "I believe you're both losing your wits. Here you sit, Ole, suggesting that we give up fishing when the sea stands teeming with God's plenty. And you're not a whit better, Mother Anna; you pour coffee for Ole, and pass me by, your husband, with whom you have lived these forty years!"

When old Jo by the Sea could say so much in jest all at one time, the other two had to laugh outright, and then Jo joined in; Mother Anna meanwhile hastened to correct her oversight.

That night Ole Hansen hobbled a Norwegian mile on his crippled leg, through woods and over squishy bogs, just to tell his wife that Per, their son, had become a rich man in America; he had now earned a good fifteen hundred crowns. — The letter had, to be sure, stated thirteen hundred and fifty; but since it must be immeasurably easier for Per to get ahead than for Nils, Ole had convinced himself on the way that he could, without exaggerating, add the needed one hundred and fifty. . . . Might very well be that Per had even more. . . . For Per was no dunce. . . . And he had got good pay from Jörgensen. . . .

II

It got to be high summer at Vaag. Sea and crag and mountain lay in a great light . . . pure, serene light. A peculiar joy, as of expectancy, had settled over the fisherman's cot.

248

Hearts That Ache

The catch turned out to be a rich one. First there had been the saithe in the forepart of the season; then the trawl fishing. In August the herring had come under shore in incredible numbers. Jo by the Sea and Ole Hansen had worked with the industry of the most expert fishers.

Mother Anna kept the house and looked after their comfort; on days when the mail arrived she made the trips to Vik.

And she took letters of her own to post—letters to Nils, composed with great pains, and laboriously, because of her having to sound out the words. They were long letters, too, for there was so much to be said.

But she brought none home, for none came that summer from either Per or Nils. Nor did any come that fall.

They took little thought of it—yet. The men were busy with the fishing, and Mother Anna had her hands more than full; moreover, last winter nearly five months had gone by without a letter.

"There'll be a letter at Christmas, you may be sure," comforted Ole.

"Aye, of that we may be more than certain!" Mother Anna agreed.

Whenever the subject came up, which occurred at least once every week, Jo had little to say. He had begun to withdraw into his old silence once more.

Christmas came and passed. New Year too. Epiphany and Hilarymas followed, with no letter from the boys.

Jo continued his silence, and Mother Anna began to grow fewer of words. But on days when Ole Hansen came to visit, she might let loose and talk a steady stream with him, basking in the sunshine of his optimism; for his faith was so bright and implicit that all doubt must vanish before it. Even Jo went peering for glimpses of Ole on the days when he might be expected.

There being no fishing in midwinter, Ole had moved home

again; but he came to Vaag every post day, always taking two days for the trip. And then he chatted, and had faith for all three.

"It's likely this, you see, that they haven't the time to write; you'll have to admit that they can't have much time for letters the way they're laying up money—that's plain to be reckoned! Besides, what difference does it make, as long as we know that they're doing well and that nothing's amiss? You may be sure we'd have heard, if there was; misfortune always gets noised about—we all know that! And they take a lot of money, too, these America letters; I really don't understand how your Nils could afford to send so many last fall. There my Per really was much more sensible!" he added, naïvely.

"A-y-e," said Jo, slowly.

"Aye, that he was!" asserted Mother Anna.

"And it's a great distance, you know," continued Ole. "When a letter can get lost between Lofoten and here, what might not happen between America and here? It's a wonder to me that as many get here as do. Besides, 'tisn't at all certain they can read Norwegian in that big city; so how can they get the letters started in the right direction?"

Which Mother Anna thought very sensibly spoken of Ole; it helped her exceedingly for a while. But then there was this about it: last fall the letters had come with the regularity of the weeks; apparently not one had gone astray.

When she mentioned this to Ole, he merely said:

"But what if there'd been a Norwegian in their post office last fall? And he'd left when summer came? And there was no one else there who could understand Norwegian? I'll tell you, Mother Anna, our letters may have gone to Russia or Palestine, for all we know."

Ole knew in his heart how Jo and Mother Anna felt, and on the long tramp to Vaag his imagination was very busy deducing reasons why no letter came. Otherwise, he did think them somewhat unreasonable in their expectation of letters—good and sensible though they were in all other matters.

One day he had found a new excuse to advance, but because of the difficulty of uttering it he didn't get it said till just before he was ready to leave.

"You see," he hesitated, speaking to Mother Anna, but fixing his eyes on the ground, "your Nils lives in the same house as our two boys; and with them so careless he likely gets out of the habit, too."

Resentment flashed out of the eyes of Mother Anna as she looked at him.

"Well, Mother Anna, you must know that it can't have gone amiss with all three of the boys. That's simply unthinkable, you see. Let's suppose now—just suppose, you understand—that some ill luck had happened to your Nils; you know very well that one of our boys would have written about it. Otto wrote several letters before Per went over, and he sent the ticket! And if there was any trouble about Per, Nils would be sure to write; he promised me that the night he left. And as I said, not all of them can have drowned at once."

One day late in March when Ole came to the cottage he assured them that they would be getting a letter as soon as the boys had returned from the woods—no question about it!

"And then you'll be hearing that each one has his three thousand crowns; Otto, who has been there so long, will, of course, have much more. I have, as a matter of fact, figured out this winter, that he'd have considerable more—but we'll never mind about that. Maybe they'll be here next Christmas. Your Nils, now—well, didn't he always talk about coming home? Don't suppose he'll be going to Lofoten again, do you?"

But Jo sat uncomforted and silent over the net he was knitting, notwithstanding.

The Boat of Longing

Mother Anna talked loud and excitedly, her unbelief and apprehension protruding noticeably.

"It's all the same about the money," she said, "if only they'd come themselves! Wasn't Per talking of buying a steamship and coming home in it?"

Ole lifted his sou'wester and scratched his head.

"Well now, to be sure," he said, deeply thoughtful, "I did hear him speak of that before he left; and it certainly isn't unlikely that he'll be doing it too. At the rate he's saving money, it won't take very long before he can buy one of moderate size. Much that's more incredible than that has happened in the world I'll tell you, Mother Anna. Isn't that what you say, Jo?"

III

The steamship proved a veritable gold mine of ideas for Ole Hansen's imagination. On the way home that day he had to stop every now and then to count on his fingers; in the evening he sat down with paper and pencil, drew the lamp close, and figured and figured.

— If Nils, now, had three thousand, Per probably had three thousand five hundred; at that rate Otto would have at least ten thousand; in all, that would make sixteen thousand, five hundred. . . . Ole Hansen rejoiced like a child at the stupendous figure which he could make it net.

— For that matter, it was only reasonable to suppose that the second year, when they were used to the new conditions and had learned the language, they would do twice as well. According to those calculations, they ought now to be having close to thirty thousand crowns among them—that is, the three of them together, of course. "A blessed sight of money!" hummed Ole to himself, immeasurably pleased.

Then he began to add to the amount, giving the boys the

Hearts That Ache

benefit of every possibility he could think of, until he got their estate up to forty thousand.

— "No question but that," he said, half aloud, "they could, with that amount, get a steamship adequate for crossing the Atlantic. And Nils by the Sea is an uncommonly fine sailor; it happens real fortunate for Per and Otto that he's with them!"

— "Well, now I can give you the figures," he announced on his next visit to Vaag; "got 'em all in my head. I know why the boys don't write; they intend to surprise us, that's what; they're coming home in a steamship of their own! With the three of them putting their earnings together they'll manage it nicely. But where the deuce do you suppose they can dock when they come? They can't get into this cove of yours, Jo, with that big a boat!"

"Are you daft, Ole Hansen?" exclaimed Mother Anna, striking her hands together, scepticism and happiness running riot.

"Daft? Now you shouldn't be the one to say that, Mother Anna!" retorted Ole, taking umbrage.

"Well, where would they get that steamer?" Jo thrust in gravely, more to stave off a tiff than for any other reason

"Get it?" shouted Ole, thumping his stick on the floor. "That a man of your sense can sit there asking so ridiculously, Jo! They'll get it themselves, of course; they've certainly the means!" Ole Hansen fairly grew powerful.

"But do you really think they can have earned as much as that?" asked Mother Anna, melioratingly.

"Aye, that I do! You're the one who's refusing to believe!" Ole corrected her. "I've never heard such doubters as you two, even though you don't lack evidence. Just suppose that you now, Jo, or you, Mother Anna, sensible folk that you are, had estimated what Nils had laid by last year? What would you have guessed, Mother Anna?"

"Well, that isn't so easy to say offhand," deliberated

253

The Boat of Longing

Mother Anna; "I might possibly have said five hundred crowns."

"Nonsense!" interrupted Jo, with a flash. "How could you have said that, Mother? That would have been too much! We couldn't have said above four hundred."

"Aye, there you see!" beamed Ole. "There you see! But the fact remains, nevertheless, that he actually had more than three times that much."

"A-y-e?" began Jo.

But Ole didn't permit him to finish.

"I've got it all figured out, and I think I've done it correctly. Here it is: The reason the boys haven't written is simply that they've earned so much they can't write about it; they don't want to let it get out, that's all, on account of taxes and the like. Those things spread very easily. And what, besides earnings, would there be for them to write about?" cried Ole, triumphantly, thrusting his stick straight into Mother Anna's chest.

"There you have the whole explanation," he continued. "We'll never hear another word from them till they steam into Vik—they'll have to anchor in Vik, of course. 'Twill look best there, too, as far as that goes. You can imagine it'll be jolly with boats on the bay then! First Jørgensen's schooner, and then our boys' big American steamer."

Ole stood there delineating the picture until his cheeks were pink with excitement. Mother Anna gaped at him till she forgot to put the coffee-pot over the fire. Even Jo had let his work drop out of his hands and sat with them idle in his lap; his face grew brighter and brighter as Ole painted.

IV

But the sedative had no lasting effect this time.

Jo, keen of mind as he was, soon perceived that Ole's

Hearts That Ache

calculations simply didn't hold water; fortunes could not be amassed with such fabulous speed, not even in America. Mother Anna, too, detected flaws in his reasoning, though she reached her conclusion by a different route. That they might have earned this much she did not find incredible; but when she came to think of it she saw that it couldn't be the explanation of Nils's silence; she knew her son better than that!

Despair took to weighing heavily upon the minds of the two.

And Ole himself was far from being as certain as he had been, when he reached home that evening.

On the way he had stopped at Jörgensen's in Vik. The skipper had, fortunately, been alone on the quay; which had made it easier for Ole to strike up a conversation with him. He had begun to quiz the skipper about various matters.— What, approximately, did Jörgensen think a steamship would cost, similar to these coastwise ones on the regular routes— that is, roughly speaking? Ole reached the question by a devious course, involving numerous other questions; he talked about the mail and the dispatching of it, about the speed of the mail packets, and the danger of the lane here in these sheltered waters.

When Jörgensen had estimated that a boat of that type would cost a hundred thousand crowns or more, Ole had disputed him, saying that 'twas impossible it could cost so much. But Jörgensen had held to his own, insisting it couldn't be less.

The journey home from Vik became dismayingly long for Ole that day; he sat on rock after rock, figuring, but no matter how he estimated or how many possibilities he gave the boys the advantage of, he simply could not get the sum up to one hundred thousand crowns.

— No, not unless one of them should have married a millionaire, he thought as he rose and hobbled on.— And if

The Boat of Longing

that was the case, then it would most likely be Per; one never could tell what he might be up to. And he was certainly the boy to command the words, so he could, for that matter, have anyone he pleased!

But then another thought came, which made the journey still more wearisome; a boat of that size simply wouldn't be large enough for crossing the Atlantic.

Late in May Ole came moving back to Vaag; he was again to fare the sea with Jo for the summer.

He seldom mentioned the steamship now. And when he did, it was as though it were so settled a matter that it wasn't worth arguing about any longer; not having yet been able to hit upon any other solution, he had had to hold stubbornly to this one.

He was aware of how Jo and Mother Anna went about tormented by anxiety; and he would so gladly have spoken a word of comfort to them and to himself; but he could not find one to speak.

Every post day in June dawned in hope and closed in the bleakest despair; neither June nor July brought tidings. Finally, it became too piteous for Ole to endure; he must seize upon something. At last the idea came:

One day while they were out pulling in the trawl lines he took a round-about way and mentioned it to Jo:

"Just about how old are you now, Jo?"

Jo hauled, puzzled, and replied that he was sixty-two.

"Are you daft, Jo?—You're not that old?"

Jo asserted its correctness; he would be sixty-two next Michaelmas.

"But you look so young; and you're as hale and hearty as though you weren't a day above fifty."

"No, I can't complain of my health," answered Jo, continuing to haul.

"You certainly could undertake whatever you pleased so far as health and age are concerned."

Hearts That Ache

Ole manœuvred the boat, holding his peace for a moment. Presently he blew his nose into his mitt and looked at Jo: "Know what I'd do if I were you?"

"Be hard for me to know that."

"I'd travel, that's what, if it weren't for this pesky foot."

"You would travel?" Jo had to cease hauling and gaze at him.

"I certainly would."

"And where to, may I ask?"

"Aye," asserted Ole, emphatically, "I'd make a trip to Minneapolis to see those boys of ours. I'll guarantee you'd get a welcome."

Jo could only stand and stare at him; the line hung slack on the roller.

Ole continued unperturbed:

"I certainly would, this fall when the fishing's over. You're chipper and hale as any young man, so that wouldn't stand in your way. Besides, we can afford it. I'll give my share of the summer's catch. Though we need have no fear but the boys will stand the expenses when they hear that you've come expressly to see how they're getting along."

It looked as though Jo was urged to speech; but nothing came of it; instead, he fell to working again.

"Swing the boat better in line, will you? The current's strong today," he said, quietly; but that was all.

Ole obeyed, taking a few strokes with the oars.

"Do you think it's a foolish idea?" he asked.

"Foolish?"

"Aye."

"Swing the boat nearer. Don't you see how the trawl lies?" corrected Jo.

"When you're as healthy and spry as you are? We certainly can afford it, with the boys doing so well." Ole scrutinized him closely, wondering if he dared advance his other ideas; but the face before him bent so noncommittal

257

over its work, that he let them rest for the present. . . . It might perhaps be better to broach the subject to Mother Anna; there at least he could depend on an answer.

They got the lines into the boat and plied toward land. Jo did not utter a single word, and Ole's mind was too occupied with the idea to find other matter for conversation.

But that evening, while Jo worked at the waterside putting up the boat for the night, Ole spoke to Mother Anna; his words came from over a net he was knitting for Jo.

"You really should get Jo off this fall, Mother Anna; you really should."

"What is it I should do?" asked Mother Anna, coming over to the table where Ole sat, unsure that she had heard right.

"I said you ought to get Jo off."

"Well, what is it you want me to do with him?" she jested, nervously. But the jest hardly succeeded; it fell about like music from a cracked fiddle.

"Do with him? Now you ought really to ask more sensibly than that, Mother Anna."

"Am I talking foolishly again?"

"Aye, that you are; you can see it's impossible for me to go anywhere with this plagued foot of mine, and we must get word to those boys. When we're through with the fishing this fall, a trip over will just be a nice little job for Jo; then he can spend Christmas with them, and play the gentleman for a while before he comes home."

"Mercy on us, Ole Hansen! Is it stark mad you've gone?" exclaimed Mother Anna, excited. "Is Jo to start out on that long journey now against the blackness of winter? Has he said so to you?"

"Well, he didn't say he wasn't going, that he didn't," retorted Ole, his cheeks colouring. "Certainly be an easy matter for him, young looking and hale as he is; and in a little better than two weeks he'd be there; then we'd know for sure how they are, and exactly how much they've laid up. You can imagine what a welcome he'll get! And, Mother Anna, you who are so good at writing, I'll have to get you to help me with a few words to Per, so we can remind the boys to pay Jo back what it costs. Though I'm sure they'll think of it themselves, for that matter."

The thought bewildered Mother Anna.

"Have you spoken to Jo about it?"

"Aye, I mentioned it today."

"Did he answer you?" Mother Anna approached the table.

"He certainly didn't say *no* outright. I'm convinced he'll go if you urge him. We've got to have word, you see; and neither one of us two can go."

"We mustn't think of it!" exclaimed Mother Anna, terrified. "Jo, who's so timid? And black winter ahead?"

"But you know, Mother Anna, there isn't a tap to do at this time of the year; and I can just as well as not come and stay with you every other week, if you like."

Mother Anna stood wringing her hands before the impending catastrophe.

"Oh, it's not that!" she moaned. "I sat here sole alone many a winter those first years, before Nils was born—in the days when Jo was fishing at Lofoten."

"But I could very easily come and stay with you," Ole persisted. "And then there's this, Mother Anna," he continued. "In case anything does come of that steamship the boys have been talking about, which I'm certain it will, then Jo would be just the man for them to have along. There's scarcely a person knows as much about wind and weather, and who knows the sea as well, leastways in these parts, as Jo does!"

"Aye," began Mother Anna, sorrowfully.

Steps sounding on the doorstone, the two dropped their talk. Jo entered; he cast a furtive glance at the two within, but maintained his silence.

The Boat of Longing

Mother Anna went into the kitchen, where she busied herself until bedtime; she had not the courage to go in and encounter Jo's face.

V

Afterward, Ole Hansen came to wish that he'd never mentioned the America trip; he could never get a decent word with Mother Anna any more, on that or on any other subject. And he soon perceived that she avoided being alone with him, for if he happened to come in when Jo was not there, she always went out. He didn't know what to make of her antics.

And Jo himself had become so reticent and aloof that he was simply impossible. Ole, deeming him touchy, concluded that the subject had better be dropped, since it needed to be discussed from so many angles. Besides, when he came to think of it, Jo was hardly the person to undertake such a journey; he was too bashful and too slow of speech.

But one day while they were baiting lines down on the pier, Ole came to mention it anyway; later he wished he hadn't. At first Jo had been silent a long time; had just gone on working; then, at last, he had said:

"If you want to go, I'll try to furnish the money. You've got two boys over there."

Jo had spoken so quietly and with such earnestness that it was useless to begin arguing with him; Ole had not been able to marshal more than a meek protest about his foot.— If it weren't for that foot now—aye, if it weren't for the foot; but it was always more troublesome among strangers!

Then Jo had remarked—rather laconically, too—that one didn't walk to America; so for that matter—"And I'll gladly furnish every bit of the money!" he had added once more.

Thereafter Ole stood in deathly fear that the subject might arise again and Jo insist on sending him off. . . .

Hearts That Ache

Gracious! *he* to America? He who always had to hide himself wherever strangers were present? The very thought of it filled him with chills; he couldn't for the life of him understand how Jo could get such absurd ideas!

Thus a mutual dread was causing each of them to withdraw more closely into his own shell.

But on every post day the two would come out of their reserve and meet in mutual waiting. On those mornings Ole perked up and was very talkative, but toward evening he was the most downcast. Finally, the anxiety brought about by the constantly recurring message of no letter bore so heavily upon both that neither could walk upright under it.

To Ole it grew intolerable. He quit the fishing earlier than last summer under the pretext that he must go home and help the wife dig potatoes; then he left.

A very peculiar relationship moved into the cottage at Vaag after Ole's departure. Mother Anna went there pinning her hopes upon equally warm but diverse wishes till she scarcely knew her own mind.

"I should hope," she said to herself, "that Jo knows enough to ignore this nonsense of Ole's. Jo's too old to undertake such a trip; he doesn't sleep well at night. Besides, he doesn't think very fast. He could easily fall overboard, or get bewildered and lost among so many strangers. No, it's plain useless to think of it, even!"

But at times another voice made itself heard, which spoke quite differently:

"There are, I suppose, people of Jo's age who do go to America? People who are much less fit? There was that crippled Ellen Berg, for example, whom they carried in a coffin after she'd lain abed for four years. . . . But Jo really is chipper. And he's been out among people before without being troubled. . . . Maybe his step isn't as springy as it was twenty years ago, but he's still well and strong, that can't be denied.

The Boat of Longing

. . . "And since we don't know what's become of the bairn, there can't be anyone nearer to finding out than the father. . . . I almost believe I shall have to speak to Jo." . . .

With the return of her senses, however, Mother Anna might become very angry with herself for entertaining such ugly thoughts. She kept them, therefore, to herself, never uttering them to her husband.

With Jo it was otherwise. He felt certain that Ole had talked to Mother Anna about the journey; it wasn't like Ole to contain himself. What now puzzled Jo was Mother Anna's strange silence. At length he hit upon the reason:

. . . "I suppose she wants me to go, but is reluctant to say it. Isn't that likely? If she thought it foolish and utterly senseless, she'd have been certain to mention it, wouldn't she?

. . . "So she does want me to go? But she's afraid? Fears I'm not man enough for it, I reckon," he reflected, bitterly.

. . . "But she has no call to think that; she shouldn't be going about with such thoughts in her mind. What she doesn't, of course, see is that if I leave she might be left without a provider. Nils is no longer here; and if I should drop away, she'll be without anyone. We don't have more than a good two thousand, all told; and that journey will take at least seven hundred. Even if she sold all we own of boats and gear, it wouldn't be much she'd get in that wise. Should her days then be many, what's left for the end will be scant enough. I shouldn't like to see any of mine faring the countryside, a public charge.

. . . "But such considerations don't occur to her. It's only this that I've become so timid and miserable of late that I'm altogether unfit." . . .

And still her silence balked him, despite his sun-clear reasonings. That she could refrain even from hinting!— And his uneasiness went mounting.

Hearts That Ache

. . . "We're bound to take some measure to find the boy, she should see that; he's her child no less than mine!" . . .

Jo speculated so hard as to Mother Anna's probable thinking that it at last became an unsolvable riddle, and came to occupy his mind more than the journey itself. At meal-time, or of evenings when each sat over his work, with thoughts so intent as almost to become audible, Jo would strain against the silence in expectation of its momently breaking: "It will be coming now. Surely she'll be speaking." But she never neared the subject.

One morning while he was dressing he felt sure that that day was the promised one; before nightfall she would have spoken. She had been so restless during the night, had lain crying so long—as had happened often of late—and evidently had slept but little. . . . "Poor Mother," compassionated Jo, as he stood there getting into his clothes, "it's hard for her now—pitifully hard. Her child is lost and her husband is too cowardly to go in search of it."— But the day passed; evening came; they put out the light and went to bed without her having uttered a word.

Thus passed day after day.

Autumn brought drizzle and storm; tempests harried, with rain and fog; sea and sky and growthless crag dislimned in murk and darkness.

In the daytime Jo busied himself on the pier and in the boat-shed; he found so much that needed attention and repair. And Mother Anna, whenever she came to call him to meals, would always enquire:

"What are you doing today?"

To which Jo would answer:

"Oh—I'm only puttering."

"You are puttering with something, I suppose?"

"No, nothing in particular."

Mother Anna thought this unfair of her husband. He could just as well take her into his confidence; it wasn't

The Boat of Longing

altogether pleasant for her, either, up there in the cottage alone.

So each went watching the other.

One day while they sat eating at noon she let slip a significant remark. It came unexpectedly, and set Jo thinking.

"If only some one were going across, so we could send word."

"You may well say," said Jo, on the verge of happiness. . . . It would probably be coming now ! . . .

"Then we could send a letter and be sure he'd get it."

"Aye—if only some one were going. You haven't heard of anyone, I suppose?"

"No, I haven't. Have you?"

Then Jo became very happy, and relieved in his mind. Apparently she was wanting him to attempt it. "No-o-o," he replied, "I can't exactly say that I have."

Catching her quick glance, he cast his own down, rose hastily from the table, descended the hill, and went into the boat-shed.

In there he had a sea chest. It was so small that it had its handle on top of the cover instead of at the sides, and was carried by the cover. Ever since Jo had bought it, it had been called the travelling-chest, for the reason that it was always taken into use on longer journeys. It was painted green, and had black iron bands around it, as have all such chests, whether large or small.

That day Jo went straight to the corner where the chest stood, drew it out on the floor, and began to examine it. A musty smell assailed him when he opened the cover; fetching a bucket of sea water, he washed it thoroughly inside, then he brought it out into the air to dry.

It may well be that Mother Anna set big eyes when she saw him lug the chest into the house that evening and place it in the middle of the floor; it bereft her of speech for a moment, the words sticking in her throat. She turned sharply away, went into the kitchen, and sank upon the hearthstone in a paroxysm of crying. "O God have mercy! . . . God in heaven have mercy! . . . Now Jo is going, too!"

— But she couldn't remain in the kitchen; the travelling-chest was standing on the middle of the floor in the other room; she'd have to hurry in again; she'd have to find words. Or what would Jo think?

So Mother Anna returned, and made as though she just that instant caught sight of the chest. Putting as much levity into her voice as she could possibly muster, she queried:

"Do you intend to travel?"

"Aye," Jo answered from the window, his back toward her. "I suppose I'll have to be starting now."

Mother Anna wished to ask when he meant to leave, but did not. Instead she asked:

"Wouldn't it be better to put it off till spring?"

"I've thought of that, too; but then we'd have to wait till he could get back from the woods, and by that time summer would be here. We could hardly justify waiting so long."

"That's true, 'twould be summer, all right."

"Besides, I'd lose a whole season's fishing, which I could hardly afford after having spent so much money."

"Aye, aye, I can see that. If—if only you're strong enough for such a long trip!"

"Well, no one can tell till he tries it; though for that matter, I should think I could do what others can do—just about, at least."

Mother Anna looked at him with great pride, her eyes beaming through the tears in them.

"That I know you can. Aye, God be praised, I know you can."

Jo swung halfway in order to cast her a furtive glance. A slight flush tinged his weathered cheeks; but he was

The Boat of Longing

standing by the window, so it may have come from the glow which hung in the evening sky.

"When have you planned to leave?"

"The boat goes south on Tuesday; it would seem I ought to get started as soon as possible. You'll be having a couple of clean shifts for me, I reckon?"

"This coming Tuesday!" exclaimed Mother Anna. "Dear me, are you going Tuesday?"

"Aye, you see, in case he intends to work in the woods again this winter, I'd better try to reach him before he leaves."

"That's true," sighed Mother Anna. "Aye, if he is going to the woods, then you must start at once."

"It's likely, though," continued Jo, thoughtfully, "that I'll be going to the woods, too. I've most made up my mind that he decided to stay there last spring; it's on that account we're not getting a letter, I suppose. If he were in Minneapolis, and in good health, he'd have written, I'm sure."

"I reckon you're right about that."

"You see, he's a dependable boy, and they may have wanted him to work the whole year. And there's likely no mail up there," Jo explained quietly and dispassionately.

Mother Anna listened to him in great wonderment. It happened now as it had so often during their married life: having discovered how he had gone about, weighing every possibility in a matter, she stood there ashamed before his thoughtfulness and clear-mindedness. The comforting thought then came to her that a man with such insight and good sense could get along in any difficulty.

And so those two lonely, kindly souls were drawn together once more in the great common decision; except that now it was Jo who grew talkative, and she gravely reverent and quiet when he spoke.

And Mother Anna fell to packing the little chest for her

husband with even greater care than she had formerly packed the bigger one for her son.

Late on Saturday evening of the same week an aged couple came walking up the lane at Dunjarness and requested to speak with the minister. They were a long time in his office; but when they came out and disappeared down the lane in the dark, they walked more lightly. They had then partaken of the Sacrament together; and the holy rite, solemnized for these two alone, had laid a sanctification and an ineffable peace upon everything. . . . No question now but that all would be blest for them. He who ruled wind and wave and high heaven was, to be sure, mighty; but it was also true that no one who would approach Him in earnestness and upright faith need come away unblest.

The night was far gone when they at last reached home. But that night Mother Anna did not cry.

VI

Now it happened thus with Ole Hansen after he moved home that he came to go limping about and speculating in all manner of ways as to why the boys never wrote. But the question baffled solution.

Compelled, therefore, to hit upon some sort of life-saving idea, if he were not to go way under in worry and despair, he took to reviving the one about the steamship. Which worked fairly well; he even got it to the stage of reality where he himself lived on board the ship a few days. One day the idea became so vigorous and looked so altogether reasonable that he felt impelled to make a trip to Vaag with it. But upon second thought he gave that up, being convinced that neither Jo nor Anna would have faith in it, anyway; at least, not in their present frame of mind; besides, Jo might start that insane notion of his again. Peculiar with these persons who talked as little as Jo did; never any telling what they might think up and suggest when they opened their mouths.

Ole Hansen had never heard so preposterous an idea; it surely must be the worst that had ever been born. Merciful Heavens! he to America? And it had actually seemed that Jo was in earnest. No, he didn't think Jo had been jesting that time.

Worst of it was he couldn't get free of the thought. He tried in every conceivable way to escape it; and then, happening to look about when he felt secure, he would see it again. Aye, there it was, and it meant to stay! And once more, before he was aware, he might have become completely lost in it.

Every now and then as he went limping about he would find himself on board an Atlantic steamer, America-bound. And really, you know, it wasn't bad. Thus far, all had gone well. He had paid for himself like the rest, and was receiving exactly the same treatment. No one knew him, though for that matter there were none but kind persons on board; no one laughed at him, which seemed the strangest of all. And if it did chance that some passenger enquired concerning his foot, he would commence to explain, very circumstantially, that this foot, aye—this foot, well, he had broken it once in a fall. That was now a long time ago. And there'd not been a doctor near by, so one of the neighbours had put it in splints, and most likely he'd not known just how to do it; not but that the break had healed all right; but the foot wasn't quite straight; besides, it had become just a trifle shorter, though not enough to embarrass him any. They mustn't think it was a great misfortune to have it like this. No, that it wasn't. On the contrary, it was good, actually indispensable at times: for it warned as unmistakably as a foghorn every time a change in the weather approached. It probably sounded queer, but he could rely on that foot as on a barometer—aye, that he could!

Hearts That Ache

This and much more Ole went telling folks on board the America boat, and there wasn't a one that laughed at him. Now, wasn't that strange?

Or, Ole might be sitting on board a fast train, whizzing across the broad American continent. He always sat by a window. And he rejoiced at the sight of the big cities, the many people, and all the wealth. The foot, being on the side nearest the wall, wasn't the least bit in the way. Marvellous how jolly it was beside this window; there was so much that was novel to see. . . . And Ole knew exactly where he must get off the train: it was in Minneapolis, Minnesota, North America. . . . Danger in such a trip? Laws, no! Not the least!

But upon being aroused from these incursions and coming to his senses again, it might happen that he would be drenched with perspiration and shaking like a leaf.

Still he could not escape the thought.

Otherwise he kept up a ceaseless search after an explanation for the boys' failure to write, one that might give comfort and encouragement to them all.

One day it occurred to him that a couple of boys from over yonder at Öivaagen had gone to America a few years back. Öivaagen was a large farm, and lay in a rather populous neighbourhood. So on the Sunday before Jo left, Ole rose long before daylight and set out on the fourteen-mile jaunt to the place; it might very well be that the folk over there had got word, aye, the Öivaag boys might have met his boys and written about it. He was almost certain that they had been acquainted over here.

But he learned little for his pains. One of the boys had drowned off the Pacific Coast while fishing; the other had taken to studying for the ministry. Not much that was known concerning him, either; for it was now more than a year since they'd heard from him.

The latter tidings made Ole's heart leap with joy. Wasn't

it just what he had always said that in America folks didn't have time to write? If, now, he who was preparing to become a minister didn't find time, what in the world could they expect of boys working in the wild woods and elsewhere? . . . So that boy was to become a minister! Well, well! And his father only an ordinary cotter, like himself. Aye—wasn't it just like a fairy tale over there? . . . Goodness! how jolly it would be to find out what those boys were up to.

Evening had come on, for Ole had had much to talk about with the parents of the boy who was to become a minister. Several times he had risen to go, only to return and sit down again.

Finally, he had torn away. It was a beautiful starlit night, with enough of frost for the bogs to bear him. Well, sir, walking wasn't bad at all.

As he trudged along under the stars, a great kindliness took him. He longed to see his boys again. Especially Per. Gracious! that Per! What a hold he had on him! And what a joy he had been when little. . . . Ole limped along over the hills and frost-baked bogs in the starry evening, remembering this incident and that in Per's childhood, what he had said and what he had done, how they had laughed and told others. Many times he had averred to the wife that that child was far above common; she, too, could see that, he had hoped. For the likes of him for wondering and asking strange questions couldn't, he supposed, be found. This evening he remembered it all.

—Aye, Per was the child of his heart. Different with Otto. Though tonight Ole remembered that he, too, had been a great joy; 'twould be a sin to say otherwise. But after confirmation Otto had gone his own ways—aye, that he certainly had.

Tears came and trickled quietly down his cheeks. He let

them come; he thought it easier to walk when he didn't prevent them.

It was while he strode along across Grand Bogs that night that he reached the momentous decision; thinking came so easy this evening, especially if he let the tears fall unhindered.

. . . "Today I've walked twenty-eight miles," he mused. "For two summers now I've carried on fishing like any able-bodied fellow and got a full man's share. I'm far from being as decrepit as I've let out that I am. This foot is the cross put upon me by the Lord to humble me. But what becomes of the humbling, when I go about, hiding the foot, I should like to know. Can anything but hardening come of such? . . . You'll need to have a care, so you will, Ole Martinius Hansen, lest you go dodging too long with that foot and neither it nor you get into Paradise!

. . . "And Jo said: 'You have two sons over there; I'll furnish the money; one doesn't walk to America.' That's just what he said; and whatever Jo says, he means.

. . . "And then what do you do, Ole Hansen? Set up that miserable foot as an excuse, that's what. And here it's no worse but that it's carried you twenty-eight miles and isn't a bit more tired than the other.

. . . " 'He that maketh flesh his arm,' says the Scripture. But there's never a word about the Lord's excusing anyone because one foot is a couple of inches shorter than the other. Merciful Heavens! here I go evading my duty and not looking after my own flesh and blood for so trifling an excuse. Well, if the likes of me are let in, there'll be plenty of sinners in Heaven." . . .

Ole limped and limped. The thoughts came so easily:

. . . "And America is so free and large and all. Over there no one will know me. And they'll scarcely laugh at an old man like me, even if I do limp a little. All that matters over there is, I presume, what one has in his head.

And my head's all right—really, as I might say, uncommonly fit." . . .

Ole now glided into a brighter train of thoughts; and then like a flash came an idea which caused him to see more stars than there actually were that evening:

. . . "People accomplish such wonders in America, and it is said they have unusually skilled doctors! What if I got over," he reflected, getting so excited that he stood stockstill, "and found a doctor who could cure my foot? The boys will, of course, know of the best ones, and will help with the money, I'm sure. And then I could come home and walk as steady as the best of them." . . . Ole had to sit down on a knoll and rest awhile, for he was trembling violently all through his body.

. . . "Aye, that isn't at all impossible," he mused further. "Originally, that foot was as long as the other, and I've not grown since the accident. It's only this that it didn't grow together properly; that's how it got to be a trifle crooked. One of their ablest doctors could correct that, I'm sure. 'Twouldn't take much, either—really only a matter of three inches or so." . . . Ole thrust his foot straight out to study it.

Then he rose and resumed his journey. The thought was so bright and possessed him so completely that he was home before he knew it.

But he withheld the idea from his wife when he entered, thinking it might be advisable to speak to Jo and Mother Anna and get their opinion first.

The next morning saw him up early again and hobbling off to Vaag. The pure radiance of childhood beamed in his furrowed cheeks as he stepped into the cottage.

Jo and Mother Anna, long since up and their breakfast over, were seated, work in hand; the industrious fingers could not be idle, even though it was the last day before the departure. A fire burned in the grate, and the room had newly been tidied. It looked very cozy within. Close to the door stood the chest, packed and ready.

Ole shook hands with both Jo and Anna; his voice was unnaturally loud.

"Well, Jo," he said, "I'm ready ——"

The two looked at him.

"Packing myself off now," he continued, uninterrupted. "You've got the money, I presume?" He turned to Jo.

"What is it that ails you, Ole?" asked Mother Anna, deeming there was somewhat amiss with him in one way or another.

Ole rubbed his hands and laughed, tickled.

"I sort o' thought it would take your breath. But I'm off to see the boys. If a fine steamship happens to come sailing along next spring, you'll know who it is."

"Are—are you going to America?" stammered Mother Anna, gasping for breath. Jo only stared; he had let his work drop; his hands lay prone on the table. Never in his life had he felt such admiration for any person as he now felt for Ole Hansen.

"Now I've never heard the likes! Are you going to America?" cried Mother Anna once more, sinking back in her chair.

Jo continued silent.

"Aye, now I'm starting out," Ole answered, laughing. "Somebody has to go and see how the boys are getting on. And I have two, you know, and little to look after at home of a winter."

Jo by the Sea gave his throat a thorough rake round. His face glowed. "You mustn't forget to put the coffee-pot over the fire for Ole, Mother," he said.

Ole looked plainly disappointed; this wasn't at all what he had expected to hear from Jo. So he asked straight out:

"What do you think of it, Jo?"

The Boat of Longing

Jo continued to gaze at him—with the same admiration. "But how about your foot?" he asked.

"Oh," responded Ole, with a certain superiority, "it won't do, you know, for one to 'make flesh his arm.' And lately the foot's been extra fine, so to speak. Yesterday I walked twenty-eight miles on it, and it stood it just about as well as the other."

Thereupon Ole related the whole story of his visit to Öivaagen, keeping his eyes fixed on Jo during the course of it. But he grew more and more dissatisfied with Jo. Now this happening was about as remarkable a one as there had been in these parts of recent years. Certainly Jo ought to have some comment to make. He wasn't going to go back on his promise, was he? If so, well then **Jo** wasn't the man he had thought him, that's all.

"What do you think of it, Jo?" he asked again.

Jo rose to his feet, and coming straight to Ole, he said: "I think you are the most courageous man I have ever known."

Thereupon he walked right out of the house.

Ole stood following him with his eyes, his face about halfway between laughter and tears.

"Can you tell me what is the matter with Jo?" He addressed himself, excitedly, to Mother Anna.

"What is the matter with him?"

"Aye?"

"Oh, I suppose he's thinking about tomorrow."

"Tomorrow? What's happening then?"

"Jo is going."

"Going? Where?"

"To America, I wot!" said Mother Anna, proudly.

"Jo?"

"Aye."

"Is Jo going to America? Are you daft, Mother Anna?" cried Ole.

Hearts That Ache

"Certainly he's going; he's starting tomorrow. Can't you see that the chest stands ready?" Mother Anna's voice sounded a bit irritated.

Ole commenced staving about the room.

"Oh, Mother Anna, Mother Anna!" he moaned. "He mustn't—he mustn't go. Don't say you're letting him—he can't—I'm having to go myself with this foot."

"Are you going to America with the foot?"

"Of course I am! What in Heaven's name became of Jo?" He took out through the door after him.

Jo had gone down to the pier and was inside the boat-shed, moving aimlessly about, unable to recover from his amazement; there was, for that matter, no task for him to put his hands to, all having been set to rights before.

Ole intruded.

"Can you tell me what it is you are thinking of?" he called from the doorway. "Are you going to America?"

"Aye, I suppose I'd better be doing it now." Jo returned him a sober look.

The joy of victory over himself which had so possessed Ole now dispersed like smoke before a stiff breeze. He sank down on a tub, completely undone; somewhere within, a light had been snuffed.

"You see we can't both go," expostulated Jo. "I'm perhaps the more able of us two; and some one'll have to stay here to look after the place. If you could come out off and on, 'twould be fine."

But Ole sat there wordless and would not be comforted. It was so wholly incomprehensible that Jo was going to America. And tomorrow! It was positively the worst he had ever heard.

"Is it long since you decided?" he asked, glumly.

"Aye, now it's a long time. I'd been thinking about it for a good while when you spoke."

The Boat of Longing

"Do you—do you think you'll be able to find your way to Minneapolis?"

"We'll have to see; no one can say till he's tried it," said Jo, quietly.

"That's true," answered Ole, as dejected as before. "No one can tell that beforehand, that's reasonable."

Jo by the Sea felt compassion for Ole Hansen. He began talking to him, slowly, making many pauses, as was his wont. At first he met no response; but gradually he coaxed him along. It got to be a long while that they sat thus; and when Mother Anna came to call them because the coffee was getting cold, Ole had advanced so far that he could see it was wiser that Jo make the trip and he remain at home.

VII

The sea. The boundless sea. Unfailing source of all unrest. Unquiet in quiescence, rolling on in unquiet. . . . With what it once takes wholly within its strong grasp it presses ever onward, always and ever onward, round the wide girdle of the earth. Who has ever heard that the sea held still, that stillness reigned in its cavernous depths? No, the sea never rests; it never gives back, not even the mind once lost in its reaches. It bears ever onward, and yet farther onward, rocking in unrest into itself. Out of itself, into itself—touching the heavens, sweeping the abysses, restlessly, endlessly into itself.

The sea . . . aye, the unresting sea. It is a being wondrously strange. It tells no tales, gives up no secrets; it wanders its way, mute and contained. Sees all and understands; hears all and comprehends; takes all and holds its peace. Do not the winds confide to the sea? Do not the billows look down from the stars? And does not the sea feel of the depths? What deem you the billows are thinking as they steer on the evening star? Careless the sea, and icily

Hearts That Ache

silent. . . . Impassive it rolls, never rejoicing, never complaining, never feeling an instant's pity—even the chill of its cold waves' washings against all that approaches to meet them. . . . Never yet has the sea been made to break silence.

Upon its crests . . . wide over its peaks . . . in the midst of the eternally restless, Loneliness dwells. Where else should it dwell? All the chill unrest which it needs to thrive and be happy is there. Fit home of Loneliness these tops of the unquiet waves. The gull sails wide-winged and silent far through its reaches. At the verge of the spaceless he dares not go farther; turns and hastens in terror till once more he sees the dashings of breakers on a kelp-clad coast. There on the outermost point he may sit scanning the unquiet tops, till, drawn by Loneliness, he once more lifts wing. At night, when darkness broods over the sea, he will hear its heart-throbbing. . . . No creature under heaven knows the sea so well as the gull—mute bird of the Loneliness.

The sea . . . the great wide sea . . . it is so cold, so cold! How indeed could that be other than cold which eternally rocks Death in its lap? Death has its abode on the sea. There stand its chambers of the morning, both the red and the golden, and there spreads its sable pavilion of night. Ought it not, then, be chill on the sea? And desolate? From heaven's beginning to its ending it stretches, away from itself, in toward itself; spreads itself wide between the sun's rising and setting. Yet no life dwells upon it. Never has it been heard that anyone sought to dwell on the sea. All that moves over it hastens. Nothing will linger.

For there is no terror like that instilled by the sea, with its abysses above and abysses below. Who has seen its angry crests when the sun shimmers sallow at nightfall—who has seen darkness descend on the wings of the storm—and not felt the anguish of terror? What soul would not cower when the chasms above and the chasms below step forth to hold tryst?

The Boat of Longing

And its might? . . . Aye, its might! When the great sea begins washing the cloudbanks down from the welkin, when it lashes itself into fury, and heaven-high mountains of blackness roll against the fortress of storms, then all life quails before it. Or when it lays bare the abysses that the winds may dry them!

The sea . . . the boundless sea . . . nor is aught like its longing. No, naught is like its longing. Beginningless. Endless. Restless as its heart; wakeful as its spirit. Whither, pray, should it go? It touches the heavens; it descends to the bottoms—where then should it go? Have you seen a billow rise, stretch, and rock chillily onward? And followed its cold wandering from skyline to skyline? . . . The billows, they are the sea's longing. . . .

VIII

Evening was fast settling upon the autumn day. The *Hellig Olav* glided into quarantine in New York Harbour, where it was to anchor for the night.

It had had a successful voyage; the weather had been seasonable, and every one, crew and passengers, had been in as excellent health as human beings could hope to be.

Now that the destination had been reached, a satisfied, happy mood lay upon the minds. Yet there was uneasiness in it, too, excitement concerning what they might experience tomorrow. . . . Tomorrow! Aye, tomorrow was the great day!

Jo Persen Vaag leaned upon the railing in the bow. It being a vantage-point, he had kept that place throughout the voyage; the view from there was so free of the ocean and sky, and of the floating clouds. He was now gazing at the water, especially at the waves which the ship cleaved and flung recklessly off. He had not spoken many words during the crossing; there hadn't, as a matter of fact, been time, because there had been too much to look at and wonder about.

This evening he didn't budge from the rail, not even when the supper gong sounded and the steerage flocked *en masse* to the deck below. He couldn't afford to miss the scene which now opened before him. He had wanted to fetch his chest, but when he had heard passengers say that there would be no landing tonight, he had decided that he might better let it stand where it was.

But then darkness fell at a stroke. It had delayed in appearing, but having begun to come, it closed over the earth with a suddenness almost startling. Jo thought this extraordinary.

With the dark came a myriad of blinking lights; high overhead, they went together, becoming a dim luminousness which lined the night and blotted out the star-sheen.

Countless towers reared themselves in the luminousness ahead; some of them were dreadfully high, and appeared to touch the heavens; and there were some that, going beyond the luminousness, went up among the stars, where they lost their tops in deep darkness.

On the water a multitude of boats, big and small, all with red and green lanterns, darted hither and thither in every direction. As Jo now stood there alive to all the life teeming about him, he had to wonder if it could all have come about through the handiwork of man. He hardly believed that it could. A sense of insignificance began to impress itself on him—he felt so infinitesimally small; he might possibly have become altogether despondent had it not been for one thought which came and gave comfort.

This, then, was the country where Nils was. Aye, Nils was here! Jo had heard people on board say that it took only two days from New York to Minneapolis. Today was Monday; perhaps, then, he would be with him by Thursday night. Aye, in two days he might be seeing that dear blessed

The Boat of Longing

boy of his—if—if—he were alive yet. And Jo did not doubt that he was.

The lights and the teeming world around him were forgotten; he saw only Nils—wondered if he had changed much, if he was bigger, stronger, if he would know him when he saw him. Which Jo thought he would.

— When he went back now—and he couldn't stay long, with all that gear needing repair and what not, and Mother Anna, poor woman, sitting there sole alone—Nils would have to come with him. Every time he had begun to think about that homeward journey of late, Nils had always been with him.

— And they would arrive for Christmas. For Christmas, aye. They'd be getting there late in the evening, Nils and he. But Mother Anna would probably be up yet, spinning. Before they walked in they'd stamp the snow off their feet on the doorstone.— There she was, sure enough!— Jo knew exactly how the light from the lamp fell on her face.— And there they stood, Nils and he. And then Mother Anna would look up at them!

— Jo himself had to dry his eyes; he didn't wonder at all that she had to cry. But hereafter she'd not need to. And now she might sleep securely at night.

— But the first day the weather permitted, Nils and he would have to go out and provide halibut for Sunday. He knew where they would set the lines. How cozy it would be with the three of them together once more!

— Nils would, of course, remain at home this winter, that went without saying; then they'd put the gear in fine shape. They'd have to exert themselves not a little now in order to make up for all the outlay they'd had.

— 'Twouldn't be long before spring would be arriving, and then would follow the best part of all—he and Nils would be lying out on the sea together through the livelong

Hearts That Ache

luminous night. And when they returned Mother Anna would be sitting there, waiting for them, happy as could be. At meal-time, Nils would be telling about all the wonders he had seen. 'Twould hardly be quiet at meal-time hereafter.

These scenes had often bobbed up when Jo had stood in the bow gazing out over the sea; and always he had taken great care not to hinder them.

Such a hubbub set in up on the fore deck after the evening meal that it was almost impossible for Jo to stay there. The dancing on previous evenings had never been so noisy and unrestrained as it was tonight; land had been reached; the great Atlantic lay far behind in the darkness somewhere. . . . But what could Jo do about it? He might as well like it. Even the older folks seized one by the hand and hopped away into the whirl.

It got to be a restless night in the steerage. The watch relaxed its vigilance; there might be a few extra tips tomorrow. There was laughter and talk in the cabins and in the passageways. Many seemed not to care about sleeping at all. Some had danced together the whole way across and had become surprisingly well acquainted; these must use whatever time remained to advantage. Laughter and whisperings came from every corner. Not even the ship's rats got much peace that night.

Jo tossed in his berth. Being along in years, he needed to have it more quiet if he were to get any sleep. He must have turned a hundred times. So he was thankful when the time finally came that he could get up.

He was the first passenger on deck. He had brought his chest up with him; but that the steward compelled him to take below again as soon as he got his eye on it.

Breakfast he did not feel he could take time to eat; day was coming apace, revealing more and more of what it was novel to see. And as the great metropolis now loomed before him in the mounting daylight his courage again faltered. . . . "I'll never," it shrank within him, "never be able to find my way through this welter, unless God Himself comes and takes me by the hand."

It turned out to be an untoward day for Jo, and for many others as well; when night dropped its curtain upon it, there were many who questioned if they had done wisely in coming at all.

First there was the medical inspection; though that, to be sure, had its humour, too. There stood the whole steerage in a tight row, like seeds in a pod, young and old, sticking their tongues out, while a brisk, uniformed individual peered into their mouths and down into their throats. Not even the dazzling uniform nor the stern mien could stop the line which strained up the companionway from the deck below from laughter; young people who looked brightly on life laughed till they doubled.

Later they were herded into the custom-house. Here Jo felt still greater fear; and now the sea was gone, too, the sea which he knew so well and which he knew understood him. In there people ran around crazily. New droves kept arriving; the hubbub of strange tongues was enough to make one dizzy.

Jo stood guard beside his open chest. Just what advantage it could be to anyone to look at his shifts was a dark matter to him. But they were clean, that he knew. Finally he grew tired from standing and sat down on the chest.

By and by an officer came and stuck his nose into the chest—that was all. Then he shut it and put his mark on the side.

That eased Jo's mind. It must soon be time for the Minneapolis train to leave; perhaps he ought to pick up his chest and start. This was taking a long time and it was too bad to delay. In case the train was leaving soon, and he didn't get on board, well, then it would be Friday before he reached Nils.

As he sat there thus forlorn on his chest, pondering what he ought to do, an officer came along and bundled him off on a ferry. This encouraged him . . . "As long as they're looking after me, there can't be any need of me worrying," he said to himself. When they once more set out across the water, he felt certain they were now on their way to the train.

But then they weren't going to the train, after all. The ferry was taking its cargo of grist to the mill—that is to say, to Ellis Island, because the human stuff had to be sifted before it could go into the dough.

There Jo's many trials began. The chest grew very burdensome to carry, on account of the great press of people in the big house; moreover the heat was suffocating . . . the fires must have been well stoked.

Here they were let one by one into narrow stalls, to be examined and crossexamined, and again inspected by physicians, who looked into their hands, eyes, and mouths.

Jo felt tired and faint. Anxiety mounted in him; time was lengthening and he wasn't getting in; moreover, the jam was increasing and the din of panicky minds becoming intolerable.

At long last he stood before the bar of the examining officer. The questions began raining mechanically.

"Your name?"

"Jo Persen Vaag." Jo took his time in order to be sure to get it right.

"Occupation?"

"Fisherman."

"Where are you going?"

"To Minneapolis."

The Boat of Longing

"Got any relatives there?"

"Aye."

"Who?"

"A son."

"How much money have you got?"

Jo hesitated a moment before entrusting the information; then he answered:

"Three hundred and fifty crowns."

"How old are you?"

"Sixty-two; a little past."

"Sixty-two!"

"Aye," said Jo. "I was sixty-two last Michaelmas."

"Have you an affidavit from your son that he will support you?"

Despite the question's being so soberly asked, Jo had to smile a little. Were they now wanting an affidavit for that, too?

"Nils and I intend to go back soon."

"Show me your affidavit."

"Affidavit?" Jo looked at him bewildered.

"Hurry up!"

"I haven't any," stammered Jo. "Nils doesn't know I'm coming. It's a long time since we heard from him. But we'll be going back soon as I can get to him."

The heat of the place was intolerable. Jo felt faint and worn; he exerted himself to speak distinctly.

"One more!" sang the cold voice. "Take him out!"

A young man in uniform came and took Jo by the arm. He wanted to hurry him; but the chest caught everywhere; Jo couldn't look out for it as he should, now that events had got going so badly.

Their way led through passageway after passageway, out across an open space, down another passage and in through another door, where a key was turned upon him. But he had gotten the chest along with him.

Hearts That Ache

IX

In that room Jo remained until the liner on which he had
come was ready to return; the day of its sailing he was
brought on board.

But it was not the same Jo; no, not altogether. This was
an old man, stooped and broken, whose eyes seemed to have
become set while in the act of hunting for something. It was
this strange admixture of the stifled and the tense in the
face which got people to turn and look at it. The man had
aged several years in the few days since he stepped off the
boat.

He now came up the gangplank with his chest in his
hand, stepped onto the deck, and stood there. He drew the
air, sniffing it like an animal scenting; then the dead look
in the eye was forced aside by what resembled an interest
in objects about him. Others followed him up the gangplank, happy persons who pressed eagerly forward. He
crossed the deck to his old place in the bow. There he set
down his chest, leaned over the rail, and looked at the sea.
Green slime, driftwood, and other rubbish floated about in
the water. The heavenly smell of sea came up from below—
of rotten sea—about as by the pier at home. . . . Jo's face
got more life.

But when toward evening the ship pushed free of its
moorings and began gliding out of the harbour, and the
waves purled cheerily along the ship's sides, he could no
longer stand still; he had to move. He drew himself up to
his full height; and the look which now ran out across the
sea was searching, like that of an old sea dog gauging the
sky and the atmosphere.

It was by mere accident that he got any supper that evening, for when the gong sounded and people began flocking
toward the dining-saloon, he did not stir; he was not aware

of what went on about him. Just then a young man came bolting down from the forecastle; he had discovered the place from which he could really command the highest and most pleasurable view of the ocean; the wind blew so stiff in the stairs that he had to hold on to his hat. Catching sight of the solitary old man at the rail, he hastened over and, slapping him on the shoulder, reminded him in an imperfect Norwegian:

"They're eating downstairs; we'll have to hurry if we want our share of the supper. Isn't that a magnificent scene?"

Then he waited till Jo had pulled himself together sufficiently to go with him. The tables seemed already to be full when they entered.

"You stay here," said the young man, "and I'll find you a place. We're entitled to our meals as well as the rest, and we'll have them even if we have to make a row."

Before long he returned, having found places for Jo and himself.

That night it was late before Jo went to bed—it wasn't, as a matter of fact, until after the watch had spied him leaning against the deck rail, gazing at the sea. A breeze blew fresh across the starboard quarter; the waves rose and fell along the ship's side; the sea-fire lay soft and ember-like in the long white crests which the ship rolled back. Jo's face now wore a wholly natural look, save that it was tired and preoccupied. . . . When the watch discovered him, he got him a berth.

At night in the cabin all the anguish of the days just past returned to him; the ship's joyous progress and the murmur of the waves made his mind so clear that he lay there recalling all that had happened up to the other day, when the Norwegian immigrant missionary had come to inform him that his telegram to Nils brought no answer. Efforts to locate him through the Minneapolis authorities had likewise proved futile. For that reason the immigration officers would have to send him back with the ship, the law forbidding them to admit old people into the country who didn't have money, unless there was some one to guarantee their support. They had, unfortunately, no choice in the matter.

That night a fog had settled over Jo's mind, and for an interval of several days his mind had been blank; during that time he had only pottered aimlessly about, talking to himself. It was not until this afternoon, when he had stood at the rail and smelled the sea, that he had been able to recollect what had happened.

Now he relived it all, clear from the time that the door of the great room had been closed upon him:

Two Danish women had been there when he entered. He had thought they must both be insane, for he would never have believed that so much obscenity could have existed in human beings as he saw and heard in those two. He shuddered as he lay there in his berth, remembering it all. But then they had been taken out of the room.— They too had been excluded. Though he didn't wonder in the least that they had.

And then there had been three Russians—three old men. They, poor fellows, were probably sitting there yet. He knew they were Russians, for he had been with people of that kind in Finmarken. He understood why they had been locked up with him; they, also, had been too old. There was one in particular whom he could not get off his mind—a very aged, long-bearded man who moaned so dreadfully of nights. It was terrible the night he had tried to hang himself from the bars in the window. But luckily the attempt had miscarried and they had taken turns in watching him after that.

And they had brought in an Italian woman who had a little girl. What sorrow!

Jo could not sleep, only tossed in his berth. The picture

The Boat of Longing

of the dark-tressed child struggling with death stood vividly before him. She had lain there repeating the word *fiori*[1] so long that he remembered it. It had put him in mind of a wave rising and falling, falling and rising, the way she said it. *Fiori, fiori!* He thought of the night she died, remembering both her and the mother. Pitiful how hard it had been for that mother! He could endure being reminded of it now that he felt the sea rocking beneath him. He had never thought that a human being could reach the degree of grief where it would tear the hair from its own head; but that's what that mother had done. Jo was very wide awake.

He, too, had had a strange experience that night—it came back to him now. Only he could not understand how it had happened. When the child was breathing its last and he saw how the mother was acting, he had gone over and seated himself on the edge of her bed. And he had touched her with his hand; he remembered distinctly that he had placed his hand on her. Though that wasn't the strangest; he had folded his hands and begun singing to her. The melody now came back to him, and the words he had sung:

> "O Jesus, draw near my dying bed
> And take me into Thy keeping.
> And say when my spirit hence is fled,
> 'This child is not dead, but sleeping.'
> And leave me not, Saviour, till I rise
> To praise Thee in life eternal."

While he sang, the Russians had stood kneeling, making the sign of the Cross upon themselves.

Twice he had sung the stanza, though it wasn't his habit to sing at all, except in church when he could join with others. In the morning some one had come and taken the dead child away. But the mother hadn't been permitted to go along; she had then keeled over in utter senselessness. And Jo had

[1] Flowers.

taken upon himself to care for her; nor had he been at all embarrassed before the three Russians.

— The hymn now coming into his mind, he lay there listening to its melody till he slumbered off, and slept quietly for the remainder of the night.

In the morning he lay in a doze, struggling with a song. His efforts to dismiss it and to get back to sleep with the thought that it was the one he had sung to the Italian woman were, however, vain; instead he came wide awake. Then he realized that he was hearing an actual song.

The door of his cabin stood slightly ajar; the song came from out in the passage somewhere.

And there was a peculiar sadness in it, likely because the voice which sang was cracked and was having some difficulty in keeping the tune. Jo listened hard; after a little he got hold of a few words:

> "— —— home, home
> Over the white-crested billows
> I am borne home,
> Home, home ——"

"It must be morning," concluded Jo. So he got up, dressed, and left the cabin. Some of the passengers were already up; the stewards had begun setting the tables.

On the hatchway sat an elderly woman, garbed in black; her hood was of black silk. Jo knew the song had come from her, for after he came out she repeated the refrain. He took a place on the hatchway a little distance from her.

Soon the passages swarmed with people; some went into the dining-saloon and waited breakfast. After a while the woman too arose and went in; she took a seat next the wall. Jo cast a glance about, then followed and sat down beside her.

"Are you Swedish?" he asked.

"Oh no. I'm Norwegian."

"That was a pretty song," he said, quietly.

The Boat of Longing

"Dear me, did you hear it?" she asked. "I couldn't sleep this morning, and singing helps to pass the time away." The voice was sad. "I didn't dare try it inside, for fear of waking the others, and I thought no one could hear me out there. I haven't been disturbing people's sleep, have I?" she asked, half worried.

"I don't think so."

That, manifestly, comforted her.

"Where are you from in Norway?" she asked.

"Oh, I'm from Helgeland. What about you?"

"From Solőr; there are, no doubt, people from almost every part here. But I presume I'm the only Solung," she mused.

The food was brought in. Outside it was beautiful day. The genial mood of travel seemed to dominate the crowd, even though it was still early morning; people desired to strengthen the acquaintanceships of last evening and to make new ones; most of them were eager for as many romantic experiences as a trip across the Atlantic could afford. The two old ones over by the wall came, therefore, to constitute a world by themselves.

"There seem to be only kind people on board," remarked the woman. To this Jo did not find a fitting reply, so the woman spoke again:

"I suppose you've been in America a long time?"

"No—not very long. Have you?"

"Oh no, it didn't get to be long for me, either; it's just six weeks since I went across."

"Six weeks?" Jo's face grew deeply thoughtful. "Wouldn't they let you in?"

"Let me in?" The woman set wondering eyes upon him and laughed.

"You had an affidavit, then?"

"That I don't know; but there wasn't anybody who tried to stop me."

Hearts That Ache

"But you must have had some one to go good for you!" insisted Jo. "Who was it guaranteed for you?"

"Oh, of course I had; there was no difficulty there. You see, I have two sons in America, and they both sent me letters to take along; but they were written in English, so I didn't know what was in them."

Jo was mum; what the woman related gave him much to think about. It now began to dawn on him how stupidly he had proceeded when he set out on this trip.

Breakfast was over; people streamed to the decks; but since the old woman continued to sit, Jo did, too.

"What's the name of the place where your boys live?" he asked.

"Duluth. They both live there."

"I presume they've done well?"

"No one can complain about that, I guess; I'd call it little less than a wonder. You should have seen our cottage at home, and now they live in houses that look like palaces!"

"Were there many Norwegians around there?"

"Oh, I'm sure there must have been, though I couldn't say for certain, of course. Duluth is a big city, you see."

"You don't happen to have been in a city by the name of Minneapolis, I suppose?" asked Jo.

"Goodness me, I should say I have!" she waggled her head. "I had to go through that city, you see. Jacob took me—that's my youngest son. We spent three days there."

Jo was visibly agitated. He moved nervously about on his chair, his hands clasping and unclasping the edge of the table.

"Was it—was it beautiful there?"

"Beautiful? Well, I should think so! I never expect to see such grandeur again."

"And were there houses there, too, that looked like palaces?"

"Aye there? Jacob and I lived in one. And it's as true as

The Boat of Longing

I'm sitting here that the walls were of pure marble; and there were thick, soft carpets on the floor; you might have thought you were walking on down. You never saw such riches and luxury among human beings! The moment you stepped inside the door, servants in livery bowed to you!"

"Was—was that in Minneapolis?" exclaimed Jo, his whole body in a violent tremor.

"Aye, surely. Jacob and I were there three days. I couldn't begin to describe all the wonders we saw. Jacob seemed to know every place! One afternoon he hired a man to take us around in an automobile and show us the lakes and the palaces and the big parks. You never saw such splendour! They say it's only rich folks who live there."

Jo's excitement grew more and more intense under the woman's talk; tears began trickling down his cheeks. Unable to check them, and feeling embarrassed, he was forced to get up and leave.

For the rest of the crossing these two were companions. They sat next each other at table, and usually remained to talk afterward; she had so much to tell; he so much to ask about; and both glided into a great fellow interest. Because of their venerable appearance the other passengers named them Grandpa and Grandma, and they became the objects of general attention and solicitude.

Since Jo was constantly putting new questions about Minneapolis, she enquired the reason for his interest. This he did not answer until one day they happened to sit longer than usual over their after-dinner coffee; then he revealed the whole story.

"Oh, my! there you acted foolishly!" she cried. "That you shouldn't have done; you should have waited till a letter came."

"But there weren't any letters," replied Jo, tonelessly.

"How you talk! A couple of years? What's that to people in America? You see—well, likely it isn't so easy for them to write Norwegian, either, when they speak only English. Take those boys of mine, now; there was once it got to be over four years that I didn't hear from them. But I kept on writing a couple of times a year all the same. So this summer they took a notion I should come over and see them. It was Jacob's idea, I might say; he has always been more thoughtful of his mother than Mathias."

That day Jo also learned that she was a cotter woman whose husband had died several years ago, that she lived alone in a cottage far up on a hillside, and that she was going back there to live.

"Why didn't you stay in America?" Jo then asked.

This she hesitated to answer at first, and sat downcast and silent, only rocking her head strongly. After a while she explained that it wouldn't be easy for an old woman in a strange land; and then it had seemed lonesome and queer not to be able to talk to the children of her boys, those blessèd children that were so pretty and who were in a way her own.

— Couldn't she talk to them? To her sons' children?— Unable to comprehend, Jo had to question further.

— No, for they couldn't, of course, talk Norwegian!

— Couldn't they talk Norwegian? Her own children's children?— Again Jo failed to understand.

Nor was she able to explain how it came about that Norwegian children couldn't speak Norwegian. She had supposed that it just happened to be that way in America—that was the only explanation she could see.

"But it seems to me you should have stayed longer when you had travelled that far and your boys lived in palaces!" observed Jo.

She didn't answer immediately, merely fingered the buttons on her coat.

— Well, it might sound reasonable enough. But it was

queer with old folks, you know; they had their habits. And it wasn't so easy to move from a cotter's hut into a rich man's palace, even if one's own children did live there. There was so much that could happen.

Then, as if she had been guilty of some wickedness, she hastened to add that the boys had been as kind to her as they possibly could. They had paid her fare both ways, and had dressed her from head to foot like the grandest lady— she didn't know what she was to do with all the finery when she got home—and had given her three hundred dollars apiece, besides. And now that she had seen how they lived she could die with a peaceful mind. If only the Good Lord would be kind and not let her live too long, she would have all she could ask in this world.

She was, notwithstanding, reticent and downhearted that day, and Jo hesitated to question her further.

— How had they gone about amassing such great riches? he ventured later. But she couldn't enlighten him fully. She only knew they had begun in the woods; which was work they had been accustomed to from home.

Jo's mind was working less rapidly now than it had on the previous crossing. Ideas, when they came, hooked themselves fast, banded together and grew into thoughts; these he revolved, turned over, and examined as he lay in his berth at night, and took with him when he stood at the rail by day, watching the furrow which the ship ploughed.

However it came about, his face grew happier and happier as the days passed. He might stand on deck for hours at a time, coatless in the bitter blast from the Atlantic, and finally come below with a visage so cheery as to be fairly aglow; or again he might appear at breakfast with a face looking like that of a child newly returned from play.

On one occasion he had sounded her out as to whether she hadn't seen a young man in Minneapolis who was medium tall, light-complexioned, and had broad shoulders and blue eyes. One who she could tell at a glance was a kind person?

She sat pondering awhile, trying to recollect; she had seen so many in Minneapolis. Aye—now that she thought of it, she seemed to remember such a man; she was sure she had seen him. He lived in the same house that she and Jacob did; he was very well dressed, she had noticed, and seemed to be unusually busy. "Not a bit unlikely," she added, "that that was your son."

"Was he light-complexioned?"

"Aye, quite fair."

"And broad-shouldered?"

"Aye, he was that, too," she believed.

"And did he look like a good person?"

"That he surely must have been!"

"And you think he lived in the marble palace?"

"Aye, this man lived there—I saw that."

"Have you ever!" cried Jo, getting up. He had to go off by himself and think; but he was so happy that it sang within him.

All the fairy-like in what she had from time to time told him, now glided into his own distorted impression of New York, an impression which allowed of many possibilities. The series of strange pictures which passed before his mind gave more life to his thoughts.

Upon the ship's arrival in Norway, Jo was the happiest passenger on board; people had to turn and look, for the aged one walked as in a transport of song!

X

The weeks passed slowly for Mother Anna, and it grew very lonely out there in the cottage by the sea. Ole Hansen's weekly visits were a real diversion, cheering her greatly; but,

The Boat of Longing

after all, it was a short-lived cheer, since he always had to leave the next day.

After Jo's departure Ole's imagination again lifted its wings, soaring now to unprecedented heights, from which it descended with the most chimerical ideas. But best of all he had regained his happiness; it was as though all worry had been dismissed from his life. What, in fact, was there for Ole to worry about any more? Jo had gone to see after the boys, and one of them would be certain to return with him. And even if he didn't there would be definite tidings—and possibly somewhat more, reasoned Ole. So what could there be to worry about?

But when Ole set out for home and left her alone, Mother Anna's loneliness might become very great. Then she realized that she was beginning to age; had it been in her younger years, she wouldn't have minded it much. But old age was at hand—she could tell that it was.

With the passing of the days her uneasiness for her husband increased; that came because of her getting a clearer understanding of what it really was Jo had plunged himself into. He was going almost to the end of the world; had to cross sea and land, to pass big cities, and meet millions of people. It was the last she dreaded most of all. No, she didn't understand how he was to get along among all those strangers, he who was so timid, and slow to find words. They had, after all, acted unwisely in not letting Ole undertake it. Ole was a scatterbrain—there could be no doubt about that. Yet it wasn't of the kind to be serious.

Since nothing but Jo and his trip occupied her thoughts by day, neither could she get them out of her thoughts by night; there was scarcely a night that she didn't dream about him.

Every morning, her work being done, she would take her hymnary and sit down at the table; and then she would read aloud, reverently, the "Prayer for Seafarers." Nor did

Hearts That Ache

she let it do with the one, but took several of the others as well. "It can do no harm," she reflected. "If it doesn't exactly fit for me, it may for somebody else."

The cow and the sheep were a great comfort to her; with them she held long conversations morning and evening.

It had been raining all forenoon the day Jo came home. Toward noon it had stopped; but a mist remained in the air and the day wouldn't come decently clear.

Mother Anna could get no peace that day. Two nights in succession now she had had premonitions of some one's coming. It couldn't be aught but omens, could it? This morning long before she got up she had distinctly heard the outer door open and footsteps follow in the hallway. The thought of the banshee didn't alarm her, only such a queer, anxious feeling came over her. . . . Surely Jo couldn't be expected yet? No, not yet! . . .

In the morning she had taken her hymn-book and had read the "Prayer for Seafarers." To it she had added her own prayer that, if Jo was now no longer among the living, God would be merciful to him and put his spirit to rest wherever it might be. She would try to get along through the days that were left her. If he had gone, he couldn't be of any help to her, anyway; the Good Lord must be kind and help him to understand that. . . . It seemed to her that she felt better after she had got that said.

It was nearing noon. Once, when she was over by the east window, she became aware of a form down in the path. Some one was approaching through the fog! A strange feeling seized her. Who could it be?

She stood gazing. That some one came didn't astonish her; today was boat day, and Ole might be expected. But—the figure didn't appear to limp. No, he certainly wasn't limping, this person.

. . . And he seemed to be carrying a pack on his back. . . . Unquestionably, he was carrying a pack. . . .

The Boat of Longing

She left the window and went to the door, turned and went back to the window; there she stood until she recognized both Jo and the chest. But she refused to believe that it actually was he coming big as life up the path, until she saw the chest; then, of course, she had to believe.

Her body grew faint; all went black before her eyes and she had to seize hold of the table and cling to it. But she pulled herself together sufficiently so that she could get to the stove and stir up the fire.

Jo stopped outside just long enough to loose the chest from his back; he carried it by the handle when he entered. Then they stood there and looked at each other. A great smile overspread his face; Mother Anna only wagged her head.

"God's peace upon the house!" he said.

"And peace be to you," she should have answered; but the words came so feebly that she wasn't sure that he heard them. She could only stand there in a helpless gaze.

"And how is it here?" he asked. His voice was loud and bright.

"Oh——"

That was all Mother Anna could muster; but she went and put the coffee-pot over the fire. The room grew almost too cramped to contain these two human beings.

Jo took the chair she had set him and put his cap on the floor beside him just as though he had been a stranger.

"Have you been well?" he asked.

"Aye, I can't complain of that." She found talking easier, now that she had turned her back toward him; but she busied herself at the stove, nevertheless, until she had regained the mastery of herself somewhat more.

"Aren't you going to change?" she asked, facing him. "Your feet must be wet."

——Change? She was right——aye, he believed he did need to change.—— Rising, he began staving about exactly as

Hearts That Ache

though he had just come in from the sea. Mother Anna moved silently to and fro, finding clothes for him and decking the table.

Jo sought the window which overlooked the sea; there he forgot himself and stood gazing, in his underwear. There was no wind, but a considerable heavy sea, he noticed. It was breaking a good deal on the skerries, though not worse than he could go out in a boat all right.

"Do you know," he asked, "whether there's anything to be had on the sea?"

"You can't begin to think of the sea until you get dry clothes on yourself!" she protested, maternally. She now became more firm and dictatorial; this man who pottered about in his drawers must be quite alive, after all. The sign heartened her.

And so Jo got into different clothes.— He must come to the table, she invited, pouring him his coffee; after a trip to the kitchen to wipe her eyes, she came back and sat down opposite him.

It was almost as though she could not take her eyes off him. He had grown so changed these last weeks that he wasn't like the same man. Had she known him to drink, she would have said he was tipsy . . . the face and the eyes looked as happy as in a man half-seas over. . . . And talk came so easy. But it was, of course, Jo! . . . God be praised that he was sitting here in the room with her . . . she didn't care a whit even if he had had both one and two drams. . . .

Jo helped himself liberally to food.

"So you haven't any idea how conditions are on the sea?" he asked again.

"They say there's plenty of fish. But the weather's been too unsettled of late for folk to go out."

"Hmn"—replied Jo, happy of voice. "As soon as I've got a little to eat into myself, you must help me put the boat on the water. I'll have to go out with the trawl this afternoon and see what the situation is like around here."

Mother Anna wasn't interested in that just now; and since he wasn't starting the subject, she supposed she would have to. . . . The way he looked though, the tidings must be good.

"How have you fared on the trip?"

"Well. Very well!"

"And you found the way?"

"Aye, that was no trick."

Mother Anna let her eyes rest on him proudly; but her mouth quivered violently as she put the next question.

"Did you find the one you went to see?"

"Do you mean if I met him?" asked Jo.

"Aye. Did you find Nils?"

"No, I can't say I met him exactly. For you see there's a law over there like this that old people—well, they're not allowed to travel on the trains unless there's some one of their own family with them to take care of them. You see, everything's so well ordered over there. On that account, I didn't get farther than New York. But that was really fortunate, when you stop to think of it. If I had gone clear to Minneapolis and then back again, it would have taken me at least six weeks; I would have had to stay with him a while too, of course. And that would have made a long time for you to be alone. But I got news of him, though!" added Jo, happily.

"Did you really hear about him?"

"Aye! Didn't I meet people who had been in his own house?"

"What are you saying? Has he really got himself a house?" cried Mother Anna.

"I should say the boy has got himself a house!" Now it was Jo who cried out. "But that's something will go way beyond your power to understand. No, you could **never**

Hearts That Ache

understand that; for those houses over there, you see, they're not like this little cot of ours!" Enthusiasm was mounting in his voice; his eyes were beginning to burn.

"But I suppose there are ordinary houses there, too?" cried Mother Anna again.

"Ordinary houses? Far from it! No, child, you can't understand it. For they are great palaces with towers on them!"

"Are you daft, Jo!"

"No, I certainly am not. Haven't I seen them with my own eyes? And Nils is now living in such a palace; it's built of marble—of white marble! And, mind you, there are carpets on the floors so soft that it's just like walking on a feather tick. Everything is wonderful over there; if I were to sit here telling you about it the rest of my life, you couldn't begin to fathom it."

Mother Anna set eyes upon him which bored him through. What he was telling was plainly impossible! Could it really be Jo who talked thus? People were not so happy as this unless they had got strong drink into themselves. Mother Anna grew almost fearful for him.

"Now you are to tell me every bit, Jo!" she entreated, in alarm. "Begin at the beginning and tell me what happened to you."

Jo looked at her. And then he understood: How could she be expected to grasp it immediately, when she hadn't seen it? That was impossible! No, he would have to explain it all circumstantially.

And so Jo by the Sea began relating. And because only certain of his momentous experiences had fastened themselves in his mind, and because he had lived these so intensely, over and over again, his whole story got the strange spell of the fairy tale over itself. None the less, it had all the realness of sober actuality. He did as she requested: he

The Boat of Longing

began at the beginning; and from there he sprang hastily from wonder to wonder, the one surpassing the other.

The afternoon wore on and Jo related.

He was quiet and joyous, but so convincing in his happiness over Nils's great good fortune that he bore her along with him. It was about the marble palace in which he now lived . . . and more about it . . . and yet more—for it was so amazingly big and wonderful!

Off and on she had to interrupt him with a question.

But he didn't get tired of repeating and explaining. All the thoughts that had entered his mind when he stood gazing at the Atlantic now stepped forth; all the explanations he had framed; all the pictures he had been vouchsafed; as well as most of what the old woman had related: this he now sat making Mother Anna believe.

The hours passed, but Jo related.

"And in that marble palace you and I are to live with him," he explained to her. "It will hardly be long now before he'll be sending the tickets; be just as soon as he gets it all arranged. But that isn't so easily done in such a big house, as you too can understand. Though I don't think we'll want to stay there the rest of our lives," he added, "since there's bound to be noise and commotion in such a house. Then, too, it will in the long run be lonesome for us when we can't understand what people are saying. But I'll have to explain that to you some other day, for now I want to go out on the sea!"

Jo rose and found his sea boots; she followed him as if transported, no longer doubting that it was as he said. . . . It must be something extraordinary the boy was striving with, since he didn't write—aye, that it must!

Now it sometimes happens on such gloomy fall days out there on the coast that the sky will brighten above the sea

Hearts That Ache

rim at twilight, a broad, crystal band engirdling the horizon. Above it the fog and rain will gather like a wall; but along the sea it will be clear. The sky will there show an almost supernatural brilliance in contrast with the pendent blackness.

This evening it was like that.

"There you see!" exclaimed Jo when he came out and noticed it. "Aye, there you can see!"

"Perhaps it will clear off during the night," observed Mother Anna.

Then the two of them descended the path to the pier and got the boat on the water. Jo wanted to shove off immediately.

"What about the trawl lines?" cried Mother Anna.

"Aye, that's right—the lines!"

She fetched them for him, begging him, as he pushed off: "Now you mustn't row too far out."

But either Jo did not hear her or his mind was too absorbed, for he gave no reply; his face beamed at the sea, and then he sat down to the oars.

He made a way for the boat over billows and skerries out toward the open water, toward the light-band. He rowed farther and farther.

The sea flowed heavily. Billows lifted themselves; hurtled over; rolled coldly on.

Whenever the boat rode high on the crest of a wave, Jo looked out and saw all the splendour yonder:

. . . Day sank; the crystal rim changed to pure gold; it was as though all the sun under heaven had gathered above the skyline.

He turned frequently on the thwart; the glow of his countenance vied with the brilliance yonder.

. . . He pulled harder on the oars. Up the billow, into the trough . . . onward . . . farther onward . . . nearer and nearer the beautiful castle west in the sea . . . the castle which lay in the twist of gold, the castle where dwelt his boy.

But the billow rolled so chill. . . .

And night closed in. That Jo did not notice. He saw only the castle where lived his boy.

. . . On he rowed, and on, farther and farther into the skyline, out to the Great Ocean itself. . . .

Jo by the Sea was seen no more. Folk thought it strange that they didn't find the boat, though the search was both long and thorough. No one could explain it. For it had been a still night. An off-wind had, to be sure, set in in the course of the morning; but even so it should have been possible to find the boat. But there was never so much as a sliver seen of it.

THE END